FINDING REFUGE IN EL PASO

THE 1912 MORMON EXODUS FROM MEXICO

Use the following link to view the documentary video:
youtube.com/watch?v=7rm_ozZ7_4M
or scan the QR code below.

Finding Refuge in El Paso

The 1912 Mormon Exodus from Mexico

Fred E. Woods

CFI
An Imprint of Cedar Fort, Inc.
Springville, Utah

ISBN 13: 978-1-9325-9721-9

Published by CFI, an imprint of Cedar Fort, Inc., 2373 W. 700 S., Springville, UT 84663
Distributed by Cedar Fort, Inc., www.cedarfort.com

The Library of Congress has cataloged the first edition as follows:

Woods, Fred E., author.
Finding refuge in El Paso : the 1912 Mormon exodus from Mexico / Fred E. Woods.
pages cm
Includes bibliographical references and index.
ISBN 978-1-4621-1153-4 (alk. paper)
1. Mormons--Texas--El Paso--History. 2. Mormons--Mexico--History. 3. Church of Jesus Christ of Latter-day Saints--Texas--El Paso--History. 4. Mormon Church--Texas--El Paso--History. 5. Church of Jesus Christ of Latter-day Saints--Mexico--History. 6. Mormon Church--Mexico--History. 7. Mexico--History--Revolution, 1910-1920--Refugees. I. Title.

BX8615.T45W66 2012
972.08'16--dc23

2012030947

Cover design by Angela D. Olsen
Cover design © 2012 by Lyle Mortimer
Edited and typeset by Whitney A. Lindsley

Printed in the United States of America

10 9 8 7 6 5 4 3 2 1

TO MY FATHER, Fred E. Woods III, who taught me how to cross borders and take care of the needy

CONTENTS

ACKNOWLEDGMENTS xi

FOREWORD xiii

PROLOGUE 1

CHAPTER 1
The Setting: Mormon Migration into and out of Mexico 3

CHAPTER 2
Mexican Revolution and the Mormons 15

CHAPTER 3
The Exodus 23

CHAPTER 4
Relief in El Paso 35

EPILOGUE 53

INTERVIEWS

- Lorna Call Alder 57
- Elias Bonilla 60
- John F. Cook 69
- Henry B. Eyring 72
- Matthew G. Geilman 74
- Fernando Gomez 78
- Patricia Kiddney 81
- Michael N. Landon 83
- Taylor Macdonald 90

Prince G. McKenzie 95
Leon Metz 96
Michael R. Mullen 98
Karl Murphy. 99
Major General Dana J. H. Pittard. 100
Gerald Pratt 102
Vera Whetten Pratt. 105
Anna Lucile Romney. 108
Florence Black Romney. 111
Joseph B. Romney 113
David Romo 122
Bernie Sargent. 126
Melissa Sargent 129
Jared Tamez 133
Richard E. Turley Jr. 137
John Ray Wall. 142

APPENDIX A: Record of the Exodus 145

APPENDIX B: "Juarez Stake Relief Committee Minutes". 171

NOTES. 253

SELECTED BIBLIOGRAPHY 281

INDEX. 291

ABOUT THE AUTHOR 303

ACKNOWLEDGMENTS

THIS BOOK WAS MADE POSSIBLE WITH THE assistance of several individuals and institutions. Gratitude is expressed to the College of Religious Education at Brigham Young University (BYU) for its support and services rendered via transcriptions made from oral history interviews transcribed by student employees in the Faculty Support Center for Religious Education. I am also grateful for the competent staff employed at BYU in the L. Tom Perry Special Collections, Harold B. Lee Library; the Church History Library of The Church of Jesus Christ of Latter-day Saints; the El Paso Public Library; the C. L. Sonnichsen Special Collections Department, University of Texas at El Paso; the El Paso County Historical Society; and the Library of Congress.

Within these institutions, special thanks are extended to Michael N. Landon and William W. Slaughter for their help with many images (CHL); Mark Jackson for creating a map of the colonies (BYU); Russ Taylor, Cindy Brightenburg, and staff for expediting research orders (BYU Special Collections); Pat Worthington (EPCHS); as well as Danny Gonzalez, (EPPL) and Claudia A. Rivers for their help with borderlands research (UTEP Special Collections). Gratitude is also extended to the Center for Oral and Public History at California State University, Fullerton, for permitting transcripts of oral history interviews to be used. Thanks are also expressed to Taylor Macdonald and Helen Carbine, who graciously permitted usage of audio tapes from their private collections, and to Jacque Craig for her excellent transcription work of the documents in the appendices as well as some of the audio and film interviews. Gratitude is also extended to the Mormon Historic Sites Foundation and private donors for their assistance with funding for the documentary.

I also want to extend thanks to my research assistant, Jacob F. Frandsen, for his significant contribution to producing this work as well as the editorial expertise of Don Norton, emeritus professor of the Department of Linguistics and English Language at Brigham Young University. Gratitude is expressed to R. Devan Jensen, Alonzo Gaskill, Nyssa Silvester, Olivia Earnshaw, Eliza Goodman, and my daughter Addie R. White for their assistance with proofreading and indexing. Thanks are also extended to Cedar Fort staff Whitney Lindsley and Jennifer Fielding, who have provided professional direction throughout the editorial process and have been enjoyable to work with. In addition, I wish to thank all the interviewees who gave of their time for the production of this joint work. Heartfelt thanks are expressed to Joseph B. Romney for sharing documents and reading an early draft of an article, which turned into a book, as well as Michael N. Landon, who also reviewed this manuscript and wrote the excellent foreword to this book. I am especially grateful to my friend and colleague Martin L. Andersen, with whom I had the pleasure of producing the documentary. We enjoyed several weeks of capturing oral history interviews on film in El Paso and in Utah. Martin also carefully read the manuscript and provided useful feedback and images used with the interviews. Finally, appreciation is expressed to my wife, JoAnna, and our family, who have been a continual support to my diverse projects at home and abroad.

FOREWORD

FOR MOST MEMBERS OF THE CHURCH OF JESUS Christ of Latter-day Saints, Joseph Smith's call as a prophet; the translation of the Book of Mormon; the beginning of the Church in New York; the years in Ohio and Missouri; the expulsion from Missouri; the creation of Nauvoo; the exodus from Illinois across Iowa; the trek of the Mormon Battalion; and the journey from the Missouri River to the Salt Lake Valley are all familiar episodes in the Church's early history. Many Church members in the United States are well acquainted with the role that their pioneer ancestors played in one or more of these epic events. Yet many other historic events in Church history are not as well known, but are equally compelling. One of these was the establishment of Mormon colonies in the Mexican states of Chihuahua and Sonora in the late nineteenth century and the subsequent exodus of Latter-day Saints from these colonies in 1912 during the Mexican Revolution. While the story is familiar to Church members whose ancestors lived in the colonies, many Latter-day Saints are completely unaware of the story of the Mormon colonies in Mexico.

In this volume, *Finding Refuge in El Paso: The 1912 Mormon Exodus from Mexico*, Dr. Fred E. Woods provides as context an overview of the history of these Mormon colonies, in order to highlight an aspect of the exodus from Mexico that to this point has been almost completely overlooked—the charitable reception that thousands of Mormon refugees received from the city of El Paso, Texas. During the 2012 centennial of the Mormon exodus from Mexico, this volume and a companion documentary film with the same title represented just part of Fred's efforts to bring belated recognition to the generous citizens of El Paso. Dr. Woods was heavily involved in a cooperative effort between the El Paso Museum of History, BYU, the Mormon Historic Sites Foundation, and the LDS Church History Department to commemorate the exodus with a new exhibit at the museum, which opened on July 28, 2012, one hundred years to the day that the first Mormon refugees began leaving the colonies in Mexico. Linked to the centennial of the exodus, Fred also participated in the "Conference on the History of Mormonism in Latin America and the U.S.-Mexico Borderlands," which included a host of Mormon and Latin American studies scholars and was sponsored by the University of Texas, El Paso history department, the Mormon Historic Sites Foundation, and the El Paso Public Library. Finally, Dr. Woods was instrumental in organizing a public commemoration ceremony of the Mormon exodus honoring the citizens of El Paso held at the University of Texas, El Paso that included John Cook, mayor of El Paso; Major General Dana J.H. Pittard, Commanding General of the 1st Armored Division and Fort Bliss, Texas; and Richard E. Turley, Jr., Assistant Church Historian and Recorder for the Church of Jesus Christ of Latter-day Saints.

In bringing to light the tireless efforts of the El Paso community to aid the Mormon refugees, Fred included in the volume transcripts of oral history interviews describing many aspects of the Mormon exodus from Mexico and the refugee experience in El Paso. Dr. Woods has also included transcriptions of Alonzo Taylor's "Record of the Exodus" and the "Juárez Stake Relief Committee Minutes," key archival documents related to the 1912 Mormon exodus from Mexico published here for the first time. Anyone interested in Mormonism in Mexico, particularly the Mormon exodus and the response by the City of El Paso to the flood of refugees, will be richly served by Fred's efforts to shed light on an almost unknown chapter of Mormon history.

PROLOGUE

THE YEAR 2012 MARKS THE CENTENNIAL COMMEMORATION of the Mormon exodus from the colonies in northern Mexico during the Mexican Revolution. It is a time to reflect on the story and meaning of these Mormons' experience, which abruptly changed the lives of over four thousand men, women, and children. The exodus was expensive in terms of abandoned homes and lost property and goods; however, keeping their families safe was worth the heavy cost for members of the Latter-day Saint colonies. The flight of Mormon women and children by train was closely followed by the evacuation of the men. At the crossroads of two nations, the uprooted Latter-day Saint refugees were received with warmth and sympathy at El Paso, Texas. Most Latter-day Saints later decided to disperse to the western states of Arizona, California, Idaho, New Mexico, and Utah, while hundreds decided to remain and

El Paso Union Depot, early twentieth century, courtesy El Paso Public Library

build their lives in the friendly city of El Paso. Most would never return to Mexico.

This book and documentary combine to tell the inspiring story of these Saints, who subdued the soil of northern Mexico, making the desert states of Chihuahua and Sonora blossom as a rose. They also explain reasons why the Mormons entered this southern region and suddenly departed. This work is offered as a tribute to the great citizens of El Paso, who opened their arms to receive the thousands of Mormon refugees who poured over the border onto the free and secure soil of the United States.

CHAPTER 1

The Setting: Mormon Migration into and out of Mexico

ALTHOUGH THE CHURCH OF JESUS CHRIST OF Latter-day Saints was established in and grew out of firmly American soil, its branches were destined to reach into countries flung far outside of the United States. These Mormon colonists were a mix of European converts, mostly from the British Isles and Scandinavia, as well as Americans who emigrated from the eastern and southern United States. Each of these groups had experience with immigrating and emigrating prior to their migration south to Mexico.[1] Mexico early on felt the influence of the Latter-day Saint religion. The first Mormons to leave footprints on Mexican soil were members of the

Mormon Battalion reenactment, courtesy Church History Library

Mormon Battalion, who passed through Mexican territory on their journey to California. Later, as Church members emigrated en masse from Nauvoo, Illinois, to escape crushing persecution, they established a new home in the Great Salt Lake Valley, which at that time lay within Mexican territory.

This story, however, follows a group of Mormons mainly from Utah and Arizona who entered Mexico in the late nineteenth century in answer to a call from their church leaders. With their celebrated Mormon industry, the Saints tamed the barren wilderness in the northern part of the country. Then, in the midst of military revolution just decades later, the colonists abandoned their beautiful homes and flourishing towns.[2] They had come in part to Mexico to seek religious tolerance, being forced from the United States because they were Mormon polygamists. When they were driven from Mexico, however, it was because they were Americans.

PLURAL MARRIAGE AND PERSECUTION

Polygamy as a Mormon doctrine was first publicly announced in 1852.[3] Four years later, this practice drew heavy national attention when Utah applied for statehood. That same year the Republican Party announced its official stance against what they termed the "twin relics of barbarism": slavery and polygamy. The Morrill Anti-Bigamy Law, signed by President Abraham Lincoln in 1862, was the first law passed by Congress to punish polygamists; it allowed for transgressors to be fined up to five hundred dollars and imprisoned for up to five years. Fortunately for the Latter-day Saints, the law was not enforced at the time of its passage, thanks to the nation's preoccupation with the Civil War. President Lincoln viewed Mormonism much as he did the burdensome tree stumps he encountered in fields as a farm boy: "It was too heavy to move, too hard to chop, and too green to burn"; therefore, Lincoln said, "We just plowed around it."[4]

As the controversy surrounding slavery softened at the conclusion of the war, some politicians renewed their attack on polygamy. Yet the crusade against plural marriage was mostly fruitless until the Edmunds-Tucker Act passed in 1882. As an amendment to strengthen the Morrill Anti-Bigamy Law, the Edmunds Act barred polygamists from voting,

George Q. Cannon and other polygamists at the Utah Penitentiary, courtesy L. Tom Perry Special Collections, Harold B. Lee Library, Brigham Young University

holding public office, and participating in jury duty. The act also declared "unlawful cohabitation" to be a misdemeanor and made it unnecessary for Utah territorial authorities to obtain proof of a plural marriage before prosecuting suspected polygamists. This concession was deemed necessary because records of plural marriages were inaccessible to non-Mormons, and therefore, polygamy previously could not be proved and prosecuted. Under the Edmunds Act, Mormon men found living with, supporting, or caring for more than one woman could be charged with unlawful cohabitation. Five years later, the Edmunds-Tucker Act was signed, further stiffening the penalties and causing both the Church and the Perpetual Emigrating Fund to be disincorporated.[5]

More than thirteen hundred polygamous Mormon men served prison sentences, most for unlawful cohabitation, in pentitentiaries in Utah, Michigan, South Dakota, Arizona, and Idaho.[6] Others were forced to abandon their families and go into hiding on the "underground," as it was called, and they simply outfoxed or outran the law.[7]

MEXICO BECKONS

As persecution in the United States intensified, Church leaders began to consider expanding colonization efforts into foreign nations. But relief from persecution was just one of several reasons the Saints began looking to expand outside the nation's borders.[8] Missionary work was another important motive. Several months before his death, Church President Brigham Young spoke of a need to both strengthen the Mormon stronghold in Utah and expand proselytizing efforts elsewhere: "We intend to hold our own here and also penetrate the north and the south, the east and the west, . . . and to raise the ensign of truth."[9]

A Latter-day Saint colony in Mexico had been an objective of Young since at least 1874, after his secretary, George Reynolds, was sentenced to prison for unlawful cohabitation. That summer, Young directed that passages of the Book of Mormon be translated into Spanish in anticipation of missionaries entering Mexico.[10] In the fall of 1875, the first Mormon missionaries left for Mexico and commenced a ten-month journey that would take them a distance of three thousand miles.[11] One of these missionaries, Anthony W. Ivins, would later play a pivotal role in the Saints' colonization of and eventual evacuation from Mexico. The purpose of the mission was twofold. First, the men were to preach the restored gospel to the natives of Mexico. One of the missionaries, Daniel Jones, reported that President Young had told the elders that "the time had come to prepare for the introduction of the gospel into Mexico; that there were millions of the descendants of Nephi in the land, and that we were under obligations to visit them."[12]

Second, the missionaries were to scout locations for possible Mormon settlements. Apostle Orson Pratt charged the missionaries to "look out for places where our brethren could go and be safe from harm in the event that persecutions should make it necessary for them to get out of the way for a season."[13] The missionaries were to keep a careful record of their travels and report on any potentially suitable settlement locations.[14] These missionaries traveled as far south as Chihuahua, Mexico, and returned to Utah with a report in July 1876. President Young also sent Daniel Jones and later Apostles Moses Thatcher and Erastus Snow to northern Mexico to look for places to colonize,[15] though nothing came of either expedition; President Young died before ever seeing the Saints colonize Mexico.

Mormon missionaries in Mexico, source unknown

Then, in late 1884,

intensifying persecution against the Saints in Arizona for their plural marriage practices caused President John Taylor, Young's successor, to counsel the Saints there to flee to Mexico if conditions became unbearable.[16] At the same time, President Taylor continued to remind Church members of the vision of Church founder Joseph Smith that Zion would occupy all of North and South America.[17] Thus the Saints' move across the southern border was motivated in part by a desire to perform missionary work and colonization; however, according to Anthony Ivins, "The condition of marriage existing among the Latter-day Saints was the main factor in bringing the Saints to Mexico."[18]

President John Taylor, ca. 1880, by C. R. Savage, courtesy L. Tom Perry Special Collections, Harold B. Lee Library, Brigham Young University

Conveniently, the Saints' desire to move into Mexico fit perfectly with the agenda of many officials in the country. Mexican liberals, particularly, believed that Mexico's greatest unexploited asset was its vast tracts of land, and they were eager for laborers who could develop and improve it, even if this meant bringing in foreigners to do the work.[19] Consequently, the Mexican government actively enticed foreigners to immigrate and colonize.[20] One politician, José María Romero, even went so far as to assert that "the current of European immigration is [a] river of gold that brings wealth and power."[21]

Even Porfirio Díaz, the president of Mexico, personally encouraged the Mormons to settle in his country, although, strictly speaking, polygamy was illegal in Mexico.[22] In Díaz's opinion, the development of the soil and the much-needed Mormon industry outweighed any legal technicalities. At times Díaz even implied to the Mormons that plural marriage was tolerable: he reportedly told Church leaders, "It does not matter in Mexico whether you drive your horses tandem or four abreast."[23] President John Taylor reported that "President Porfirio

Díaz assured the church there were no laws against polygamy" in his country.[24]

CROSSING THE BORDER

At the dawn of 1885, President Taylor decided that the core of the southern gathering place would be in the Casas Grandes area in the state of Chihuahua.[25] And so the gathering began, with Mormon colonists entering Mexico in early 1885. In January 1886, the Church purchased thousands of acres of land in the states of Sonora and Chihuahua.[26] Between 1885 and 1906, nine major Mormon colonies were founded in the two northern Mexican states of Chihuahua and Sonora. In Chihuahua, Colonia Díaz was established along the Piedras Verdes River, just twenty miles from the international border. Farther south but also bordering the river were Colonia Dublán, Colonia Juárez, Colonia Pacheco, and Colonia García. Colonia Chuichupa lay farthest south, about one hundred eighty miles from the border. In the state of Sonora to the west, Colonia Morelos, Colonia Oaxaca, and San Jose were established along the Bavispe River.[27] The colonists converged to build up these settlements on wild and untamed land; but the Latter-day Saints had caused the Salt Lake Valley and other inhospitable areas to blossom as a rose, and it seemed that if any people could do the same in northern Mexico, it was the Mormons. Many of the settlers were accustomed to moving from place to place. Colonist Isaac Turley, for example, had moved with his family from Canada to the United States, then relocated to Missouri, Illinois, and then to Utah with the Saints. After settling in Utah, Turley helped colonize San Bernardino, California; Washington, Minersville, and Beaver, Utah; and settlements along the Little Colorado River, in Arizona.[28]

Their first year in Mexico, the colonists faced a sweeping variety of challenges, including water and food shortages, lack of sturdy clothing, and insufficient shelter. A cemetery had to be established quickly in Colonia Juárez as a smallpox epidemic rolled through the population.[29] But despite these hardships, the Saints began making headway in the empty desert.

Colonists' homes were initially rough but were soon replaced by adobe and then brick dwellings, with furnishings mostly imported from the United States. Other buildings sprang up in the colonies—churches, tithing houses, schools, and even a beautiful Relief Society building. At least one building, the Juarez Academy in Colonia Juárez, built in 1897, is still in use today. The Academy was the center not only of education in the region, but also of cultural refinement in the areas of music, drama, and athletic programs.[30] Gristmills, sawmills, mercantiles, and even a candy factory helped support the growing population, while saloons were outlawed.[31] Canals and irrigation ditches, carved into the vast empty territory,[32] soon gave way to orchards, fields, and cattle pastures. The Juarez Cooperative Mercantile Institution, based on the model of Salt Lake City's Zion's Cooperative Mercantile Institution (ZCMI), was established in 1889. It was "the only institution in the nation [of Mexico] so organized and said to be the first of its kind attempted by Americans in a foreign country."[33] Patrons traveled to

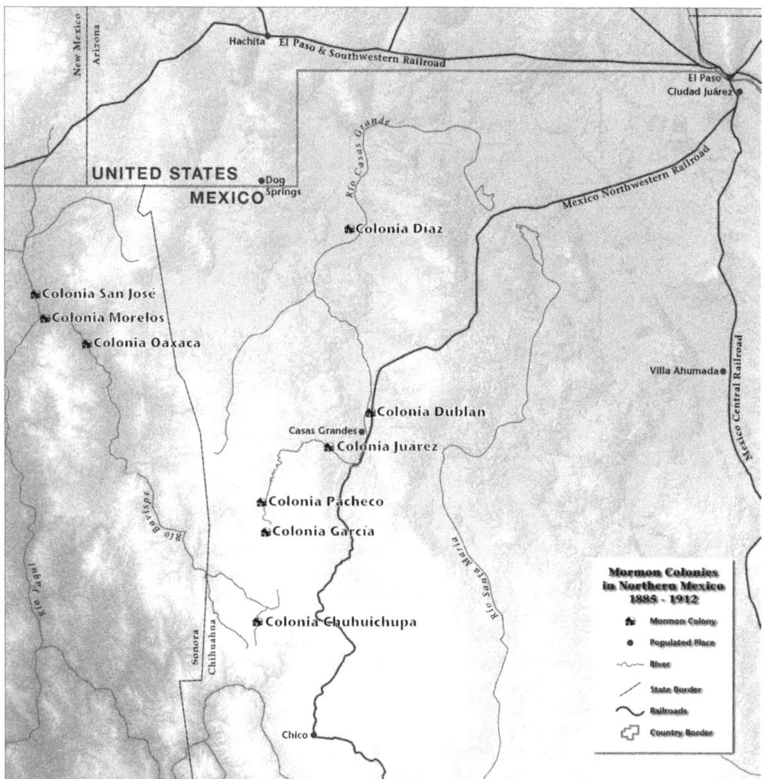

Map of colonies, courtesy Mark Jackson, Brigham Young University Geospatial Services

Porfirio Díaz, by Otis Aultman, from El Paso Public Library

the store from all over Chihuahua and Sonora.

Interestingly, when the Saints had first begun settling in Mexico, their situation took a sudden turn. With seemingly no provocation, the Secretary of the State of Chihuahua issued a letter to the Mormons, stating, "I hereby command you, together with other families which you represent, to leave the state within the period of 16 days from this date, April 9, 1885." It appeared the colonies would have to be abandoned before they were even fully established. However, Mormon leaders acted quickly in response to the expulsion order, traveling to Chihuahua City to request an annulment of the declaration.[34]

The situation had still not been settled a month later, so Latter-day Saint Apostles Brigham Young Jr. and Moses Thatcher traveled to Mexico City to put an end to the matter. There they met with President Porfirio Díaz, who not only overruled the state's decision but also informed the Apostles "that the Mormons were not only welcome as colonists in Mexico, but that the Government was anxious to have them help in the development of the country."[35] Díaz was quickly becoming the Mormons' most powerful Mexican ally. He consistently made it clear that he wanted the Mormon colonists in Mexico, even stating, "When the Mormon people first came to Mexico, I felt impressed to receive them. I believed them to be industrious, moral, and progressive, and that they would greatly aid in the development and progress of the country."[36]

With the sanction of Mexico's president, the colonies continued to grow. Each was formed under its own political structure within the Mexican system. The president of each colony acted as town sheriff and administrator. The respective presidents, town councils, and other local officials acted under the authority of the larger Mexican municipalities. Though most did not become Mexican citizens,[37] the colonists often celebrated Mexican holidays, including the country's national holiday on September 16. During one such celebration in Colonia Juárez in 1896, a parade, including several floats—each featuring one of the town's industries—preceded renditions of the Mexican National hymn and shouts of "Viva la independencia! Viva Mexico!" from the crowd.[38]

Anthony W. Ivins home, courtesy Church History Library

Mormon homes, courtesy Library of Congress

The colonists' great material prosperity came at the expense of missionary efforts. Proselytizing took a backseat as the colonists worked to establish themselves in Mexico, although full-time missionaries preached elsewhere throughout the country. The Latter-day Saints believed that the Mexican natives were the blood of Israel, but cultural issues, including sensitivities regarding the practice of plural marriage, seem to have divided the colonists from their Mexican neighbors from the beginning. The colonists' efforts, therefore, seem to have focused more on supporting their American families who had sought refuge in the colonies than on bringing additional sheep into the fold. In fact, historical evidence reveals that although friendly relationships existed with a number of local Mexican citizens, the Mormon colonists, as a general rule, did not go out of their way to socialize with their foreign neighbors. Agnes Scott Bluth of Colonia Juárez recalled, "We didn't associate with the Mexican people. They didn't want us to do that because they didn't want [us] to intermarry. . . . We were not allowed, we didn't go to their dances and we didn't allow them at our dances. We didn't mix with them socially."[39] According to Bishop W. Derby Johnson Jr. of Colonia Díaz, "Those who come to join us must have recommends. Parties in School House Mexicans must not be invited [n]or we go to their dances. . . . [We] keep our mouths shut."[40] That the assimilation was difficult in the colonies can be ascertained from a general conference address given by Elder Anthony W. Ivins after the twentieth century had already dawned: "We are surrounded by a strange people, with a strange language, with customs and manners entirely foreign and distinct from ours."[41]

Yet within a few years, Mormon industry in the colonies was in full swing and was recognized by outsiders, with reports such as this from the *Mexican Financial Review*:

> Hundreds of industrious Mormons have purchased lands and they have everywhere built neat and comfortable adobe cottages and windmills for raising water for home use as well as for irrigation. They have built and are building barns, and their vineyards and orchards are rapidly coming into bearing. In fact, they have changed this once wild and almost uninhabited region into comfortable and productive farms.[42]

By 1896, the Mexican government invited the Mormons to participate in a national fair in Mexico City. The government paid to ship specimens of Mormon industry to the fair, including leather goods,

Mormon women at loom, courtesy Church History Library

Sawmill near Juárez, courtesy Church History Library

Small Mormon store, courtesy Library of Congress

brooms, dairy, clothing, rugs, produce, and photographs of the thriving colonies. So great was the skepticism of fairgoers that the Mormons had accomplished so much in so little time that "an ambassador was therefore dispatched to the colonies to verify the authenticity of the pictures."[43] President Díaz, who personally examined the Mormons' displays at the fair, reportedly praised the Saints for achieving fifty years' worth of industry in a single decade.[44]

Praise for the colonies came from the United States as well. Charles W. Kindrich of the US State Department described Colonia Juárez with admiration in 1899: "The capital colony is a beautiful village comparable to any in New England. There is every evidence of thrift, cleanliness, industry, comfort, and good management. There is an absence of the vices common to modern communities. There are no saloons, tobacco shops, jails, nor houses of ill fame in the colony."[45]

Citizens ready for a play, courtesy Church History Library

Juárez Stake Academy baseball team, courtesy Church History Library

Juárez Stake Academy Band, courtesy Church History Library

CHAPTER 2

Mexican Revolution and the Mormons

NOTWITHSTANDING THE COLONISTS' GREAT efforts over the course of several decades to establish peace and prosperity in the colonies, in 1912, reverberations of the Mexican Revolution would begin to shake the tranquility of the idyllic settlements.

During the course of Díaz's presidency, Mexico saw huge economic growth and improvement; however, greed, corruption, and social favoritism left the country's lower classes feeling neglected and unsatisfied. Many also felt that Díaz was "giving the country away" to foreigners like the Mormon colonists.[46] In the face of increasing criticism, Díaz announced in 1908 that he would not run for reelection; however, he went back on his word and won the presidency in 1910. A vocal opponent of Díaz, Francisco I. Madero, claimed that Díaz's election was invalid and called for Mexican citizens to rise up in rebellion. Particularly in Chihuahua and other northern states, where

Francisco Madero, courtesy Church History Library

Anthony W. Ivins, courtesy Utah State Historical Society

American land holdings were most extensive, citizens reacted to this call to arms, and revolution began to sweep across the country.[47] Though Mexico had been ravaged by a number of previous revolutions, this war was to escalate into a massive conflict came to be regarded as the Mexican Revolution.[48]

Francisco "Pancho" Villa,[49] Pascual Orozco, and others led the rebellion in the north, where most of the initial fighting took place. The rebel leader with whom the Mormons would deal the most was General José Inés Salazar, who coincidentally had been educated at the Mormons' Juárez Academy.[50] Early on, the Mormon colonies remained largely unaffected by the intermittent skirmishes,[51] and the Saints were confident that the rebellion would die away or be stamped out quickly, as Díaz had fended off opposition countless times before.[52]

As the rebels, known as "red flaggers" or "colorados," clashed with the armies of the Porfirio Díaz regime, the United States government urged American citizens living in Mexico to remain neutral. Church leaders also counseled the Mormon colonists not to take sides. Former Juárez stake president[53] Anthony W. Ivins, who was now an Apostle, admonished the Saints to "remain perfectly neutral; take no part with either side. Solicit judiciously the protection of whatever faction is in power. Explain carefully your position, and strive always to be at peace with them. Accede to their demands in reason, and give or deny with all the wisdom in your possession." He further counseled, "Be humble, seek diligently the help and protection of God. Do this, and though you may lose property and animals, I promise you you will not lose your lives."[54]

Juárez Academy, courtesy Church History Library

By October 1911, Díaz had been unseated and had fled the country, and with his fall the Mormons lost their most powerful supporter. Madero replaced Díaz as president, and in turn Madero's former ally Pascual Orozco defected and raised his own rebel force against Madero, continuing the conflict.[55]

José Inés Salazar, by Otis Aultman, from El Paso Public Library

Revolutionary combat, by Otis Aultman, from El Paso Public Library

As Mexico's political situation deteriorated, so did conditions in the colonies, despite the Mormons' efforts to maintain neutrality. Even though both government officials and rebel leaders alike had promised the colonists that they would not be harassed as long as they avoided taking sides, rebel soldiers began converging on the Mormon settlements, setting up camp, and confiscating food, livestock, and merchandise. At first, rebels issued receipts for the seized supplies and property, promising to pay the Mormons back.[56] But the receipts went unpaid, and soon the rebels began stealing property outright. At one point, rebel General José Inés Salazar offered to reimburse the Mormons for the stolen goods, but the colonists were not willing to receive compensation, fearing that if they accepted payment, they could be perceived as selling supplies to the rebels, thereby breaking their neutrality. "We felt that the only way in which we could maintain a clear course would be to refrain from anything which bore the semblance of aid being rendered to either side," said stake president Junius Romney.[57] Yet maintaining neutrality became increasingly difficult as the war progressed. Soldiers constantly demanded horses, cattle, saddles, food, and other supplies, and they plundered cash and merchandise from businesses and homes.

Joseph T. Bentley, son of Bishop Joseph C. Bentley of Colonia Juárez, said, "I can remember many nights that we went to bed without taking our clothes off because the bandits and the revolutionaries nearly always got into town before daylight. They just walked up to a house and walked right in. If the door was locked, they would just break it down. Many, many mornings before daylight bandits would come. . . . If we were in bed when the bandits came in, they would just take the covers and blankets, then go through the house looking for anything, money, blankets or saddles."[58]

Several events in 1911 and 1912 further strained the fragile relationship between the colonists and the local residents and authorities. During the trial of four Mexicans accused of stealing Mormon property, local citizen Juan Sosa threatened the sitting judge, Jesús José Rodriguez, and the Mormons with death. In response, a group of deputized Mormons attempted to apprehend Sosa outside his home. One of the deputies, Jesse Taylor, recalled that when Sosa saw the men, he "just began calling us everything that a human could think of. . . . And . . . Frank [Lewis] started to crawl through the fence and when he did old Juan just tiptoed and hit him with a shovel just kind of a glancing blow, you know, and just opened up his skull."[59] The blow knocked Lewis unconscious. Thinking that Sosa had critically injured their comrade, and as Sosa lifted his shovel to strike Lewis again, the other deputies were ordered to shoot him, which they did. Fortunately, Lewis was not killed and eventually recovered from his injuries, but the Mormon deputies were later arrested for killing Sosa. The men

Rebels in Juárez, courtesy Church History Library

were eventually set free, but not before permanent damage had been done to the Mexicans' and Mormons' strained relations.[60] "That . . . was the beginning of the end," remembered colonist Hazel Richardson Taylor. "We never had peace after that."[61]

Junius Romney, courtesy Church History Library

During this time, according to H. I. Miller, an El Paso businessman, "Mr. O[rson] P[ratt] Brown, who is looking after the interests of the Mormons, is corresponding with Senetors [*sic*] Smoot and Fall, and Brown is doing everything possible to get intervention and there is hardly a day passes but what a story is started about some depredation occurring, laid to the Rebels, either in the Mormon Colonies or in some other of the State of Chihuahua."[62]

In the atmosphere of heightened animosity and increasing threats, colony leaders decided to attempt to import powerful new firearms from the United States. Although President Madero flatly denied them permission to do so, the colonists smuggled arms in and distributed them among the colonies, "to be used only in cases of emergency."[63]

In 1912, General Salazar commanded stake president Junius Romney to take an inventory of all firearms contained within the colonies, assuring him that the weapons would not be confiscated and that the purpose of the inventory was simply to assist in locating smuggled arms and ammunition.[64] The Mormons complied but for obvious reasons did not include their newly smuggled weapons in the inventory. Not long afterward, another rebel commander demanded that the colonists' firearms be turned over to the insurgents' cause. When Romney appealed to Salazar, the general overrode the order, saying that no such demands were to be made of the colonists—not yet, anyway. Salazar's apparent slip of the tongue alerted Romney to the precarious situation the Saints now faced. It appeared that their firearms—their only means of protection against the frightening depredations they confronted—were safe only temporarily.

Freshman orchestra, courtesy Church History Library

Indeed, the scenario Romney dreaded played out just weeks later. In late July 1912, General Salazar demanded a meeting with Romney. At the meeting, Salazar's "opening shot was to the effect that he had determined to withdraw all guarantees heretofore given the Mormon people and that no longer would he give protection to their lives or property."[65] The general then demanded that the colonists surrender all of their guns and ammunition to the rebel army. Coming from Salazar, a former student of the Juárez Academy, the demand must have caused intensified anger and frustration in Romney.

With six of Salazar's cannons trained on Colonia Dublán, President Romney instructed the residents to surrender their weapons—though they gave up only their old and unreliable arms and secretly kept their best.[66] Though the outdated weapons appeased Salazar at least for the moment, the situation had finally come to a head. Romney and other leaders decided that conditions were perilous enough that the women and children of the colonies should leave the country immediately. Word spread to Juárez and the other colonies that the Dublán colonists were evacuating. The Juárez colonists, who had enjoyed relative peace and were unaware of Salazar's command to surrender weapons, were surprised by the seemingly baseless decision to evacuate. However, when Romney arrived at Juárez and recounted the last few days' events, the colonists voted to flee to the United States.[67] Bishop Joseph C. Bentley of Colonia Juárez, one of a few Mormons who had become naturalized Mexican citizens,[68] was one who opposed the idea of

Joseph C. Bentley, courtesy Joseph Bentley family

evacuating. However, he stated that "if our Stake President's advice is to move women and children to a place of safety, mine will go right along with the others and I'll instruct my ward members to do the same. No matter what private opinions I may maintain, I know that safety lies in obeying the priesthood and I am as always subject to its direction."[69]

John Jacob Walser, from John Jacob Walser, *My Life*, compiled by Bonnie Simon

John Walser, who lived in Colonia Juárez, wrote in early April 1912: "My family are all well, and we feel grateful to God for His great Blessings, and His protection over us. Colonia Juárez looks like a flower garden. The fruit trees all blossoming." However, in his next entry, recorded just months later (July 28, 1912), he wrote, "We were compelled to deliver up our arms to the rebel forces, in consequence of this we sent our wives and children to El Paso."[70] This same abrupt shift in circumstances is described by seventeen-year-old Willard Whipple, who recalled "how fast things were happening, I had played my violin in an orchestra for a dance in the Juárez Stake Academy celebrating the 24th of July," but four days later, the exodus had already begun, and the Saints were beginning to pour into the United States. [71]

Another colonist illustrated the sweeping shift of emotion that accompanied the sudden evacuation. Hyrum Albert Cluff describes the heights of joy felt at a Pioneer Day celebration and the apparent depths of despair experienced at the time of departure: "July twenty-fourth, we held a dance and had quite a good time. July twenty-eighth, we received word to leave our homes. We spent the twenty-ninth packing what few things we could take and cooking. We just walked out and closed the door and left everything."[72]

CHAPTER 3

THE EXODUS

EVACUATION OF THE WOMEN AND CHILDREN

AFTER NEWS OF THE EVACUATION REACHED Colonia Dublán, Bishop Anson B. Call, father of youngster Charles Call instructed his family to pack their bags immediately. When Charles asked his father where they were being evacuated to, his father replied, "I don't know. Maybe Jackson County, Missouri."[73] The implication that Jackson County would be a safer haven than Mexico is telling, since the Mormons had been driven from that place years earlier amid severe persecution, yet they still planned to return one day.

Mormon colonists gathering for departure, courtesy Church History Library

Catherine Aurelia Carling Porter recalled: "The Bishop sent a runner over to our place to tell us to be ready to leave on the next train that would take us to El Paso, Texas. . . . We

Edward Christian Eyring, 1893, image in public domain

Charles McClellan, courtesy Church History Library

Louise Skousen, courtesy Helen Carbine

had to walk out of our home and leave everything we could not pack into two trunks—cows, horses, chickens, all our food and household things."[74] John A. Whetten, who was living in Colonia García at the time, noted, "We were given less than 24 hours. . . . We were only to take clothes and bedding for a short stay. . . . Most everyone worked all night to be ready to make the 30-mile journey in wagons over mountain roads to Pearson, where we would get [the] train for El Paso, Texas. My women washed, ironed, and sewed all night to have clothes ready for the children."[75]

Vaneese Harris Woffinden remembered, "Each family was told to pack one trunk and make a roll of bedding in preparation to leave at a minute's notice."[76] Charles E. McClellan recalled that "words cannot fully describe all that it meant to these people to abandon their homes and all the cherished accumulations bought so dearly with toil and sacrifice through a quarter of a century."[77] The evacuees took few possessions, both because of the suddenness of the evacuation and because they were hopeful that their absence from Mexico would only be temporary and that they would return to their homes once federal troops arrived in the north and established order once again.[78]

Edward Christian Eyring explained, "At the time of leaving we had not the slightest idea we were making a permanent move. The families going out on the train took only a few necessary articles to last for a couple of weeks when we expected we would return." Yet most of the departing colonists would never see their homes again.[79]

For many of the colonists' children, the evacuation was an exciting adventure. Louise Whipple Skousen, nine years old at the time, recalled, "I stayed up all night watching my mother make cookies and pack, and you could only take one trunk and a few bedding. . . . And mama was crying and crying and crying and I was sitting there just tickled to death."[80]

The first leg of the colonists' journey was traveling to the nearest train station—for the Juárez colonists, this was in Pearson, ten miles away. Enos Wood's experience showed that just getting that far could be dangerous. As he escorted his wife, mother, and sister to the depot, two drunken Mexicans stopped Wood and "poked a high powered Mauser rifle into [his] stomach." Wood was able to make friends with the men and go on his way; however, other less-fortunate evacuees were robbed as they tried to make their way to the rail line and head north for the border.[81] Annie O'Donnal recalled that to keep her children calm, the family joined in song as they bid farewell to their home and departed.[82]

LDS men loading the train to help the women and children departing for El Paso, by Otis Aultman, from El Paso Public Library

The *El Paso Herald* noted, "Like the exodus of the Jews from Egypt, or the hegira of the pioneers . . . from Nauvoo to the great Salt Lake Valley, . . . pioneers in another country . . . are streaming into Pearson." The article also observed that "three women gave birth to children while en route from Colonia García to Pearson with the hard, bare boards of the wagon beds for their natal beds."[83]

The women and children of Colonia Chuichupa, the southernmost colony, boarded trains at Chico station. Of the tender farewells that took place at the Chico train station, Bishop George T. Sevey recalled:

> I think that never had I experienced such emotional upheaval as I did during that period of good byes. As I stepped onto the platform of the car and down the aisle, and looked into the faces on either side, and saw the tear dimmed eyes and the grim, bewildered expressions, I suddenly turned all soft inside, and a tight knot rose in my throat that seemed to threaten strangulation. I . . . struggled for composure, and managed somehow to force a smile, which at best was a feeble, g[h]astly grin. As I passed through the cars shaking hands, it suddenly occurred to me that some of those dear eyes that I looked into, I never again would see during this life.
>
> As I stepped down to the ground after the last hand shake, . . . I stood like one in a trance, from which I did not recover until a long poignant wail emerged from the engine[']s steam whistle. . . . I came to with tears rolling down my cheeks. This was indeed embarrassing, I hesitated turning around, but as I stole a peek through the misty environment I could discern that stronger men than I were all but sobbing, all I think wept unashamed.[84]

Jesse M. Taylor recalled that upon arriving at the Pearson station, the colonists found themselves in a "ticklish" situation: revolutionaries on horses were darting horses back and forth along the rail line in an apparent attempt at intimidation.[85] The Mexican Northwestern Railroad had agreed to send as many train cars as possible for use in the evacuation, including boxcars and cattle cars. When the northbound trains began to arrive, women and children

LDS men loading the train to help the women and children departing for El Paso, by Otis Aultman, from El Paso Public Library

colonists, eager to be free of the revolutionaries' presence, packed into whatever space they could find. The few men who accompanied the evacuees for protection rode on top of cattle cars.[86] Men over fifty years and boys under sixteen also departed with the women. All others stayed to guard their homes and property.[87] Many young men, such as Henry Eyring, wished they could stay with the older men rather than depart with the women on the train. At age eleven, Henry felt confident riding a horse and firing a gun.[88]

Camilla Eyring, seventeen years old at the time, recalled: "Our family was in a third-class car with long, hard benches . . . and baggage piled on top of one another. Buggies and wagons were left standing empty at the station. When passenger cars filled up, boxcars and even a few cattle cars were attached. We all suffered intensely . . . in the stifling July heat."[89] Sarah Jones Payne remembered that "suitcases, trunks and bedding were put in first and packed to a depth of four feet. The people found seats as best they could on top of these."[90] One passenger car was so crowded that the conductor had to walk on the seat backs to pass through to the next car. In an attempt to cheer the overheated and anxious passengers, Viva and Ivie Huish played their mandolin and guitar as they traveled toward the border.[91]

"There was considerable anxiety over the possibility of the bridges

Boarding the trains, courtesy Church History Library

being burned ahead of the train," recalled Bishop George Sevey, "as the blowing up of tracks and burning bridges was a sort of set pattern for the [red flaggers]." According to Hazel Richardson Taylor, 'dgers told the Mormons, "'You won't get any farther than the bridge.' They said, 'We will blow that train up. ' But we thought, 'We just as well be blowed up on the bridge as farther down the line. ' So we just all got on the train and came along."[92]

Lagging under the weight of their human cargo, the trains crawled slowly across the barren landscape. Frequent stops at water stations were needed about every twenty-five miles to take on water for the steam engine.[93] The trains were so slow that Willard Whipple, a youth at the time of the exodus, remembered that some of the children passengers, who unlike their exhausted parents had energy to spare, leaped from the sluggish train and ran alongside for a time.[94]

In one car, a young man who wouldn't stay put "stepped into a five gallon can of honey . . . and strung honey all over people, bedding and luggage," greatly adding to the passengers' discomfort.[95] On top of all this, the passengers soon ran out of drinking water and were left parched and miserable.[96]

On July 29, 1912, the front page of the *El Paso Morning Times* announced that five hundred American refugees had crossed the border into El Paso at midnight, with two thousand more expected soon. Traveling on a special train over the Mexico North Western Railroad, the evacuees came in from Pearson and Casas Grandes.[97] Another article in the *El Paso Herald* noted that General Salazar had given "hysterical speeches" in both Pearson and Dublán, letting foreigners know that "their room is preferable to their company." Most took his words as a hint to vacate as soon as possible.[98]

In Salt Lake City, the front page of the *Deseret Evening News* carried the headline "Mormons Flee From Mexico": "Driven from the colonies in western Chihuahua by threats of violence by rebels under Gen Ynez Salazar, 350 American 'Mormon' colonists reached El Paso early today. More than 400 more arrived this afternoon on special trains, and all of the women and children in the colonies will come during the next 24 hours if trains can be secured to bring them. Refugees from the colonies tell of threatening conditions there. All colonists were yesterday deprived of all arms and ammunition by the rebels.

Homes were searched and colonists warned that resistance would result in severe treatment. Stores in the colonies were relieved of all arms, ammunition and supplies."[99]

Two days later, it was reported that the cause of the expulsion of the Saints from the colonies was "not because the colonists are 'Mormons,' but because they are Americans, and because they have valuable property. The blow, the insult is aimed at the United States and not at the Church . . . and the expulsion . . . is to be regarded as a measure of retaliation for the refusal of our government to recognize the insurgents [and to render them aid]."[100]

EVACUATION OF THE MEN

In the meantime, the men returned home, forming "a sad procession, scarcely no one spoke a word on the return trip except to occasionally remark that they were returning to a desolate and lonely spot that only a few days before had been the scene of happy and contented homes filled with women and children."[101] Upon their return, many of the colony's men began gathering at Brig Whipple's confectionary store to pass the lonely hours. "There the idea of a special treat began to blossom. There were eggs, ice and freezers in the shop, there were cows that could be milked . . . and there were willing hands." Soon the men were enjoying fresh ice cream and watermelon, but this would prove to be a short reprieve preceding the trying experiences that soon followed.[102]

The Stairs, by John Edward Wall, courtesy Church History Library

The men received word on August 1 that the women and children had arrived safely in El Paso. George T. Sevey recalls that when the men heard the news, "imagination alone could draw a picture of the vast feeling of relief that swept over us, letting down tension to a point where we could catch a few winks of sleep; the first in over forty hours for most of us."[103]

Even as looters pillaged homes

Camp in Stair Canyon, by John Edward Wall, courtesy Church History Library

and businesses in Dublán, the men in Colonia Juárez temporarily enjoyed peace and hoped that their families would be able to return home soon. However, the situation soon changed dramatically as a detachment of rebel soldiers marched into Juárez and set up camp. The Latter-day Saint men had determined to stay and protect their homes "as long as life was not in absolute danger,"[104] but as it became clear that the rebel troops were not fond of the Mormons, the situation began to appear precarious. As more soldiers moved into town, President Romney called the men of Juárez to meet and discuss the situation. It was decided that they would promptly adhere to the plan of following their families in abandoning the country. Though some differed in their opinions, the men were unified in following the counsel of their ecclesiastical leader. Word of the decision was carried to the other colonies, and the men prepared to leave. They "propped open the chicken house doors, kicked the boards off the pigpens, turned the calves out to suck

Hiding Juárez Stake records, by John Edward Wall, courtesy Church History Library

Breaking camp at Stairs, by John Edward Wall, courtesy Church History Library

their mothers, and let down the pasture bars."[105] Goods were stashed away in hiding places outside of town.[106] All the men were to gather at the Stairs, a rugged area in the mountains about ten miles west of Colonia Juárez.[107] The men from Juárez and Dublán were first to arrive at the Stairs, where they set up camp and carefully buried the Juárez Stake records to keep them safe.[108] Within a few days, the Pacheco and García men arrived, but the García group reported that the Chuichupa men had been detained and were several days behind. The others decided to depart without them.[109] Before beginning their journey, the men were organized into six companies of home guards and nine companies of scouts.[110] They traveled in military formation, with four scouting parties at the front escorting a main column of wagons. This group was followed by the home guard companies, and loose horses and wranglers brought up the rear. The entire caravan formed a mile-and-a-half-long column that moved steadily north toward freedom. The group left the Stairs on August 8 and reached the United States two miles east of Dog Springs, New Mexico, the next evening.[111] As the group approached the United States, they stirred up a column of dust that was spotted by a detachment of about twenty American soldiers who were guarding the border against marauding Mexicans. Suspecting the Mormons to be Mexican belligerents, the American commander had his soldiers hide behind rock walls and observe the approaching group. "Having crossed the border . . . , the colonists felt greatly relieved, abandoned their military order of march and their discipline and marched straight toward the muzzles of the waiting soldiers. Just as the officer was to issue the command to open fire, one of the soldiers recognized Ammon M. Tenney Jr., one of the colonists, and shouted that the approaching men were Americans. Having been reprieved from death by a shout, the men were welcomed by the soldiers and pitched camp a short distance further inside the United States."[112] By August 11, the men had joined their families in El Paso.

In the meantime, the Chuichupa group were also advancing toward the border. Days earlier, having word that they were to evacuate, they began making preparations to depart. Local businessman Sam Brown divided goods from his local store among the men, with the understanding that he would be repaid for the supplies at a future date. All the horses in the colony were gathered so that each man had a mount.[113]

Before setting out for the rendezvous point at the Stairs, the Chuichupa men stopped momentarily just outside of town. George Sevey recalled, "I with two or three others stopped at the point of Temple Hill where we could see clearly all that went on within the valley. Supplied with a powerful pair of binoculars we were able to pin point all that went on. We had hardly gotten located when the Reds began stringing into the valley along the regular wagon road. They took lodging in the most prosperous looking houses. Shots were heard, which we learned later were aimed against hogs, beef and poultry."[114]

Commissary and packers, by John Edward Wall, courtesy Church History Library

Breaking camp in Tapicita, by John Edward Wall, courtesy Church History Library

Wagons to Hachita, by John Edward Wall, courtesy Church History Library

When the Chuichupa men arrived at the Stairs, they found it abandoned. Sevey recalled that the group "walked through the deserted camp grounds and saw the litter of camp garbage lying around, noted the heaps of dead ashes, quarters of beef hanging from limbs in the trees. One pitifully lonely dog crouched under a tree; some discarded cans of fruit and other parcels of food stuff was in evidence. Evidently, the move from camp had been a hurried one, and we wondered what were the circumstances that

Entering the United States, by John Edward Wall, courtesy Church History Library

precipitated the flight." The men had no choice but to continue northward alone. The group traveled in military fashion, with a lead and rear guard and companies of ten headed by captains.[115] The advance guard bore a large white flag.[116] In hopes of remaining undetected by militants and bandits, the company refrained from lighting fires, posted guards after nightfall, and moved as quickly as possible during the day.[117] Notwithstanding their precautions, on August 10 the Chuichupa group were spotted by a detachment of federal troops and were soon surrounded. The Mormons explained their situation and to their great relief were allowed to continue.[118] The next day, two days behind the main group, the Chuichupa men crossed the border and continued on to Hachita, New Mexico.[119] From there they took the train to meet their wives and children in El Paso.[120]

EVACUATION OF COLONIA DÍAZ

The story of the evacuation of Colonia Díaz follows a somewhat different course than that of the other colonies. The colonists of Díaz were already on edge when the schoolhouse bell pealed out an urgent alarm during the dark morning hours of July 28, calling for an immediate gathering. "When the people heard the bell they knew something must be wrong," remembered resident Maude T. Schofield.[121] At the meeting, it was announced that stake president Junius Romney had directed that the colonies' women and children depart for the United

States as soon as possible. Díaz was about twenty miles from the New Mexico border, and men, women, and children abandoned the colony together on horseback and in wagons and buggies. The group arrived in "the Corner," New Mexico, that night, and proceeded to Dog Springs, New Mexico, the next day. After a week in Dog Springs, they moved on to Hachita, New Mexico, where they set up camp with one hundred government-issued tents and other equipment.[122] Maude T. Schofield, who was fifteen at the time, remembered that "one of the most unpleasant things about [the camp] was we had no real milk, we had to drink condensed milk. . . . I think everyone in the camp contracted diarrhea, which had its effect on our already low morale."[123]

With the Church's assistance, the Díaz colonists were gradually able to leave Hachita to put down roots in other places. Maude Schofield, along with her mother and siblings, moved to Utah for a time until her father found a home in Columbus, New Mexico. While the family was in Columbus, Maude's father obtained a permit from General José Inés Salazar to return to Colonia Díaz to collect some of the furniture the family had abandoned. He found that the home was now occupied by natives who refused to allow him to take the furniture until they were shown the permit from Salazar. "Still quite reluctantly [they] gave him permission to take a few things," Maude remembered.[124]

Hachita, by John Edward Wall, courtesy Church History Library

CHAPTER 4

Relief in El Paso

FOR THE MAIN GROUP OF MORMON EVACUEES—men, women, and children—the immediate destination was El Paso, Texas.[125] Eyewitness Orson Pratt Brown, who had been assigned to assist the incoming immigrants, said, "I have never witnessed such heart rending scenes, as with the anxiety of women and children who left their husbands and fathers behind to look after the cattle and property."[126] The August 1, 1912, *El Paso Morning Times* described the pathetic sight of Mormon women and children arriving at the local train depot: "The scene in the Union Station . . . as the train pulled in was a pitiful one. Children of all sizes and ages streamed from the coaches, tugging at the skirts of their mothers and looking in wild-eyed surprise at the evidences of the city about them."[127]

Orson Pratt Brown, 1914, image in public domain

With the city's inhabitants estimated at about forty-one thousand at this time, the Mormon refugees would swell the population to capacity as thousands crossed the border.[128]

EL PASO CITY ADMINISTRATION AND CITIZENS

To the colonists' relief, the citizens of El Paso had come to meet them, eager to render relief and assistance. Twenty-six refugees would be housed in the home of Church member Arwell L. Pierce,[129] while the *El Paso Morning Times* noted that Church leader Anthony Ivins sent out agents all night to find lodging for the refugees and that one hundred fifty of these Mormons were "quartered in private homes."[130] Five families were taken into a small house by a compassionate *El Paso Herald* employee. A former *Herald* newspaper carrier was also found among this party. Others would be sheltered in the local Odd Fellows Hall or other temporary lodging; however, the majority were transported to the nearby Long lumberyard.[131] "As fast as the colonists gathered in the [train] station lobby, the San Antonio street auto stand drove up to the side entrance of the building where the refugees were driven out to the lumber yard. . . . All the automobiles are furnished free of charge by the drivers."[132] Other El Pasoans "met them with carriages, buggies, whitetops, and autos, and unloaded everything from the train onto these vehicles and took the lot of them over to the Odd Fellows hall. . . . Then the kind people had brought them over unloaded those bundles. . . . Some thoughtful folks from town brought galvanized tubs with water and ice in them, because it was so dreadfully hot."[133] Lucille R. Taylor recalled, "The El Paso people were very kind. They provided water and food and everything we needed because we had taken very little."[134]

El Paso train depot, by Otis Aultman, from El Paso Public Library

El Paso Union Depot, from Union Depot

Immediately upon their arrival, some pregnant women were whisked off to a hospital, where they delivered healthy babies.[135] The refugees "felt like the people were just angels."[136]

At the lumberyard, located two miles outside of town, the refugees were treated to a "plentiful supper" that evening.[137] But notwithstanding the locals' hospitality, the conditions at the lumberyard were uncomfortable at best. Camilla Eyring described the "improvised shelter" as being a "corral with dust a foot deep, flies swarming, noisy, stinking, and crowded with a mass of humanity. It was enough to make the stoutest heart sink. Those in charge tried to arrange a stall for each family, and we piled in for the night, hanging up blankets in an attempt at a little privacy."[138] Upon the evacuees' arrival, local workers began installing a roof on the lumberyard. "We were so worn out we lay on our mattresses and slept all afternoon the first day while Texas men sawed and hammered over our heads," remembered Walter Frederick Hurst."[139]

Maude Cluff Farnsworth recalled that inquisitive local citizens soon began gathering, peeking through cracks in the yard's fence to get a glimpse of the Mormons packed in like "wild animals."[140] Vaneese Harris Woffinden said, "I felt as if I were a circus animal on parade and . . . shut behind the bars of a cage."[141] However, as the *Deseret Evening News* explained, "to the credit of the El Pasoans and others active in the relief work, it must be said that everything possible is being done for the refugees."[142]

Some refugees, like Lily O'Donnell Whetten, had small babies who required extra attention. Infants were particularly susceptible to the mosquitoes that invaded the lumberyard in swarms. The mosquitoes were so bad that mothers were willing to try anything to keep them away. Whetten's mother-in-law speculated that kerosene might ward off the insects, so desperate mothers smeared their baby's faces, arms, and other exposed skin with kerosene, which apparently brought relief.[143]

The refugees' food, provided by the government and local citizens, consisted mostly of bread, milk, cereals, and canned goods.[144] The refugees took turns preparing meals for the entire group, cooking food in a six-gallon lard can over an open fire.[145] Later, after some locals brought in a stove along with some meat and vegetables, "the women within the enclosure cooked hugh [*sic*] pots of stew where each refugee might come and receive hot food."[146] Hazel Richardson Taylor recalled, "I shall always be grateful for the good old USA. They really did take care of us—they fed us, they housed us, they paid our doctor bills. . . . They gave our men employment. Morning after morning they brought truckloads of good food. Otherwise we would have suffered to no end."[147]

"Soon after our camping in the lumber sheds we had a heavy rain and the yard became a mud puddle, making it very unpleasant for several days," remembered William Morley Black.[148] Some elderly Saints like Black had taken part in the Nauvoo exodus over sixty-five years earlier,[149] although at their advanced age, the exodus from Mexico in some instances exacted a heavier toll. For example, one elderly refugee, Byron Harvey Allred Sr., made a trip to town to purchase a much-needed tub and washboard, but upon his return he died of a heart attack.[150] Allred was thus described as being "the first martyr to the Mexican exodus."[151]

As the weeks drew on, newspapers in El Paso and Utah chronicled the plight of the Mormon evacuees. In Utah, the *Deseret Evening News* reported on July 30, 1912, in a front-page article titled "Refugees Are Fleeing North," that "the majority of the refugees are being housed under sheds in an abandoned lumber yard, although many have been taken care of in hotels and rooming houses." Culling from the Associated Press, this same article observed, "The city has put in water

Henry Eyring Bowman, courtesy Church History Library

sewerage and lights and the Mormon Church is furnishing food to those unable to buy it. Many of the refugees are without clothing or utensils for cooking, but these are rapidly being provided and they are being made as comfortable as possible."[152]

The same day, the *El Paso Morning Times* reported on a meeting in the Chamber of Commerce in which El Paso businessmen were told of the terrible plight of the fleeing Mormons by one of the refugees, Henry Eyring Bowman, "as tears coursed down his bronzed face." After hearing a portion of this report, Walter S. Clayton, president of the local chamber of commerce, asked local businessmen "to devise ways and means to care for the families of the American settlers . . . who are being driven from their homes. . . . The call was responded to by a large number of the leading men of this city."[153]

The article also noted that Clayton assigned a committee to work with Bowman, "who had delivered the most stirring, heart compelling, yet simple story of human outrage ever heard within the walls of the El Paso Chamber of Commerce." Further, county judge A. S. J. Eylar[154]

El Paso Chamber of Commerce exterior (left) and ambulance (above), by Otis Aultman, from El Paso Public Library

Long's Lumberyard, by Otis Aultman, from El Paso Public Library

and Mayor Charles E. Kelly "instructed both the city and the county physicians to care for any of the refugees that might need medical aid. They had arranged that all refugees now in the city would be housed at Magoffin Avenue and the Texas Pacific crossing and orders were issued to see that sanitary arrangements were made there at once."[155]

According to the same report, at Long's abandoned lumberyard, "everything was rushed to these temporary quarters, . . . and the refugees were told that they would oblige the people of El Paso, if they would make out a list of what they wanted—nothing would be lacking. Tears coursed down the cheeks of the women and children at the hospitality extended to them." Finally, Mayor C. E. Kelly remarked, "As the city's chief executive I did what I could. What I did as a citizen I refuse to permit you to mention. These people are El Paso's guests and it is our pleasure and our duty to take care of them."[156]

Evidence reveals that the El Paso citizens went the extra mile to take care of both Mormon adults and children as their special guests. For example, the *El Paso Herald* ran an article stating, "Books and magazines are greatly desired at the camp of the Mormon refugees in the Long lumber yard, and any contributions of such reading material will be greatly appreciated. The refugees have no occupation and a great deal of time on their hands, and books will fill a great want."[157] Further, the *El Paso Morning Times* reported that the Latter-day Saint children were given free tickets to Saturday movies at the Unique Theater.[158] Melissa Sargent also recalled that during this same time,

Mayor C. E. Kelly, courtesy El Paso Municipal Clerk's Office

"a gentleman came with a buggy, [and] took children for rides around the city of El Paso, took them to see the alligators in San Jacinto Plaza."[159]

Unique Theater, by Otis Aultman, from El Paso Public Library

Back in Utah, in another report, the *Deseret News* again described the turbulent events for the refugees: "While their homes are being looted, their fields and crops devastated, and their cattle stolen and killed, [they] . . . are fleeing for safety . . . and are being huddled in quarters in this city [El Paso] with scanty provisions and only few comforts. To the credit of the El Pasoans and others active in the relief work, it must be said that everything possible is being done for the refugees."[160]

William Morley Black remarked, "I feel thankful to our government and to President William H. Taft for the prompt appropriation of the magnificent sum of one hundred thousand dollars to be used in giving aid to the American citizens who were expelled from Mexico."[161] Funds were used for food, which was distributed at the Long lumberyard, while Church officials from the northern Mexico region established temporary offices in El Paso's American National Bank building to oversee the needs of the refugees.[162]

Much of the Saints' assistance had been arranged by LDS Church leader Anthony W. Ivins, who had been responsible from the beginning in arranging provisions, temporary lodging, and rail transportation into and later out of El Paso.[163] Ivins had served a mission to Mexico (1882–84) and had been called by Wilford Woodruff to serve as the stake president of the Colonia Juárez Stake, the first stake in Mexico (1895–1907). During those years he also served as the general manager and vice president of the Mexican Colonization and Agricultural Company. At the time of the Mormon exodus in the summer of 1912, he was a member of the Quorum of the Twelve Apostles and continued to have some responsibility in overseeing the Church throughout the colonies in Mexico.[164]

FORT BLISS AND MILITARY AID

Fort Bliss, located just five miles northeast of downtown El Paso,[165] played an important part in the relief effort for the displaced colonists. At the beginning of the Mexican Revolution in 1910, Fort Bliss was a small, four-company post, a single link in a chain of American military posts near the Mexican border.[166] However, as fighting in northern Mexico spilled across the Rio Grande into the United States, Fort Bliss began to play an important role in local, regional, and even national security for the first time. The fort expanded into a major cavalry post as it was suddenly thrust into national prominence.[167]

Mormon colonists in lumberyard, courtesy Church History Library

Brigadier General Edgar Z. Steever, courtesy Library of Congress

Fort Bliss barracks, by Otis Aultman, from El Paso Public Library

During the revolution, Fort Bliss served several important strategic and logistical functions. The fort served as base camp for patrol operations, monitored the flow of weapons into Mexico, detained Mexican prisoners of war, acted as supply point for troops throughout the southwest, and received Mexican and American refugees from across the border.[168] As soon as the Mormon refugees crossed into the United States, officers at Fort Bliss, particularly Brigadier General Edgar Z. Steever, began coordinating aid.[169] On July 30, as the initial one thousand refugees entered El Paso, Steever telegraphed the War Department in Washington, DC, saying that "if Government desires them sheltered, tentage should be rushed here from nearest Depot and authority for expense incident to water sewerage, sanitary, etc. authorized."[170]

Soldiers from Fort Bliss were posted at the gates of Long's lumberyard to guard the refugees and help ensure privacy.[171] Church officials petitioned Steever for aid, and he secured one thousand dollars from the adjutant general's office in Washington, DC, to install plumbing and sewerage facilities at the lumberyard and the tent city being installed east of town.[172] In addition, the Fort Bliss 22nd Infantry Band, led by C. F. Waddington, played for the refugees at benefits held at Cleveland Square in downtown El Paso.[173]

Fort Bliss 22nd Infantry Band, courtesy University of Texas–El Paso Special Collections

The *El Paso Morning Times* reported that in addition to the Long lumberyard and another building, a third location had been set up to house refugees—a tent city located near the El Paso foundry.[174] For the tent city, five hundred class "A" military tents—enough to house fifteen hundred people—were transported to Fort Bliss, and soldiers from Fort Bliss helped set up the tents and other camp equipment.[175] Government-issued tents were also shipped to Hachita, New Mexico, for the Díaz colonists and to Thatcher, Arizona, for colonists from the state of Sonora.[176] The tents were none too spacious; despite their class "A" designation by the War Department, the

Tent city, courtesy Church History Library

Mormon woman in tent city, courtesy Church History Library

Refugee camp, courtesy Church History Library

Rowley family, courtesy Church History Library

soldiers referred to them as "dog" tents.[177]

General Steever received an additional three thousand dollars from the War Department to purchase rations, which were to be "simple and inexpensive."[178] By August 6, Steever had to request additional government funds.[179] Later, twenty thousand dollars was appropriated from the Mississippi Flood fund,[180] and on August 12, a bill was passed by Congress that provided one hundred thousand dollars to feed the refugees and pay for their transportation to other locales in the United States.[181]

Myrl Rowley Day, a young girl at the time of the exodus, remembers being thrilled about a shower the army installed for the refugees, though it took some getting used to. It was built on a wooden dock jutting out over the Rio Grande, and gaps between the boards allowed water to drain into the river. "The shower itself was in a tin can with nail holes in it," Day remembered. "I had never seen a shower before so we thought that was great. We had always taken a bath in a washtub before that. There were cracks all over, and we could see the river water under us. . . . I was scared and afraid I was going to fall through into the river. We could see dead dogs floating down the river."[182]

THE CHURCH RELIEF COMMITTEE

Shortly after the exodus from Mexico began, a Church relief committee was established in El Paso with Henry E. Bowman as chairman. Other committee members included Guy C. Wilson, Orson Pratt Brown, and Joseph E. Robinson, who was then serving as the president of the California Mission.[183] President Robinson, along with O. P. Miller of the Presiding Bishopric, had been sent by Church President Joseph F. Smith to assist Elder Ivins in administering relief to the Mormon refugees.[184] Upon his arrival in El Paso, Robinson wrote a report to President Smith: "The strained, frightened look in the eyes of the children, the haggard faces of the women and the gaunt-silent men, all called up vivid memories the aftermath of the quake and fire at San Francisco [in 1906]. . . . It wrings my heart to see them in such a hapless condition, yet it thrills me with pride to note the devotion to God, their unbounded faith and good cheer."[185] The arrival of Robinson and Miller must have been a boon to Elder Ivins, who had fallen ill under the weight of his responsibilities.[186]

American National Bank, by Otis Aultman, from El Paso Public Library

The relief committee met often at their headquarters established in the American National Bank building in El Paso to evaluate the situations both of the refugees in the United States and the few colonists who chose to stay in Mexico.[187] In its first meeting, the committee resolved that "all those [refugees] who were indigent, aged and in ill health, or those who desire to go to Utah or other remote points, to be sent away at once; whilst those who desire to return to the Colonies should be encouraged to remain here or in the immediate vicinity and not get too far away."[188]

Another order of business the committee attended to during that meeting was to draft "a card of appreciation for the help so generously tendered by the Auto Club, Transfer Companies, and people of El Paso," which was "ordered printed in two daily newspapers."[189] The next morning, the *El Paso Morning Times* carried the notice, titled "Colonists Express Their Thanks to Citizens" and signed by Anthony W. Ivins and four other committee members:

> To the Times: In our own behalf and in behalf of the many refugees from the colonies of Chihuahua, who are now in El Paso, permit us to express, through the column of your paper, our appreciation, and the deep gratitude we feel, for the spontaneous and universal expression of

> sympathy, and the ready assistance, which has been rendered in this hour of trial and distress.
>
> The city and county officials, businessmen and people have responded as Americans are wont to respond when danger threatens, or calamity comes to human kind.
>
> To the military department, who have desired to do more than discipline would permit, we are grateful.
>
> We are especially grateful to the Mexico North Western Railroad, whose representative[s] have been untiring in their efforts to transport our people from the danger zone to this city of refuge.
>
> We thank the transfer companies for the service rendered, and desire particularly to express our gratitude to the owners of automobiles who rendered such valuable assistance in carrying our people, without charge, from the Union depot to the places assigned to them.
>
> May He who rewards all men according to their works do unto you and yours as you have done unto us.[190]

As the initial evacuation came to an end and the Saints were safe and settled, the relief committee had time to reflect on the recent events. The committee was aware that many within and without the Church had expressed personal opinions about the decision to leave Mexico. According to Elder Ivins, "The matter had been discussed in the papers, pro and con, as well as on the street corners by our own people and strangers and that the action of the leading Brethren in the Stake in bringing the people out had been questioned and designated by many, as unwise." The committee determined to examine all available facts and thoroughly evaluate the decision to evacuate Mexico.

Accordingly, the committee reviewed in subsequent meetings the climate in Mexico that had precipitated the evacuation and also appraised feelings and opinions of the evacuees.[191] On the matter of the colonists' attitudes at the time of the exodus, President Romney remembered that "some showed bitterness, others were sad. The attitude was not uniform."[192]

Committee members' opinions about the decision to leave were likewise divided. After much discussion, on August 14, the committee drafted the following resolution:

> RESOLVED:—That it is the sense of this meeting of representative from the Mormon Colonies in the State of Chihuahua, Mexico, that the abandonment of the Colonies from which we come was the only

> course that could have been pursued to have avoided open war with the rebel forces, which are in full control of the section of country where the colonies are located.
>
> That it was the manifest intention of General Inez Salazar and other rebel officers to force intervention by the United States, by attacking the "Mormon Colonies" and that, in our opinion, there was no means by which a conflict could have been avoided except that adopted.
>
> We, therefore, endorse the policy which has been pursued on the abandonment of the colonies and in bringing the people to the United States for safety.[193]

Still, some committee members felt that the colonists ought to be free to return to their homes in Mexico. To that end an agreement was made with the Mexico North Western Railway to give half-price tickets to Mormons to return to the colonies.[194]

Several displaced colonists made visits to Mexico to evaluate the conditions there, and the committee paid close attention to the reports they provided. However, these accounts conflicted greatly and did little to help the committee choose a course of action. For example, while Miles A. Romney wrote from the colonies that things were in order and he felt it was safe for the Mormons to return,[195] others reported that the colonies had been ransacked and were not safe.[196]

Bishop Albert D. Thurber of Dublán even reported that an American "who had been a prisoner with the rebels for five days, had claimed that the rebels were very much disappointed through the Mormons coming out as they did, and thus thwarting a deeply laid plot against the Mormon people, and the rebels threaten to get vengeance."[197]

The relief committee also followed a disturbing story that they pieced together from reports trickling in from Colonia Pacheco. The Stevens family was one Mormon family who declined to evacuate with the other colonists, and then experienced a tragedy soon after the other colonists had left for the United States.[198] While they were out picking berries, two daughters of the Stevens family spotted an armed duo of local Mexicans who were apparently trying to stay hidden. When the girls alerted their father and he confronted the trespassers, a struggle ensued that left the two Mexicans and Brother Stevens dead.[199] This and other reports from the colonies served to convince the relief committee that the country was not a safe place for the colonists to be.

On September 5, the committee reported that "after reviewing conditions in detail in the Colonies, Pres. Romney declared emphatically that it is not safe for families to go yet into the colonies or to be there."[200] Yet despite this declaration, dissention still marred committee meetings. On September 22, the committee held a special meeting. "The purpose of the meeting was to come together in fasting and prayer to seek earnestly the Lord to know his will, to know whether the attitude of the Committee in the past has been wrong, with a determination to change our attitude if the Lord will manifest that we have been wrong; or to continue our stand if the Lord inspires us to con[t] inue to do so."[201]

After kneeling together in prayer, members of the committee took turns expressing their opinions on the matter, with the vast majority supporting the decision to stay out of Mexico.[202] Later, the refugees at the lumberyard held their own fast and testimony meeting where branch president Hyrum S. Harris read a letter in which the First Presidency noted that they completely sustained the counsel given to the people by President Romney to evacuate Mexico.[203]

SOME REMAINED IN EL PASO

As the colonists began to realize that their absence from Mexico was to be extended or perhaps permanent, many started making plans to make a new start in El Paso or elsewhere in the United States. On August 2, 1912, even before the last of the colonists had exited Mexico, the *Deseret Evening News* reported that the "western railroads have granted a rate of one cent per mile to colonists who want to leave for places of refuge and safety in the United States. Two hundred women and children will leave tonight for the Gila valley. Many others have left, or are preparing to leave for Utah, Arizona, and other points."[204] On the other hand,

Camilla Eyring, from *A Biography of Camilla Eyring Kimball*, by Caroline Eyring Miner and Edward L. Kimball

some colonists returned to Mexico within a few weeks. On September 11 a trainload of Mormons crossed the border back into Mexico.[205]

While some Mormons left El Paso almost immediately, others made more permanent arrangements in the town. The *El Paso Times* dated August 2, 1912, reported that the realty company of Juan B. Creel was doing "a good business in real estate among the local refugees. Mr. Creel reports that he has just made two rooming house deals which amounted to $1300 and has rented eighteen houses during the last week. The firm has also found accommodations in the city for more than sixty refugee families."[206]

Camilla Eyring's mother, Caroline Cottam Romney Eyring, got straight to work finding for her family a home that was more suitable than the lumberyard. "She was expecting her ninth child in a few months. She finally took one room in a small hotel for the fourteen of us. . . . We stayed there about a week. We then moved to a tenement way down on Talles Street near the Rio Grande."[207] Camilla got a job as a maid for a well-to-do family in town. "I was the first-floor maid, with a white cap and apron. . . . For my services I earned four dollars a week—and was very proud of the earnings."[208] But just weeks later, Camilla moved to Provo, Utah, where she completed high school while living with her uncle.

Lucille R. Taylor recalled finding temporary El Paso lodging in a local neighborhood known as Highland Park: "Some of the people who were fortunate enough left that lumber yard and went to a hotel . . . and stayed that [first] night. . . . Father got a house the next day in El Paso for our two families. . . . There was nothing in it. We had our bedding, and we slept on the floor."[209]

Henry Eyring Bowman and his family lingered at El Paso for four years with the hope that they would be allowed to return to Mexico when conditions improved. The family, who had always enjoyed playing basketball, formed the Bowman Brothers team and established a reputation in the area, eventually winning a regional YMCA tournament.[210]

David Brigham Brown and his family erected a livery stable in El Paso and later rented a five-hundred-acre farm in the Rio Grande Valley before finally returning to Colonia Chuichupa.[211] Calvert Lorenzo Allred stayed in El Paso and found employment building roads.[212] Brigham Young Whipple got a job and rented a house for his family. They sublet part of the home and also took boarders to supplement their income.[213] Teenager Willard Whipple found employment as a stock boy at a local department store called the White House.[214]

According to Richard Turley, "The reason my grandfather [Edward Vernon Turley] remained in El Paso for virtually the rest of his life was because he had a warm welcome there and was able to find employment and contribute to the economy himself. My father subsequently was born and raised in El Paso and I spent time in El Paso as a child. So we have fond feelings towards the people of El Paso and the way they greeted the Latter-day Saints when they were driven from Northern Mexico."[215]

Eventually Church President Joseph F. Smith formally released the displaced Saints from their church assignments in the colonies. In the October 1912 general conference, President Smith directed that they get a fresh start and relocate wherever they desired. During his address, President Smith summarized the experiences of the colonists for the benefit of the whole Church:

> We have had some very sad experiences of late,—a large number of our colonists in Mexico have had serious cause for the exercise of faith, patience, forbearance, hope and charity this year; and many of them, I have no doubt, have found it difficult under circumstances which prevail around them to see how the hand of the Lord could ever be made manifest for their good. They have been robbed, plundered and driven from their homes, their rights have been denied them, their property taken away from them, the safety of their wives and daughters jeopardized and their lives threatened, and at last they found it necessary to abandon their homes and possessions, and come away from that land of riot and murder, brigandage and robbery in order that they might escape at least with their lives; and quite a few have not been fortunate enough to get away with their lives, but have fallen by the hands of marauders and assassins.[216]

Joseph F. Smith, courtesy Church History Library

To the evacuated colonists, President Smith said, "You have proven your worth, your intelligence, that you are men and women of high standing among men. You have been patient and forbearing; and when you have had to suffer indignities, you have taken it patiently; when you have been smitten you have not smitten again; when your brethren have been shot down in cold blood you have restrained your passion, you have withheld your wrath, and you have exercised your patience and have been willing to leave these things in the hands of God."[217]

President Smith further noted, "I could not advise our people going back to Mexico. . . . Indeed, I would advise them not to go back, if I should give advice at all to them, but we wish our brethren to feel at liberty to do just what they feel in their hearts will be for their best good."[218] Though President Smith said he could not foresee whether Mormons would venture back into the Mexican colonies, he believed the time would come when conditions would improve and possibly allow for a return. In the meantime, many displaced colonists attempted to claim redress from the Mexican government for their loss of goods and property, and some small payments were indeed made. However, the Mormons received little compensation for their losses, which were estimated at seven to eight million dollars.[219]

EPILOGUE

THE MORMON EXODUS FROM MEXICO IN 1912 was a costly venture in terms of lost homes, property, and goods, not to mention the heavy emotional toll exacted of the evacuees. However, in other ways the exodus had invaluable consequences. The demanding transition served to strengthen the character of the Latter-day Saints who had dwelt in the Mexican colonies for decades.

El Paso chapel dedication, 1931, courtesy Utah State Historical Society

Descendants of the more than four thousand Church members who migrated back into the United States have blossomed into hundreds of thousands of faithful Saints who have left their mark on both the LDS Church and many communities throughout America. For example, George W. Romney, who was five years old at the time of the exodus, later became governor of the state of Michigan; his son Mitt won the Republican Party nomination for the 2012 U.S. presidential election. Further, President Henry B. Eyring, descendant of the Eyring family who lived in the colonies, now serves in the First Presidency of The Church of Jesus Christ of Latter-day Saints. Many other Church leaders and community servants could be mentioned as being descendants of the Mormon colonists in Mexico.

Of the Mormon experience in Mexico, Latter-day Saint Mexican historian Fernando Gomez observed:

> The Mexican colonies were really very useful to the Republic in later years, even though it was very slow in getting started. There were several [LDS Church] branches here and there in the Republic, but as time went on, there are hundreds of people, men that have served the Lord throughout the world in different positions in their calling, priesthood callings that they have received. Today, there are now twenty-five missions in Mexico. There are two hundred and twenty-two stakes in Mexico. There are twelve operating temples and one under construction, and over one million members today in the Republic. So the value of the initial colonies going into Mexico was not only the economic welfare but the spiritual blessing that has been generated for now decades. [220]

Looking back at the Mormon exodus from the Mexican colonies decades later, the *El Paso Herald* reported that about two hundred of the Mormon refugees had permanently settled in El Paso. By the spring of 1931, a beautiful Latter-day Saint chapel had been erected on Douglas Street, designed with Spanish Colonial architecture. [221] Local Latter-day Saint historian Mike Mullen related that "after [the Mormons] had been [in El Paso] for twenty years, they built this beautiful chapel. Actually my grandfather, great-grandfather, and my other grandfather's cousin were all members of the building committee that built this chapel. I've had five generations of my family that have attended church here in this meetinghouse."[222]

President Henry B. Eyring, courtesy Martin L. Anderson

Karl Murphy, currently a stake president of one of the two Latter-day Saint stakes in El Paso, stated, "As I think about the exodus of the Saints in 1912 until today, the Church has almost doubled in size. We have around nine thousand members in both stakes that are here, spread throughout the city of El Paso, and our members are ingrained in the community. Whether it be in the military or whether it be in the large businesses here in El Paso, or even in the school districts, and so we feel as welcome today as I'm sure the Saints did in 1912."[223]

Reflecting upon the great service rendered by El Paso a century ago, President Henry B. Eyring, a member of the First Presidency of The Church of Jesus Christ of Latter-day Saints and a descendant of the Mormon colonists, said:

> On behalf of the many people who descend from these 1912 refugees, may I express my own profound thanks to your parents and grandparents, the noble and great citizens of El Paso. What they did for our people was gracious, kind, and benevolent. A century ago, Latter-day Saint members of the El Paso Relief Committee expressed their thankfulness in an article prepared for the *El Paso Times*. They wrote, "Permit us to express . . . our appreciation, and the deep gratitude we feel, for the spontaneous and universal expression of sympathy, and the ready assistance, which has been rendered in this hour of trial and distress." Along with this Relief Committee, I too say, "May He who regards all people according to their works do unto you and yours as you have done unto us." Thank you to the people of El Paso for all that was done. It is not forgotten, nor will it ever be. [224]

INTERVIEWS

Regarding the Mormon Exodus from the Mexican Colonies in 1912

LORNA CALL ALDER

RESIDENT OF COLONIA DUBLÁN IN 1912
PROVO, UTAH, JULY 29, 2012

GROWING UP IN DUBLÁN WAS A HAPPY THING, recalled 106-year-old Lorna Call Alder, and she is still full of joy. "I wake up every morning glad I am alive," she said during an interview conducted exactly one hundred years from the day the Mormons left the colonies and entered El Paso. She remembered pitching horseshoes and watching dances, such as the Virginia Reel, in her Mormon community. She also recalled several songs that were sung and she even sang a few. Her father, Anson B. Call, was the bishop of Dublán, and "he was a bishop supreme," said Lorna. She was the daughter of Julia Abegg Call, one of Anson's wives.

"I was born May 28, 1906, in Colonia Dublán. . . . We had to herd cows and take care of chickens. We had two corn cribs we had to work on and build. . . . We used to play in the corn cribs. . . . It was quite an interesting childhood. I was happy doing the work." Lorna also mentioned that part of her work as a little girl was "tending the babies." She remembered, "We also had prayer in the morning, and we held hands in a circle while the prayer was being said." Lorna further noted that their Mormon family (Bishop Anson B. Call and his wife Julia) "were separated" from the Mexicans while living in Dublán.

Her family had to leave Mexico because they "wanted to keep away from the rebels, and Pancho Villa . . . Salazar." Yet she added that their Juárez stake president, Junius Romney, "was a man we all looked up to, a leader, a divine guider." Of the image taken of her soon before she would leave Dublán with her mother and younger sisters, she said, "I used to hold still while they braided my hair. . . . I was always glad when they were done."

Lorna Call Alder, age 6, courtesy Francis Call Alder

Lorna and her family took the train from a place called "The Station," which was just south of Dublán. "The passenger car was full. . . . Several of us got on the train. . . . The passenger car was loaded, and we had to sit in the freight car, and I was afraid my feet would get hurt because the train was going too swift." It was the first time she had ever been on a train, and she sat in a boxcar, because, she said, "at Pearson, they filled the cars up before they got to us." She explained, "We had to stop to get water . . . real often," and the train went slow. "As a little girl, I used wish they would not stop but keep going. . . . Some of the big boys would hold on and run with the train, being careful not to stub their toes."

Her father and the men stayed behind to take care of homes and property. "We left the house . . . in charge of Mexicans to take care of the pigs and chickens and things like that. . . . We said to Father, 'Come and go with us,' but he said, 'I can't, I have things to take care of here.'"

Reflecting on her arrival at the El Paso Union Station, she said, "I remember as if I were there today how we arrived, how we picked up chips—pieces of wood—if we needed a fire to keep warm." Concerning Long's lumberyard, east of El Paso, she said, "I can see the place where we stayed. . . . There was not a place to sleep. They pulled a blind to separate us from the other families. . . . A drape separated us from some of the other people. We knew they were there, but we had a little privacy."

People came to Long's lumberyard with food, but "it was hard to chew the hard tack." The children played down by the Rio Grande River; and the children used to "pick up rocks and hit targets." Lorna and her family were not long at the lumberyard. Soon they went to Bountiful, Utah, then only later returned to Colonia Dublán.

When asked if she would like to say anything else at the conclusion of the interview, with a twinkle in her eye, Lorna began to sing: "Way down in Mexico, there lives a people they call the Mormons, you'll learn to love, I know. You say they labor, for home and neighbor, . . . working for the cause they love."

ELIAS BONILLA

CO-CHAIR OF THE MEXICAN REVOLUTION CENTENNIAL OUTREACH SUBCOMMITTEE, LOCAL EL PASO HISTORIAN
EL PASO, FEBRUARY 16, 2012

PRESIDENT DÍAZ HAD BEEN A HERO OF THE WAR against the French invaders. He got into politics, turned on his former mentor, Benito Juárez, and became president. There was nothing really notable about his first term. He allowed another person to become president; unhappy with that, he decided to run again. But this was all against the Mexican constitution. Presidents are only supposed to have had one term, but he started the business of the continuous reelection, and that was one of the reasons for the Mexican Revolution. People grew tired of the "eternal president," as they called him, the point being that in his later terms of office, he had done quite a bit for Mexico. He's not often given credit for all that he did. In fact, he did do a number of things. But there was one large swathe of land of states that were not fully developed, or were practically undeveloped.

These were the northern tier of Mexican states right up against the southern border of the United States, Chihuahua being one of the largest states. It has a vast, expansive desert and not much water. The mountains, of course, cross it, outlining the western portion of the state. The situation was such that the Mexican president and his cabinet knew they had to develop the northern tier. . . . They couldn't depend on the agricultural products being raised in the center of the country. They needed more, and they needed to get closer to the market of the United States. What they decided to do, then, was to throw open this area, the northern tier of states, to foreign investment. . . . We had something like six Mormon colonies in Chihuahua, and about three more in the adjoining state of Sonora. . . .

The reasons for the Revolution were many, but basically the populace was really in a position of servitude, and the business of bringing in foreign investors with tremendous advantages in which the Mexican population did not participate was appealing. For example, the railroad labor was furnished to the Americans, who were the investors and builders, and at a fixed rate, something like sixty-five centavos a day, and no allowance for improvement in status. The Americans had all the top jobs and the Mexicans had all the laboring jobs at a set fee. This didn't go well with the Mexicans, and this was brewing—the witch's cauldron was brewing.

Another thing was resistance to this group coming from out of the country. When the Mormons, for example, were brought in in 1885, there was resistance against them. Here was a group of white Americans coming in from out of state, from out of the country, and they were being given, or it was being negotiated, to purchase land alongside the waterways in northern Chihuahua. The group who were native to, for example, Casas Grandes and Dublán and those towns and had been there for many years—these people resisted the Americans. They in fact forced the government to move the Mormons from their original locations they had decided on and pushed them further north where the water was not as plentiful. Of course, the reason that the Mexican government dealt with the Mormons was because their prowess and reputation as great agriculturists had preceded them. They knew how to make the desert bloom, and this is what was needed in Chihuahua, and the Mormons did it. But again, there were people like José Salazar, a native of that area, and his family, who didn't care for this at all. As a matter of fact, he was one of the earliest revolutionaries.

The early revolutionaries were actually focused around the ideas of the Flores Magon brothers, who were anarchists, who were really bomb throwers. It's often said that the intellectuals start a revolution and the politicians then steal the revolution from them. You can actually make a case for this in Mexico. The intellectuals were the Flores Magon brothers. They attracted a group of socialist-minded people. They call themselves "colorados," "the red flaggers," and they were tied in, for example, to the IWW, the International Workers of the World, known as the "Wobblies" in the United States. There was that tie, and of course that went on across the ocean into Russia, so there was a tie-in there. These people were really the early Communists. What transpired then was that the Revolution began due to the leadership of Francisco Madero, and shortly after, his family. Francisco Madero and his family financed the Revolution. . . . There was a lot of this kind of corruption, and . . . that contributed to the dissatisfaction of the Mexican population and fueled the Revolution. The bringing in of the Mormons, who actually dug the earth with their hands, was different from the investors who merely put money in and had other Mexicans do the work, again at a fixed rate. . . .

The Revolution was gathering steam, if we can put it that way, and by the time Francisco Madero placed himself at the head of the Revolution, Mexico was itself in bad shape. The Mexican government was literally bankrupt. It had poor credit, and the finance minister . . . spent a lot of time in New York and also in Europe trying to improve finances for Mexico. The Díaz administration depended on him to be able to gather finances to keep the country going. This was a problem, a continuous problem. The government didn't have enough money to have a strong army in place. . . . The army was only brought in to do the heavy work, like moving Indians around, which was often done in order to take away from them their ancestral lands.

The Mormons were between a rock and a hard place. They had to get along with the people like the socialists, led by, in that particular area, Salazar. Salazar was a big fellow who wore boots and was very quiet, almost morose, but he was very intelligent. When he needed to, he could give a speech and fire up his people. He was a natural leader, and as such, people followed him. But he was also hard to deal with, as far as Orozco was concerned. Pascual Orozco had been named the general of the Revolution by Francisco Madero, and he had a number of followers, who were merely colonels, including . . . Pancho Villa. But Orozco was a general, and under his orders his people came back and forth as the Revolution started gathering force outside the city of Juárez. There you had the buildup. . . .

The Revolution was brewing; a lot of it was being formed in the state of Chihuahua, always a troublesome state for the Mexican government. The people were inclined to rise up, and they did. The Mexican government had a real problem. They knew there was a lot of unhappiness. They knew there were a lot of problems in places like Sonora, Chihuahua, and the other northern states. The people in those states were actually fomenting. The earliest socialists, the Flores Magon brothers, were being displaced, and they were quickly displaced when the Madero revolution began. The actual firing . . . of the first shots had occurred at other places and at other times, but basically the Mexican Revolution took place in Juárez. This is where it caught fire.

The socialist army was incorporated into Madero's army. Madero gave up the idea of being the leading military general and turned leadership over to the professionals because he himself was not capable of leading the people into battle. It just wasn't part of his makeup. He was an intellectual, and although he was a brave fellow, he had no real training or inclination to be a military leader. So he found his place, moved over, and allowed people like Orozco to be the leading general. Pascual Orozco had a lot of ambition, though. He wanted to be in the cabinet, as secretary of war—that sort of thing. But it was not to be; neither was Villa and neither was a lesser general like Salazar and a number of others. They really were nothing but soldiers in the Revolution to Madero, and that's where he wanted them. He didn't want them interfering with the provisional government he was forming; he didn't need them there. He needed trained intellectuals, educated people who could handle the international scene; they would be able to handle and solve problems. He didn't need these soldiers.

Consequently these soldiers turned against Madero, feeling that he had made promises to them and failed to deliver on them. Pascual Orozco turned against Madero not very long after the Revolution was completed. Francisco "Pancho" Villa was paid a certain amount of money and opened a chain of butcher shops; that's all he wanted to do. Later on he became the international celebrity, but that's further along in our story. . . .

One of the reasons for the Revolution, of course, . . . was that

Americans were being given preference over Mexicans in Mexico. That was hard for the Mexicans to take. This was the sort of reason why Pascual Orozco had raised up and joined Madero—to fight off preference for foreigners. All his army felt the same way. This was actually taking place in Chihuahua. The general feeling was that the Mexican army was there to protect the foreigners more than it was to protect the Mexican citizens. As a consequence, the people turned on the government. After Orozco rose up against Madero, there occurred another war, which shifted alliances here and there. The Mormons now became very hard pressed.

They represented not only foreign investment, they had actually been given title to rich farmland and well water, and they had done well with it. They had put in orchards and fields, they had made a community, and they had even invited Mexican Catholics to join them and work for them. This was fine if you were a subsistence laborer with a family, but to military-minded people like Salazar and his group, this was surefire fuel for the Revolution. He wanted the Mormons out, but at the same time these colonists were providing the army with the things they needed to continue their revolution. The embargo against the importing of American guns and ammunition into Mexico throttled the revolutionaries in Chihuahua at that time. They couldn't get the rifles they needed, nor the ammunition. They had a mixture of arms and ammunition for themselves, including a lot of very old, rusty weapons, like the very early lever-action Winchesters. The Mormons, on the other hand, had modern weapons and ammunition. They kept them at home under the beds, so to speak, but they had them nonetheless, and word of that got out.

This is what Salazar was after. He knew that Mexico needed development. He knew that the Mormons were doing well, putting in orchards, mills, and good fields, and providing labor jobs for Mexicans. He didn't really want to interfere with that, but he was going to get his hands on what the Mormons had hidden away. This was not necessarily what Pascual Orozco wanted him to do, but he was hard to deal with, hard to handle. He had the backing of hundreds of his . . . hometown people. As their leader, he spoke for them, pointing out how the Mormons were maybe not actually working against the Revolution, but they weren't friends of the Revolution. They were trying to be neutral. So the Mormons had to provide whatever the group of riders would come up to the community and lay out demands for—"Bring us your rifles, . . . brings us your ammunition, . . . we need money, we need some cattle, we need to eat"—and the Mormons obliged. The revolutionaries would go from community to community and take what they were given. Many times, of course, the Mormons gave them the oldest weapons they had and kept the good ones. Still, all in all, this was plain extortion.

The revolutionaries were also doing the same thing to the large Mexican haciendas. They would visit the hacendados (landowners), who were absent but usually had an overseer, usually a Spaniard, who would, in modern parlance, make them an offer the landowners couldn't refuse. That is to say, they would tell him, "Here is a list of the things we want from you. Now, either you give them to us or what we are going to do is burn down every structure on your land, including the people inside. What's it going to be?" Naturally, in order to preserve what he could, the superintendent would usually give them ten or fifteen cattle, saddles, ropes, ammunition, money, and arms. Whatever they wanted, they got. In this way, the overseer would buy time. After all, these were just material things. No one could afford to lose people, crops, and all that had been built up. But this is the way revolutionaries were operating. They were living off the land, not only that of the hacendados—Mexican citizens—but also the Mormons.

When it got down to brass tacks, they wanted more and more, and the Mormons had to evacuate in order to protect their women and children. That's what forced the Mormons out of the country.

The group that came to El Paso came on the railroad. The group that went straight up into the southern borders of Arizona and New Mexico simply went any way they could, because there was no railway connection. The only real connection for railroads was from the Casas Grandes area to Juárez and into El Paso. Our story now takes us to the arrival of the Mormons in El Paso. . . .

The reputation of the Mormons in northern Mexico was "No sais de haven." The Mormon men wouldn't put up with a lot. They fought back. And they did have rifles to do sniping. It's clear why the Salazar group knew they just couldn't walk in and take everything, because the Mormon men would fight back; they would shoot. They would fight violence with violence, and that is what was going on. For example, it became a matter of the women being caught off guard, being kidnapped or raped—that sort of threat against their very lives. Because some of the Mormons had been shot and the Mormon men had shot some of the raiders, the Mormons had to move the women and children out of harm's way. Where were they to go? They had certain plans afoot to do it, and one plan was to take a trainload of women and children to El Paso, and that is why they showed up there. But the city was not prepared to receive and care for an exodus of this magnitude.

It had happened in El Paso's history more than once, but the citizens were never ready; this was kind of a small, peaceful adobe town, even though there were in El Paso charity groups who were willing and who did in fact help others that needed it. But they were limited in how much they could do. They would very quickly run out of money, space, and everything else. As a consequence the people in the town had to step up and find what the Mormon women needed. We have photographs of the women existing in a warehouse on Cotton Street. . . .

The Mormons had originally immigrated into Mexico, to avoid the persecution and prosecution against polygamist Mormons in the United States; in a sense, they had been forced out. Either they renounced polygamy or got out of the country. Unbeknownst to the group who came into Mexico, who negotiated all of these arrangements, they were stepping from the frying pan into the fire, because the Mexicans, now rising up in rebellion against their government, needed supplies, and these they wanted to take from the Mormons. They especially didn't like the fact that these were American Mormons, a foreign group being treated with a good deal; the Mexican government was making accommodations for them that it wasn't making for the native Mexicans. So there was a lot of ill feeling—more than ill feeling, actual resistance, actual rebellion. They moved under Salazar and against the Mormons, taking what they could. But they also found out that the Mormon men would not put up with a lot. They were not going to roll over dead. Even today, the reputation of the Mormons in northern Mexico is . . . that they won't put up with such things. They will rebel if you attempt to coerce them or to extort from them. They will accommodate; they have to—they have to get along, but they are not going to roll over dead and allow their women and children to be molested or harassed. . . .

It came to the point where the Mormons had to make a decision. That is to say, they had to avoid losing everything, but on the other hand, the one thing that they needed above all was to salvage the lives of their women and children. They had to get them out of harm's way. They had escaped persecution and prosecution in the United States some years back; they had gone into Mexico, and now here was another wave of hazardous living coming to them—a washing over them by the Mexicans in the states of Sonora and Chihuahua, who were also against their own government. It was a problem that had to be resolved quickly, and it had to be done with as much courage and planning as possible, which was to move the women and children out of harm's way. This is why they came to El Paso—they could no longer live in peace. They could no longer accommodate the revolutionaries; there were too many great forces against them, so they had to move the women and children out of Chihuahua and Sonora, at least until things could settle down and they could return. . . .

The Mormons were in a position of great peril. The movement against them became more intense, even violent. The men, the leaders of the community, had to make a decision. They wanted their families out of a dangerous situation. The men stayed behind, for the most part, to protect their interests, at least to keep things under control: their orchards, their livestock, and of course their houses and their furnishings. This was what they were going to protect. Everybody thought they were going to come back if things could be resolved. Everybody would go back to their normal procedures. But it was not to be. They never really did come back in force. They resettled: some resettled in El Paso, some went to Utah, some went to New Mexico, some went to Arizona and parts of West Texas. Of course their land fell into disrepair. Many adjustments had to be made after the Revolution, when the land was given back to those who had lost it earlier, which had led to the Revolution.

The Mormons had come down into Mexico seeking asylum, seeking refuge, and they made a success of the lands they had been awarded. Then the Revolution started, only a short span of time between the time they arrived in 1885 and 1912, . . . a very short period of time. They had done a successful job of colonizing, but being forced out and redistributing themselves in the American Southwest is the true story of the Mormons.

JOHN F. COOK

MAYOR OF EL PASO
EL PASO, FEBRUARY 20, 2012

IF YOU GO BACK IN EL PASO HISTORY, BACK TO 1912, El Paso was a lot different than it is today. People like those from the East Coast will oftentimes think of El Paso as a dusty little border town, and back then it really was a dusty little border town. Thousands of Mormons were fleeing Mexico, trying to find refuge somewhere. They arrived in El Paso in the middle of the night, maybe midnight or one o'clock in the morning. Here they were in a strange town, wondering what the future now held for them. What kind of reception would they get? They had basically left everything behind. This story has a lot of significance in my own personal life. My wife was a refugee from Vietnam back in 1954. She knew what it was like to leave everything behind and end up in a strange city. The welcome you get determines much about your outlook on life and your ability to move on, despite some kind of an obstacle.

Back in 1912, when these folks got off this train at the El Paso Depot, they were wondering what kind of reception they would get, what kind of people were going to greet them. Would they be refugees on their own, or would they find open doors? Fortunately for them they landed in a town that opened its doors and hearts and welcomed them to the city. As a matter of fact, the mayor at that time said it was his obligation as a human being to welcome people—to open those doors and hearts. I think he was probably symbolic of the people of El Paso. He wasn't alone in the philosophy of wanting to open his heart to people in need, other folks did the same thing. People provided clothing and food, they brought water to them, and many opened their houses so they could take showers and do other things like that. It was a proud moment in El Paso's history. Today we are very much still the same kind of people. We open our hearts to people; we open our doors. Oftentimes people refer to El Paso as the melting pot, the Ellis Island of the southern border, and we pretty much are. We accept people. I know I, for example, don't judge people by whether they have the documentation to be in this country or not. If they are in need we open our doors to them and give them a helping hand. . . .

The mayor in 1912, Mayor C. E. Kelly, opened the doors to the city. He didn't look at it as just being his obligation; he looked at it as being a pleasure. It sort of reminds me of Thanksgiving, a two-part word. The first part is giving thanks, and a lot of people give thanks for the bounty that's laid on the table. But the other part of thanksgiving is even more important, the giving part. My dad had an expression when I was a little kid growing up: "Life is like a bucket: you don't get any more out of it then you put into it." When people put stuff into someone else's bucket, they end up getting more out of their own. One little tidbit of information: in 1912, when all those refugees landed on our shores, so to speak, the mayor wasn't the only person who symbolized that giving spirit. We had people like cabdrivers who spent the whole night shuttling people back and forth from the train depot to a makeshift lumberyard, and refusing to accept any money for it. That pretty much speaks for the character of the people of El Paso back in 1912, how they really responded.

I'm reminded of the same thing when we had the Katrina evacuation here. Thousands of people arrived at Biggs Army Airfield, and my wife and I greeted all of them as they came into the convention center. We shook hands with them and told them they were our guests while they were here. . . . I see some of them today, and they say, "I remember you and your wife greeted us, and we really felt welcomed." I'm sure it was very similar to that in 1912 when these folks got off of the train, wondering what God had in store for them, what life had in store for them, and what kind of reception they would receive. . . . To have a taxi cab driver say, "You know what? You need the help and I need to help you. Just get in the cab and I'll give you a ride." That's pretty cool. . . .

Speaking of the Katrina evacuees, many of them decided they were going to move on once they got their lives put back together, but a whole bunch of them also decided they had found their new home at the foot of the Rocky Mountains and a pass to the north. In 1912 not all the Mormons decided they were going to ship out either. Some of them felt so welcomed here that they found this was going to be their new home; they raised their children here and ended up having grandchildren here. There are still Mormons who can trace their roots all the way back to 1912 when they came to the sunny city called El Paso and felt such a warm welcome that they didn't have to look anywhere else for another home. They had found it.

HENRY B. EYRING

FIRST COUNSELOR IN THE FIRST PRESIDENCY OF THE CHURCH OF JESUS CHRIST OF LATTER-DAY SAINTS
SALT LAKE CITY, MAY 25, 2012

THE EXODUS FROM MEXICO BY THE LATTER-DAY Saints was very personal. Much depends on your age and your station. My father told me the story from the point of view of a boy who at the time would have been eleven years old, who saw himself as a full-grown man. He had his own horse, his own gun. He rode with his father across the grasses of Chihuahua, and he couldn't believe the Mormon leaders were sending him out with the women and children, sitting on a railroad flatcar, to El Paso, when he could be back in the colonies tending the ranches and the people. But they sent him out anyway. I can just see him as he described himself sitting sullen on that flatcar as he went to El Paso. . . . His sister, Camilla—who of course also came out with the women and children—saw it very differently. To her it was a frightening time. So the brother, the young eleven-year-old, the sister, the sixteen-year-old, quite frightened, were both very much humbled to come from the wonderful circumstances of Mexico, and Dad, feeling that he was just like the men, unafraid of anything. So their reactions were very different. You could get a different story whoever you talked to about what it was like to come out in the Mormon colonies' exodus into El Paso. . . .

In 1912, my relatives fled to El Paso from northern Mexico with thousands of other Latter-day Saint refugees. Among them was my widowed great-grandmother, Mary Bommeli Eyring, a hardworking and resourceful woman of modest means who was robbed of her savings by a bandit just before she left her Mexican home.

On behalf of the many people who descend from these 1912 refugees, may I express my own profound thanks to your parents and grandparents, the noble and great citizens of El Paso. What they did for our people was gracious, kind, and benevolent.

A century ago, Latter-day Saint members of the El Paso Relief Committee expressed their thankfulness in an article prepared for the El Paso Times. They wrote, "Permit us to express . . . our appreciation, and the deep gratitude we feel, for the spontaneous and universal expression of sympathy, and the ready assistance, which has been rendered in this hour of trial and distress."

Along with this relief committee, I too say, "May He who regards all people according to their works do unto you and yours as you have done unto us."

Thank you to the people of El Paso for all that was done. It is not forgotten, nor will it ever be.

MATTHEW G. GEILMAN

ARCHIVIST IN THE CHURCH HISTORY DEPARTMENT,
SALT LAKE CITY,
SALT LAKE CITY, FEBRUARY 17, 2012

THE MORMONS BEGIN TO LOOK SOUTHWARD AT the end of the nineteenth century for a number of reasons. First, they knew of some rising persecutions because of polygamy and accompanying doctrines of the Church. Also, . . . and I truly believe this, there was a prophetic underpinning to it. They felt strongly that there were Book of Mormon ties south of the border, and early on they felt that they were going to take the gospel to these people. . . .

In 1874 Brigham Young came to Daniel W. Jones and began to plant within him a need to prepare, to take copies/translations of the Book of Mormon south of the border to the descendants of, . . . he said, Nephi. Much preparation went on during the course of the coming year. . . .

In 1875 a small group of men, an exploratory group, headed to Mexico, whose role was, really, as explorers; they even called themselves "prospectors." They were going to pave the way, find places suitable for colonization, and also preach the gospel. Before they completed their journey, they distributed . . . a small pamphlet of about a hundred pages of Book of Mormon translations. . . .

When they first crossed the border, one of the things that took them off guard was the reaction of a Catholic priest there, . . . who laid it down hard on them, denouncing them in front of all the people. It was after that encounter that they realized, as especially James Stewart said, they needed to learn the language: "I began to study Spanish earnestly." This so they could react to the local people. But the sentiments of the Catholic ties were much stronger near the border. As the Mormons went further south, they found a much more liberal spirit, probably because more reform laws had been passed, and a little bit of power had been taken away from the Catholic Church. Also, the people were a little more liberal to hearing their message. . . .

When the Latter-day Saints finally made the decision to establish colonies, it was circumstance that led to it. There was heavy persecution in Utah with the Edmunds Act, and the Church needed to find a place of refuge for the polygamists south of the border. Yet there had been many very important antecedents to the decision to colonize northern Mexico. . . .

When the colonies first started, it was a struggle for several years. Like any pioneers, they came and had to establish themselves fresh. They soon became a very prosperous community. In just a short period of time, the Mexican government became very grateful to have them there because of how much they were producing by way of business, and even the produce they had and were sharing at the fairs. Everything looked like it was going well.

At the start, only a small group came, but there were nearly four thousand by the year 1912 when things began to change drastically. This is probably best recorded in the journal of John Walser, who wrote in April of 1912, . . . "My family are all well and we feel grateful to God for his great blessings and his protection over us." You could just feel that things were good. Colonia Juàrez looked like a flower garden. The fruit trees were all blossoming. It was far different than it had been just twenty years earlier when the Mormons came. But then Walser's very next journal entry, dated July 28, 1912, reads, "We were compelled to deliver up our arms to the rebel forces. In consequence of this we sent our wives and children to El Paso on the twenty-ninth." His descriptions go from a flowering garden to delivering the firearms to the rebels and having to leave. . . .

When the conflict started to arise with the 'dgers and the Revolution, having firearms was probably the one thing that gave the colonists a sense of security that they could protect their families. But when Salazar began making intonations that his men were going to request firearms, mostly so that they could have them for their fighting, things became very troublesome. Junius Romney, in particular, knew even weeks before they gave up their firearms that things were going to get out of control if that happened. That was the breaking point, the turning point for the decision. The Mormons might have been able to stay, but once their protection was taken from them, there really wasn't any other option. . . .

In 1879, Moses Thatcher, a member of the Quorum of the Twelve Apostles, was sent to Mexico City to dedicate the land for the preaching of the gospel. Unlike the first mission to Mexico, his was not to survey for colonization, yet that became an interesting side result of his time there. He and the missionary party with him became convinced that colonization would be necessary in order for the gospel to be preached in Mexico. . . . On January 25, 1880, Moses Thatcher . . . and James Stuart went to the upper room of their hotel to dedicate Mexico for the preaching of the gospel. As they were there, one of the things they felt very inspired about was the need for colonization in Mexico so the gospel could be spread. They felt strongly enough about it that following the dedicatory prayer, they prayed as a group, and Moses Thatcher felt that he should return to Utah prematurely from his mission to present the idea to the Brethren in Salt Lake City. He left, to return within just about ten days of the experience in the hotel room.

After making his presentation to the leading members of the Church, they decided to not colonize at that time. Instead of being crushed because he'd felt inspired and left his mission to come home, he wrote a letter back to his missionary companions explaining what had happened. What he wrote is very interesting in light of the fact that five years later, colonization would eventually happen. He said,

Regarding this matter I've reflected much since my return, and came to the final conclusion that the Spirit of God prompted us while expressing our views before I left you. But I now understand, and I think that when the Elders are inspired to have even a peep into the future, the Holy Ghost, even by a partial removal of the veil, makes things that may actually, in a natural way, be distant, seem very, very close to us. We were only a little overanxious as to the time.

One of the interesting things about colonization is the scope they anticipated having with regards to where their colonies and settlements would be. Brigham Young, at the same time that these parties are going down into Mexico, made the statement that "I look forward to the time when the settlements of the Church of Jesus Christ of Latter-day Saints will extend right through the city of Old Mexico and from thence on through Central America to the land where the Nephites flourished at the golden era of their history. And this great backbone of the American continent be filled, North and South, with cities and temples." Interesting: "Temples of the people of God. In this great work, I anticipate the children of Nephi, of Laman and Lemuel will take no small part." . . .

Although settlements as a whole did not end up spreading all the way throughout Mexico and into Central America, the fact that it was in their minds that there needed to be that presence, both in the north of Mexico and even throughout, has an interesting application with regards to the number of stakes and temples that now fill those lands "through the backbone and corridor of Latin America. . . ."

One of the wonderful things about these men that went down to survey Mexico is what they sacrificed for months. It was basically a giant camping trip for ten months as they worked their way down into Mexico. Only two of the people in the party even knew Spanish, yet they were willing to go and do whatever they were asked to do. . . . Three thousand miles on horseback all the way down through the corners of New Mexico, through El Paso and down into Mexico. They gave up the comforts of home to survey the land. One of the evidences of how seriously they took this responsibility is the level of detail they included in their journals. Most of what they wrote until they got into Mexico was somewhat superficial, but once they got to the land itself, they recorded specific details—locations, observations. They even indicated that Casas Grandes was perhaps the best place to purchase land because of available resources in the area. These men were hard workers, dedicated to their cause. They had even put their lives on the line to complete this mission.

FERNANDO GOMEZ

PRESIDENT OF THE MORMON MEXICAN HISTORY MUSEUM IN PROVO, UTAH, AND MEXICO CITY
PROVO, UTAH, FEBRUARY 22, 2012

THE FIRST MORMON MISSION TO MEXICO WAS in 1875, when missionaries left Salt Lake City and entered Mexico in January of 1876. The purpose was to go to Sonora, but there were problems with the Yaqui Indians and the Mexican government, so they diverted through Chihuahua, and entered El Paso del Norte in January of 1876. They did not have much success in the city because of the influence of the Catholic Church, but after working several months, they decided to go further south into Chihuahua, where they held the first official church meeting in the capital of Chihuahua. Daniel W. Jones gave the sermon there. From there they also sent selections of the Book of Mormon to prominent people all over the Republic of Mexico, which act later became very fruitful for the continuation of the gospel in Mexico. They then left the capital city and travelled to the mountains among the Indians, where they had much more success in their presentation of the gospel. They were well received, and they felt that the Spirit of the Lord had accompanied them. They were also able to investigate lands for colonization in the future. So that was the first official mission to Mexico. . . .

In 1885, John Taylor, the Mormon prophet, decided to go to Sonora to investigate the possibility of colonizing in the state or in Chihuahua. They selected Chihuahua, and that's where the first migrants from the Church went in Mexico. But the state government, not very pleased with them, gave them a letter telling them that they needed to get out within fifteen days. The Church reacted by sending Brigham Young Jr. and Moses Thatcher to Mexico City to talk to President Díaz about the Mormons and about colonizing in another part of the Republic. He immediately issued a letter to the state government indicating that they should leave the Mormons alone, and thus the colonies were able to be established. However, the relationship between Porfirio Díaz, the president, and the Mormons goes back to an encounter on a ship on the Pacific when Samuel Brannan, who had been excommunicated but who had earlier been a missionary, was able to land in Manzanillo, a port city on the Pacific. Benito Juárez was the Mexican president at that time. For nine days the two travelled together between Manzanillo and Panama, and it is recorded that the Americans gave the Juárez delegation a banquet for the principles they were pursuing, and thus they established a relationship that became friendly. In the 1860s, . . . Brannan helped support Benito Juárez and the Mexicans against the French by loaning them money and arms, and an army, to fight the French. Porfirio Díaz was a general during that war, and thus knew of the allocation that Brannan had made for them. Thus when the situation in Chihuahua came about, he remembered the Mormons and gave instructions for the government to lay low and let the Mormons colonize. . . .

When Díaz heard about the Mormons, he already had knowledge of their agricultural successes, and he needed to have the northern part of the Juárez country developed. Thus he felt a need for the Mormons, and also the Mexican government, to help in the growth of Mexico at that time. So he welcomed them, and he was very impressed with the quality of people and their working habits. They had participated in many of the fairs in Mexico City with their products, and they had always been well received by Porfirio Díaz. . . .

When the colonists arrived, they had problems securing land because of different problems with the documentation of the land they were purchasing, so at first they started to rent land, before the Church was able to buy land where they could settle. I'm sure that the local people around the colonies were looking for employment as well, and so the Mormon settlement was also beneficial for them. Later also, the Juárez Academy became of benefit to some of the Mexicans, who attended the school, and the school also produced members for the Church, as well as missionaries, like Andreas Gonzáles, who served as the first Mexican two-year missionary in the central part of the Republic. . . .

As far as the Revolution is concerned, the people in the colonies were neutral. They did not want to join any of the different factions in the government at that time. But because they were successful and had plenty of obvious commodities, the revolutionaries wanted their guns and their horses; they just wanted the Mormon people to help them fight for their cause, but the problem was that one faction . . . would come in, and then another, . . . and that put the colonists between the factions, a very difficult situation. That's when the Mormons decided they could no longer stay in the country, and that created the exodus. . . .

When it became very difficult for colonists, the local people were asked to take care of the properties in the colonies, while the American pioneers decided they would leave the colonies and go back to the U.S. Apostle Anthony W. Ivins sent the train down to take care of the women and children, one part of the exodus that took place. The other part was very difficult: the men went on horseback, and they had several encounters, but they were also successful in getting back across the border. . . .

The Mexican colonies were very useful to the Republic in later years, even though they were very slow in getting started. There were several branches here and there in the Republic, but as time went on, hundreds of men served the Lord throughout the world in different positions in their . . . priesthood callings. Today, there are twenty-five missions and 222 stakes (ecclesiastical units of several thousand members) in Mexico. There are twelve operating temples and one under construction, and over one million members in the Republic. So the value of the initial colonies going into Mexico was not only the economic benefit but the spiritual blessing the colonies generated for decades.

PATRICIA KIDDNEY

LOCAL EL PASO HISTORIAN
EL PASO, FEBRUARY 17, 2012

THERE WAS A LOT OF UNREST IN MEXICO IN 1912, and it was necessary for the residents in northern Mexico to flee the unrest the Mexican government was going through. So in doing that, many, many families came up to El Paso and stayed during the entire time frame of the Mexican unrest. In doing so, many people decided to stay here and raise their families, and many ended up staying here forever and being buried here. We find that many of these people went on to become integral parts of our community. . . . The Mormon plot is in the El Paso Concordia Cemetery. . . . The Mormons fled Mexico up to El Paso, which was known as "the city of refuge." There were thousands of refugees, in addition to the Mormons. But these particular Mormons ended up living here, making their living, raising their families, and . . . many of them dying here. In fact, we have in El Paso sixty-two burials of Mormon settlers and Mormon pioneers. . . .

As these settlers passed time in El Paso, many of the families learned to like the area and decided they would stay here and raise their families. Many of them even have established businesses. One family in particular is the Romney family. Another is the Pierce family, which family produced the first bishop in El Paso. . . . We're very, very proud to honor the Mormon settlers.

MICHAEL N. LANDON

AUTHOR AND ARCHIVIST AT THE CHURCH HISTORY LIBRARY, SALT LAKE CITY
SALT LAKE CITY, FEBRUARY 23, 2012

THE MORMONS ACTUALLY WENT INTO MEXICO in the latter part of the nineteenth century . . . for a number of reasons. In a way, it was a natural progression of colonization. The Mormons had been moving south from the Salt Lake Valley to Southern Utah. They had moved into the Arizona strip and into the Little Colorado area, where they had settled. Eventually they went to the Salt River, then down to the Gila and the San Pedro Rivers, where they established agrarian communities—all through the Southwest. Eventually, if you went far enough south, you would hit an international border.

The other issue that sort of brought the question to a head was the prosecution of Latter-day Saints for the practice of plural marriage. Federal marshals were putting intense pressure on the Latter-day Saints, and so they needed a refuge; and Mexico offered that opportunity because at the time the Mexican dictator, Porfirio Díaz, was encouraging foreign investment and economic development; and he viewed the Mormons as industrious and potentially advantageous to him in terms of his economic development plans. So in a way, from his point of view, although it was illegal to practice polygamy in Mexico, he apparently turned a blind eye to that issue. What was paramount in his mind was economic development for Mexico, and he viewed the Mormons as hardworking people who would further his objectives. From the Mormon side, the idea that they were not going to be harassed for their peculiar practice proved to be a boon. The issue was land—they needed land for settling. When they first went to Mexico and started looking for land, some of the issues revolved around obtaining land and how to set up colonies. . . .

Mormons had been down in Mexico doing proselytizing work as early as 1875. Moses Thatcher initially wanted to set up colonies as havens for native converts in Mexico. But the colonies actually ended up being established in about 1885, and the principal reason was as a haven for polygamists who were fleeing persecution in the United States. . . . The Saints were prosperous in Mexico, though the initial years of setting up were tough , but once they got their land established and crops in, they thrived. Being American citizens, they had some advantages. They didn't have to pay import taxes for implements, so consequently they could in some ways operate their agricultural enterprises at an economic advantage over their neighbors. Plus, there was the cooperative nature of Latter-day Saints. These colonies were so prosperous that they almost become a poster child for Porfirio Díaz. He had them bring their goods to Mexico City for display at a fair that celebrated the industrialization and progress of Mexico. Particularly the Mormon apples from the colonies were a great hit in Mexico City. . . .

Part of the reason the Mormons were so successful was the scale of the economy, because their large operations were cooperative. Many of their neighbors worked small plots, unless they were large, large landholders. The issue in Mexico all revolved around land. Many survey companies were coming in and surveying, and the Porfirio Díaz government required them to prove title to much of the traditional land that had been worked by small farmers for generations. They had to pay a sum which they obviously could not come up with. The end result was that these people were dispossessed of their land, and larger and larger concentrations of land fell into fewer and fewer hands. The Mormons, of course, were able to take advantage of this. Their land holdings increased, just as did those of some of the other landholders. But the Mormons were not interested in landholding per se. They were interested in a host of other things—among them improving their lives. They set up an educational system. They were interested in a holistic aspect to life. They weren't absentee landowners as some of the other foreign and domestic land owners were. . . .

At the same time the Porfirio Díaz policies were actually benefiting the colonies and the colonies were prospering, the social fabric of the country was unraveling. As I mentioned, the dispossession of land was creating very serious problems within Mexico. The other issue was that many of the Mexican elites were sending their children to Europe or the United States for education, and these children learned western philosophies and thoughts, including ideas about democracy. Francisco Madero, in particular, could see the disconnect between what he was learning and what he was witnessing in Mexico; the idea was basically freedom. So he began agitating for free and open elections.

Díaz had been in power for decades, and he brought no opposition to Madero. He simply did not oppose him. His economic policies on paper looked spectacular, but oftentimes there wasn't good planning. Foreign companies would be given huge contracts for, say, building a railroad. But was that railroad going to go to places where markets could be developed? Was it going to truly benefit the infrastructure of the country, or was it just being built because it was money to be made? At the same time there was economic growth, there was also, at least statistically, a burgeoning, landless peasantry; a dispossessed middle class; economic difficulties; a stark contrast between rich and poor. It was a desperate setting. Madero began clamoring for the free elections and reform, and he found very fertile ground. . . .

The Revolution started in 1910. When it finally reached the colonies in terms of actual soldiers and rebels in the area, the colonies were pretty secluded. The impact really didn't start appearing in a real sense until 1912. Suddenly the colonies were in the midst of an unfolding revolution, which was becoming more and more violent. Pascual Orozco and his forces, needing arms, began demanding them from the colonists. The stake president, Junius Romney, made the only real decision he could make, in my opinion: get the Saints—at least the women and children—immediately out of the colonies. Once he realized Salazar was not going to back down on his demand for firearms, these people had to defend themselves. What were they going to do? Lawless bands were running all over. Romney made the only logical decision—ship the women and children out, and the men would follow later on horseback.

But the colonies were their home. They may have known in the back of their minds that the Revolution might eventually touch their lives, but that wasn't a question they wanted to entertain seriously. Yet here it was, from one day to the next, right in their faces. They were given almost no time—"Pack what you can pack, less than one hundred pounds, and get out." Think about your own circumstances if you were told to do that. All the work, all the labor, all the effort that had gone in to establishing these colonies—homes, fields, everything. Not to mention their lifestyle. This was home in a larger sense. It was a very prosperous, happy, religious community. . . . In their eyes, it was very, very nice.. . . .

When the bishops of the individual wards received notice to get the women and children out, Bishop George Thomas Sevey, bishop of the colony of Chuichupa, the southernmost colony, arranged to get the women and children to Chico station, the nearest railhead, about twenty miles away. The men took them there and put them on the train, to try to escape revolutionary Mexico. Because Chuichupa was the southernmost colony, the people had to travel a long ways before they would actually reach the U.S. border. . . . Then the men had to turn around and go back to their houses to take care of matters and prepare to go out on horseback to the United States.

That had to be incredibly difficult for these men to do. The emotion is hard to imagine. In fact, I don't think any of them were able to sleep a wink until they actually knew that that train had crossed the border. It had to be a tremendous relief knowing that the women and children were actually safe in US territory, which is ironic. Their place of refuge, in this case, was the very country they had earlier fled because of persecution. They had left the United States to go to Mexico, to escape prosecution for the practice of polygamy, and then the Revolution came and they were actually fleeing Mexico to the United States, because the Revolution was impacting their lives. . . .

When the men sent the women and children out, you have to

wonder, were they thinking this was permanent? There's a lot of opinion about that. Most of them thought this would be a temporary thing; they'd come back. However, I wonder about that, because Junius Romney actually assigned an individual to be a photographer of this exodus. One has to wonder about the rationale: was this obviously to be a momentous event in their lives? Would it be temporary or permanent? Brother Romney wanted a record, so he got a photographer, John Edward Wall, who actually documented the removal of most of the men from the colonies.

The stake actually devised a plan: the men were to meet at a location called the Stairs, sort of a midway point between the mountain colonies and the valley colonies. From there they would go out on horseback into the United States and eventually to Hachita, New Mexico, where the men would pick up passage on rails to El Paso to reunite with their families. Chuichupa, being the southernmost colony, the men got the word and headed out to the rendezvous, but there was some confusion about where they were supposed to meet the García and Pacheco men. At one point, the men from all three colonies went to the Stairs, meeting up with the others and going to New Mexico from there. The Pacheco and García men did not wait for Chuichupa. Apparently they had heard that a lot of the Chuichupa men were rounding up cattle up in the mountains, and it would be some time before they were all ready to travel. So the Pacheco and García men left. When the Chuichupa men arrived at the rendezvous points, there was nobody there. At first they were a little disheartened, thinking, "Those guys have kind of abandoned us." But when Bishop Sevey sounded the opinion of the men, many of them said, "Well, no, that gives us more latitude to do what we want." They were able to take care of themselves. . . .

I view these men, in a sense, as frontiersmen. These were men who sort of bridged the generation between the earliest Mormon pioneers and this twentieth-century version of Mormonism that we have. These were men—I guess the best word I can think of to convey a sense of what they were like—were cowboys. Cattle ranching was a big industry in Chuichupa. The growing season was short, so ranching was one of the major occupations there. . . . When you listen to their language and witness their decision-making, you get the sense that these men were pretty tough, pretty wise, pretty sage men.

One of the most difficult things they had to do was make a decision on whether or not they were going to bring their cattle dogs, their herd dogs, with them. Bishop Sevey wrote about these dogs as being more than just family pets. These were companions to the men. When the men were out alone herding cattle, these dogs became true companions. Difficulty came when the decision was made to have to put the dogs down. The difficulty of doing that tells a great deal about the lifestyle, about the worldview, about what life was like in Chuichupa.

The men finally start heading out, and they did encounter some difficulties getting across the border, but eventually they did make it into the United States. They crossed at Dog Springs, . . . and when they got to Hachita, they arranged for rail passage and met their families in El Paso. . . .

One of the other issues that tells me that Romney perhaps viewed this as a longer-term exodus than others viewed it was the fact that he decided to bury the stake records. It could be that he just didn't want them to be destroyed, and he didn't know whether the colonies were going to be looted, burned, sacked, and these were important records to him. He had the photographer go with him and two others up into the mountains to the Stairs, where they buried stake records. They had John Edward Wall take a picture and scratch on the glass plate negative, "Hiding of stake records." So they actually buried these records up in the mountains. . . .

Many of the men who were with Pascal Orozco had actually been educated in the Juárez Stake Academy, as had many of his officers. They knew the Mormons; they were familiar with the Mormons and their enterprises. The Juárez Stake Academy had a very, very fine reputation as an educational facility. So Salazar arrived, and he and his men had a discussion with Romney. It was as if these men had never had any contact with Romney, that there had been no contact between the two. Romney was able to discuss the issues with Salazar, but Salazar was absolutely immovable. You have to understand that partly, he had been hammered. He had lost some engagements, and he needed to get guns for his men. So in my view, the Mormons didn't really have . . . much of a negotiating point.

George Thomas Sevey—the bishop—had to get his people out, women and children. . . . How wrenching that was to send them on the rail, and he was the one in charge. He had to make the decisions. Every decision made in these circumstances could have had a very poor outcome. The consequences could have been severe. Yet at one point he decided that he and his counselor would go ahead and scout out the way; in case they got caught, the rest of the men would have a chance to get away. A third man said, "Well, I know Spanish, and I will be an interpreter."

Bishop Sevey said he was always grateful for that man's willingness to go with him. They started out and then the bishop looked back. Here were all the rest of the men following. He said to them, "Hey, what did I just say?" They said, "Look, it's all or one, you know." It was a "what happens to you happens to us" kind of thing. He called them "ornery cusses," but he had to admire the fact that they wanted to stay together in unity. Bishop Sevey even admitted that there had never really been any orders. "We navigated by pure understanding." But the unity was so tight that these men understood one another and what needed to be done. . . .

The Mormon colonies in Mexico were actually a small group of colonies, four thousand people, more or less, but they have had a tremendous impact upon the Church. When they were forced out, most did not return to Mexico, but they remained very faithful, active Latter-day Saints, and they enriched the communities in which they ended up. Their children and grandchildren, when they talk about the great epic historical context of their ancestors, don't think about Nauvoo or crossing the plains; they talk about Mexico. . . . It's an impression on my part, but I think if you were to check the early records of missionaries throughout Latin America, a disproportionate percentage would have surnames from the colonies. . . . That eventually allowed the gospel to be spread throughout Latin America. . . . Mexico today has . . . a million members of the Church. That's . . . in a way a testament to the faith, sacrifice and obedience of these Latter-day Saints from the little enclaves in northern Chihuahua and Sonora.

TAYLOR MACDONALD

DESCENDANT OF COLONISTS
EL PASO, FEBRUARY 19, 2012

THE MORMONS WENT TO MEXICO LARGELY because it was just a natural extension of the settlement of the West. Brigham Young had always envisioned going south into Arizona and even into Mexico. The Latter-day Saints felt a need to seek out the descendants of the people in the Book of Mormon, and Brigham Young, with a broad view, was also interested in settling the West. Originally the Latter-day Saints went clear to California as part of the original state of Deseret, so going to Mexico was a natural extension of the settlement—north and south: north into Canada and the northern states, Idaho, and Wyoming, and those places; as well as south into Arizona and into northern Mexico. . . .

Almost all of my recent ancestors were in Mexico. My great-grandfather was Alexander F. Macdonald, the stake president in Mesa, Arizona. . . . He was asked and told to go to Mexico and look for possible settling places. . . . He went down there in 1879, and was there all through the early 1880s; he also made a number of exploratory trips into Mexico, all through the early 1880s; hardly a year went by that he didn't go to Mexico looking for a place to live. . . . He was one of the leaders. He was also the first counselor to the president of the Mexican

Mission. Then he was the general manager of the Mexican Colonization and Agriculture Company, on the temporal side of things, landholding and that kind of thing. The Macdonalds lived in Colonia Juárez. My other ancestors were the Taylors—Edwin and Alice Ann Taylor, who also were in Colonia Juárez. Edmund Richardson was first in Colonia Díaz, and then in Colonia Juárez. I had other ancestors, the Adamses and some of the Butlers; many others of my ancestors were in Mexico, mostly in Colonia Díaz, Colonia Juárez, but also Dublán and various other colonies. . . .

The early years were very difficult. The colonists were living in primitive conditions, while they were building. From about the early mid-1890s up into the time of the exodus in 1912 is what I like to call the "golden age of the colonies." Towns, chapels, and schools were built. Many of the people had beautiful homes, with furnishings, organs, and even a few luxuries. So they were doing well.

Colonia Juárez was a village. I don't even know if it ever had a thousand people, but it was quite a village. It had a hotel, factories, brick kilns, leather and clothing factories, fruit, and animal-breeding programs; it was a very, very busy place. And so were Dublán and some of the other colonies. Some of them were much smaller than others; they weren't all the same. Of course they were all largely agricultural, but they also were very, very involved in business and different kinds of extensions of the skills they brought with them. There were an unusual number of skilled, experienced leaders in the colonies. . . .

In 1912, most of the Mormons were still Americans, even though . . . many of them had come from Europe. They had not naturalized into Mexico, so they were not Mexican citizens. It was a dangerous proposition to take sides in what was a Mexican revolution. The official Church policy was that the Mormons remain neutral in the Mexican Revolution that broke out in 1910. . . . By 1912, the Mormons had hoped they could stay kind of out of the way of the main revolutionary activities. . . .

The Mormon colonists thought that they were in a remote, out-of-the-way place and wouldn't really be a part of the Revolution's main events; they thought it would be easy to be neutral. But then all of a sudden circumstances changed, and they found themselves to be right in the epicenter of the Revolution. Because the Revolution divided into several different factions, there were lots of internal battles. One of the factions was the so-called Red Flagger Movement, and one of their major leaders was José Inés Salazar, from Casas Grandes, right next to Colonia Juárez. In fact, he had gone to the Juarez Stake Academy, and he knew all the Mormons. But at this moment, he was the commander of an army, and in the summer of 1912, two of his enemy commanders were coming at him from two different directions. They were going to go to battle against him, and he was very short on ammunition and arms. But he knew the Mormons had a lot of ammunition and arms, so he called in the stake president and some other leaders and said, "We must have your guns and ammunition in order to defend ourselves." The stake president said, "We are neutral, we are not part of this battle. The only reason we have those arms is because we don't want to be left defenseless in the middle of the war, but we're really not part of the war." Salazar said, "If you do not deliver us your guns and ammunition, then we will go from house to house and door to door and kill every man, woman, and child and confiscate these rifles, because we must have them."

So the stake president then knew things that nobody else knew. This was told him by Salazar in a private meeting in the middle of the night. After Salazar left, The Mormons immediately realized that they were in very serious danger. The stake president went back to his people and said, "I am sending my wife and children out to the United States as soon as possible, and I recommend that you do the same." The men had a priesthood meeting and discussed the proposal, as the stake president tried to explain in detail of what was going on. My grandfather, Jess Taylor, who was present in those meetings, said that everything was spoken very frankly, very, very openly, and everybody supported the stake president, who was Junius Romney at that time. Even though they were shocked and dismayed at having to leave, they felt like that was what they ought to do. Not everybody agreed with the strategy, but they decided it would be the safest thing to do, at least to send the women and children out. That was what was the direct cause of the evacuation of the colonies in 1912. . . .

Once the decision was made that the Mormons were going to evacuate the colonies, a number of Church leaders in El Paso directed arrangements from there. They arranged for some railroad cars to be sent down to the train station nearest to Colonia Juárez, in a place called Pearson (which is now the town of Mata Ortiz). They also sent down railroad cars to be used for the Saints in Juárez, Dublán and other nearby colonies to get on the trains and go to El Paso. An actual phone line was set up between various of the colonies, up in the mountains and in places in Chihuahua. Leaders actually sent by phone some of these messages to the people, telling them, "We are going to leave. . . . Get ready to leave." My great-grandfather, Charles Edmund Richardson, was living in Colonia Díaz. He had become a lawyer in Mexico, and he was also a very successful rancher, with a large family. It is told how one night he went out with his wife for a walk on their ranch. He told her, while they were having a nice little chat, "Well, . . . we've worked hard all these years. We are now going to be able to help our children. They are going to be able to get educated; we're going to be able to help them get started, to get married. We're going to have the means to help launch our children."

The very next day they received word that they were to evacuate their town. He, his wives, and his children all had the rug jerked right out from under them. They left Colonia Díaz, went to the New Mexico State line, and crossed over. Most of them never came back. The irony is that just when he thought everything was going to go great, everything crashed around him.

Colonia Juárez and Colonia Dublán were much bigger and closer settlements to the railroad and other places, so the people got in their wagons and went over to the railroad station in Pearson, where they loaded on the trains and took off. It was very difficult—some were in passenger cars, but some in cattle cars, and there were sick people, . . . women in advanced stages of pregnancy, and people with broken legs, the normal things you would have in these towns. They had to be handled. So it was very difficult and very unnerving. The decision was made to send the women and the children out first and leave the men in the colonies to look after their homes and their ranches. . . .

One of the torturous things about this trip was that the train never could go more than five or ten miles an hour. My grandfather said that one family took a dog. The dog got restless because the train was going so slow and finally jumped off the train and started running along the side. The dog finally got bored going so slow that it ran ahead, so when the train arrived in El Paso the dog was waiting for them on the railroad platform. It was hot, it was difficult, and it was slow, and people didn't know whether they were going to be attacked along the way. They'd see plants and bushes, the ocotillo bushes and so forth, growing along the way, and at night they thought these were soldiers. So it was a long, hot, terrifying trip.

When they arrived in Ciudad Juárez, the Mexican city on the border just before crossing into El Paso, they had to wait for a long time to have all of their baggage and everything gone through. It was the middle of the night, and they were all exhausted. Once they got into El Paso, of course, the people of El Paso were geared up to help them in every way possible. Taxi drivers provided free taxi fare to wherever they wanted to go, all night and all the next day, distributing people throughout the city to where they could stay at least temporarily. Some stayed in hotels—some of my people rented a hotel room. Some just rolled out blankets in civic buildings and slept on the floor. It wasn't until a day or so later that they found temporary living quarters in the lumberyards on Magoffin Street (those yards were still there for many, many years. . .). The people of El Paso came forward and provided enormous service. . . .

There were maybe six, seven, or eight hundred people from Colonia Juárez, and probably a thousand from Dublán, plus people from a little town called Guadalupe and from other places. Hundreds of people all of a sudden hit the town in the middle of the night, and the town came to their rescue. . . .

A number of my ancestors were in the exodus: grandparents, great-grandparents, even some great-great-grandparents who had been living in the colonies. I can only say that I personally feel a great debt of gratitude to the people of El Paso for the way they treated these people, because they were refugees; they had been jerked away from their homes, and the families of many of them were split up. The people of El Paso, the U.S. government, and Fort Bliss—all of these groups in the area of El Paso gave them the kind of material help and moral support that they needed. I personally feel very grateful for that.

PRINCE G. MCKENZIE

DIRECTOR OF THE RAILROAD AND TRANSPORTATION MUSEUM OF EL PASO
EL PASO, APRIL 13, 2012

WHEN THE MORMON WOMEN AND CHILDREN boarded the train, it was in a hot, steamy, densely vegetated area. But as the train went northward and passed the Casas Grandes River, in the Casas Grandes area, the people went across a very dry, extremely hot desert. . . .

As they passed the river in the Casas Grandes area, they continued north for . . . approximately 150 miles, and the train had to stop every twenty-five miles on average to take on water at the water stops along the way. After about eight or nine hours . . . the train arrived at Ciudad Juárez, passed through the city and over the bridge into El Paso, and stopped at the El Paso Union Passenger Station, where the people detrained.

In early August the Mormon men who had been travelling by horseback across Northern Chihuahua arrived in Hachita. From there they boarded trains of the El Paso and Southwestern Railroad and headed east towards El Paso, travelling through Columbus, New Mexico. Along that way the engines also had to stop . . . on average every twenty-five miles to take on water, because they consumed about one thousand gallons of water an hour.

LEON METZ

EL PASO HISTORIAN
EL PASO, FEBRUARY 12, 2012

WHAT EL PASO WAS IN DAYS OF THE MEXICAN Revolution, we still have in streets of downtown El Paso. For instance, Juárez Avenue goes towards Juárez; St. Louis Street goes towards St. Louis; Santa Fe Street goes towards Santa Fe; and El Paso Street is right in the center of town. It's remarkable that whoever laid those streets out gave them the names they did, and invariably the streets pointed in different directions to different towns. El Paso was a way station; in other words, most of the caravans going east to west or vice versa would wind through El Paso. . . .

El Paso was a city of refuge primarily because for one thing it was the end of the earth. Many of the refugees in El Paso were people who had been maybe driven out of other places. The streets downtown were low level, everything was made out of adobe, and transportation was horseback or muleback until streetcars were finally introduced. Transportation went to Ciudad Juárez across the river, which in those days was El Paso del Norte. . . . There was a plaza downtown; I remember the alligators downtown. . . .

During the time of the Mexican Revolution, El Paso was a city of refuge. . . . As things moved along, a lot of people were killed in

El Paso—not hundreds, but people were killed or wounded by rifle fire from across the river. Windows were shot out. Everybody lived downtown then, right across the river from Juárez. The saloons were of course everywhere; stagecoaches were everywhere, constantly coming and going. The town was waiting for the railroads. It was the railroads, really, that made El Paso. I've often thought, if the rails hadn't have come through El Paso, what kind of a city would it be like today? Probably we'd have maybe fifteen thousand people and they'd all still be living downtown. . . .

As I said, El Paso was a city of refuge; over a period of time, a lot of Americans . . . were captured down in Mexico. When the Mexican Revolution ended, those people came out, and so did a lot of Mexican people. . . . They were put behind thirteen strands of electrified barbed wire out at Fort Bliss—men women and children. Roughly . . . something like a couple of thousand people spent several years behind barbed wire out at Fort Bliss, with U.S. troops guarding them. . . .

The reason the Mormons came to El Paso was because there was no other city to go to. . . . The only place they could go was downtown. That was it. Once you reached what's now the freeway or the park, you were out of town. If you went more than half a dozen blocks in either direction, you were out in the world also. . . .

Streets were laid out and buildings built, but the town really didn't come alive until 1881, when the railroads came. . . . At that point El Paso began to change. . . . The population of El Paso was increasing, as people were brought in. And as a result, if the railroads had not come to El Paso, El Paso today wouldn't be any bigger than what's downtown right now. It wouldn't be spread out like it is.

MICHAEL R. MULLEN

DESCENDANT OF COLONISTS
EL PASO, FEBRUARY 12, 2012

IN 1912, DURING THE MEXICO REVOLUTION, . . . many of the Mormon colonists left Mexico and came to El Paso. The women and children rode the trains , the men came out on horseback, and many of them took refuge in El Paso. They'd had to leave with one suitcase; they could carry only a little stuff with them as they came out. Many of them hoped to go back, but most of them never did go back. They were welcomed in El Paso. Fort Bliss provided housing, and the city of El Paso provided housing, as well as food, sanitation needs, electricity, and everything these refugees could want. Many of them moved on to other places with their families and lived in other parts of the United States. Many of them stayed in El Paso. It became the nucleus of the members of the Mormon Church in the city. As the congregations grew, in over twenty years they eventually grew large enough to build a beautiful chapel. . . . One of my grandfathers, my great-grandfather, and a cousin of my other grandfather were all members of the building committee that helped design and build this chapel. Over the years five different generations of my family have attended . . . meetings in this beautiful building.

KARL MURPHY

PRESIDENT OF THE MOUNT FRANKLIN STAKE
EL PASO, TEXAS
EL PASO, FEBRUARY 19, 2012

WHEN I LOOK BACK AT THE 1912 EXODUS OF the Saints from the Mormon colonies in Mexico, I think of the city of El Paso and the community, and what they did in opening the city's arms and allowing the Saints to come in. Mayor Kelly and his effort, as well as opening the lumberyard, and Walter Long, who owned that lumber yard, allowed the Saints to come and reside there. Also, Fort Bliss provided tents, cots and other things to support the Saints as they came from Mexico to El Paso. Some of those Saints left and went on, but many of them stayed in El Paso. We still have family members, the Pratts, Romneys, and others, who still live in El Paso. We have probably close to nine thousand members in two stakes, which is double the number of Saints who came from Mexico to El Paso in 1912. And as I look at the community today, it's just as open and welcoming as it probably was back in 1912. . . .

The members of the Latter-day Saints church are ingrained in the community, whether it be in the military, or in the large businesses in El Paso, or even in the school districts. We feel as welcome today as I'm sure the Saints did in 1912.

MAJOR GENERAL DANA J. H. PITTARD

COMMANDING GENERAL, FORT BLISS
FORT BLISS, JUNE 5, 2012

THE COMMANDER OF FORT BLISS IN 1912 WAS Colonel Edgar Steever, an 1871 graduate of West Point. . . . At the time, Ft. Bliss was going through a huge expansion from being a backwater kind of garrison post to becoming the strategic link amongst our forts along the American-Mexican border. A lot of money was coming into Fort Bliss. So Colonel Steever at that time made the call on his own initiative to do what he could to take care of the . . . Mormon refugees coming from the Juárez area in Mexico, fleeing the Mexican Revolution. . . .

Colonel Steever was originally from Pennsylvania. At that time he had been in the army for . . . forty-two years. He was a man of principle. At one time he even commanded the army marksmanship unit of all places. He had been in the Philippines and had fought in over thirty-four different battles or engagements. He was quite the professional officer, but again, he made the call to look at housing and feeding the Mormon refugees that were coming through. He worked with the local officials. In fact, one of the wealthier people in El Paso at the time, Walter Long, who had the lumber business, allowed many of the Mormon refugees to stay in the lumberyard, but he also he helped with the supplies and the tents. In working with Mayor Kelly in El Paso, . . . I think about three hundred tents were set up. . . . It was a great call on the part of Colonel Steever to do that. So Fort Bliss played a major role in taking care of the two thousand-plus . . . Mormon refugees. . . .

I think he used the equivalent of about ten thousand dollars at the time, and if you look at ten thousand dollars back in 1912, that would be like $223,000 today. So he took a little bit of risk in doing that. Then the local officials in the El Paso city and county area lobbied Congress to appropriate money to help. But the initial initiative was Colonel Steever's, and we're very, very proud of that here at Fort Bliss. . . .

The army was expanding Fort Bliss at the time, so the timing of the Mormon exodus was very, very important. There were a number of tents and other equipment at Fort Bliss because we were getting a great increase of soldiers to protect our border, because of what was happening with the Revolution in Mexico. There happened to be those kinds of supplies in the Fort Bliss area at the time, because Fort Bliss was going through an expansion. . . .

Our First Army Division Band, prior to that called the 62nd Army Band, has a great tradition at Fort Bliss. They play in concerts all throughout the Southwest and other places in the country. But back in . . . in 1912, our band used to play free concerts in downtown El Paso. Everybody used to look forward to those. We have started that tradition once again in Fort Bliss, believe it or not, with our Freedom Crossing area, the largest PX commissary complex in the world. We have concerts once a week. About every third or fourth week it's our band that's there also. So we're kind of rejuvenating a tradition from one hundred years ago.

GERALD PRATT

SON OF REY L. PRATT, GRANDSON OF HELAMAN PRATT, AND GREAT-GRANDSON OF PARLEY P. PRATT
EL PASO, FEBRUARY 17, 2012

I'M PROUD OF THE FACT THAT MY GRANDFATHER, Helaman Pratt, answered the call to make that trip to Mexico. As I was reading through his journal, he did not cross the river to Juárez, but to El Paso, because at that time Juárez was named El Paso, and El Paso was named Franklin. So he crossed the river from Franklin on the north side to El Paso on the south side, the seventh day of January, 1876.

It was interesting how the call to Mexico came. Someone got up in general conference and named off those who were going to make the trip. They were told to get ready the next day and leave. When we get a call nowadays, it says, "In two, maybe three, months from now you'll go on a mission." It was a very severe trip, a very hard trip. The group had some very difficult times to overcome. My grandfather had decided, when they were planning to go to Mexico, that he was going to learn the language. So he made a real effort to learn it. . . . His Spanish was very good. After he filled a mission in Mexico City, he was called first as a missionary, and then as president of the mission. When he was released his call he said, . . . "You need to stay in Mexico for the rest of your life," and so he did. He spent the rest of his life in Mexico.

In Ciudad Juárez on a Sunday, Helaman Pratt and the first LDS missionaries to Mexico decided, all of them, to go to the cathedral. They arrived there a little late, I guess, because there was just standing room in the doorway. The padre got up and said, . . . "God has sent us all kinds of plagues. We've had droughts; and we've had windstorms, terrible windstorms; we've had terrible flooding; we've had insects attack us; we've had all kinds of plagues; but the most serious and the most difficult and the meanest plague we've got today is those seven men that are standing there in the door, those Mormon missionaries." At that time, Brother Jones, who was in charge of the organization, said he thought discretion was the better part of valor, and they decided to leave before somebody stuck a knife up in their ribs and got rid of that plague. But later that year, Brother Jones, being a good saddle maker, finally ended up making a saddle for the padre; they became very good friends and worked to their best mutual advantage. Although the missionaries didn't have any converts in El Paso at that time, they planted some seeds that I'm sure, in later years, came through. . . .

As I understand it, when my grandfather's family came to the colonies, he had wives in Salt Lake City at the time, and one wife was expecting. He told his other wife to bring all of the kids from Salt Lake and meet him. . . . They lived in Colonia Juárez. . . . Later he built a home in Colonia Dublán, and that home is still standing, one of the only original buildings still standing in Dublán. . . .

My folks came out from Mexico single, met in El Paso, and decided to get married. They were married in El Paso before they went back to the colonies. . . .

One little story concerning the exodus. When they were in Dublán, all the people were lined up along the railroad track waiting for the train to come. At the time of the exodus, they thought the train was going to come early in the morning, but it was late coming, so they were all there waiting in the hot sun. Over two blocks across the way, my grandfather had left a peach orchard which Helaman Pratt had planted. My grandfather was taking care of my father, Rey Pratt. My mother, Mary Merrill, and my father, Rey Pratt, were kind of sweethearts. My father came by, as they were all waiting there, and got talking to her. They went over to the peach orchard, picked a bunch of peaches, and brought them back for all the people that were standing there hungry, waiting for the train. That's the last time they saw each other until after the men folks left the colonies. Of course they met again.

At the time of decision to leave the colonies, . . . my father was standing by in Colonia Juárez at the time the stake president and the high council were having the meeting wherein they decided to leave the colonies. When they came out of the meeting, they left him the word, and he drove—rode on horseback—that night from Colonia Juárez to Colonia Dublán to advise Bishop Thurber of the Dublán ward to get everybody out of town before daylight. . . . They didn't quite achieve that; but they got out all right. Later, when they did leave and got into Hachita, he left his horse and whatnot there and caught the train to El Paso.

My to-be mother, Mary Merrill, was single at the time of the exodus. She rode the train to El Paso. Mother had a great advantage because she had worked at the White House in El Paso. . . . She was a seamstress, and she had already connections in El Paso. So when she got to El Paso, she took her mother and those of her family and found them a place to live. They never did stay in the lumber sheds like a lot of them did—like my mother-in-law, Lily O'Donnell Whetten, because she didn't have any place to go. But my mother had the advantage that she already knew El Paso and had connections. My father stayed in Dublán with the menfolks, and when the decision was made for all the menfolks to leave, he was standing by in Colonia Juárez. And the high council and the stake presidency had their meeting wherein they made the decision to leave, and he rode at ten o'clock at night from Colonia Juárez to Colonia Dublán to tell Bishop Thurber to get the people together and get out of town before daylight, which they didn't quite achieve; but they got out all right. Later, when they did leave and got into Hachita, he left his horse and whatnot there, and he caught the train to El Paso. And of course they met again.

VERA WHETTEN PRATT

DAUGHTER OF COLONISTS
EL PASO, FEBRUARY 17, 2012

MY FATHER, JAMES ALBERT WHETTEN, WAS known as Bert Whetten. He was born in Snowflake, Arizona, and moved as a child to Colonia Juárez, then on up into the mountains to Kade Valley and several other colonies. My mother, Lilly O'Donnell, was born in Oklahoma and came as a young child into Mexico because the feeling against the Mormons in Oklahoma was not good; so the elders recommended that they come west. On their way west, they stopped in El Paso overnight, where they met a Brother Lake, who was in the colonies. He said, "Oh, Brother O'Donnell, you need to go to the colonies. Land is available; it's not expensive. The colonies is a good place to raise your family. So many people with your same ideals and standards." So my grandparents went to Mexico instead of going on to Utah or California, as they had planned to. That's where my father and my mother met. . . .

They lived in Colonial Juárez, . . . but at the time of the Revolution it was felt they needed to leave. So my mother and my father's younger siblings, and her in-laws, my Grandpa and Grandma Whetten, were on the train and helped her. She had a tiny baby, so she was grateful for a mother-in-law who could help her. When they got to the sheds, as they were called, in El Paso, she said it was really hard, it was bad. The only privacy they had was stringing up wires and hanging quilts, to divide off one family from another family. The city of El Paso was very good. They brought in two or three restaurant-size stoves where the refugees could cook, and they brought in groceries every day.

But this was in July, and so it was very hot, and there was no air conditioning. My mother said the mosquitoes were terrible; they would chew up the babies. My grandmother said, "There must be something we can do to keep the mosquitoes off the babies." (This was before mosquito repellant.) "Kerosene smells so bad. I wonder if we put kerosene on the babies, it will keep the mosquitoes off?" And it did. So they would rub kerosene on the baby's faces and arms and cover everything else, and it did help with the mosquito problem. . . .

My mother, Lily O'Donnell Whetten, was with the group that came out on the train, and my dad was one who stayed to try to rescue some things. But because they lived in the mountains, they had to come by wagon, eight hours down, to get to Pearson, where they caught the train. . . . That was quite a ride before they joined the people who caught the train in Dublán. She said they were able to take very, very, very little. She tells one story of being on the train; my dad had a couple of teenage sisters who were a little embarrassed about Grandpa being with all of these children and women and the polygamy thing and whatnot. So these teenage girls were in the back of the train, not with the rest of the family. One of the little brothers, like a ten-year-old, said, "Hey, Candy, what are you doing back there? Why don't you come up here with the rest of the family?" She was embarrassed.

It was a long, hot ride. They took lunches with them, such as they could. But because it was hot, they couldn't bring . . . meat. They talked about taking biscuits and making jelly sandwiches out of biscuits. They also had bottled fruit, which they opened up and enjoyed. But it was just a long, hot, miserable ride. Mother, who had a tiny baby, was really miserable. When they got into El Paso, they felt like the people of El Paso were just angels to send them ice and food and meat. . . .

Mother said she felt like the people of El Paso were trying hard to make them comfortable in an uncomfortable situation. One thing was bathrooms. There couldn't be enough bathrooms for all of these people, and little outhouses were set up. But that was awful, because she got dysentery. She said, "And there was always a line and I would just get back to bed and I'd have to go again, and there was always a line." She said it was miserable. Then the people of El Paso wondered what Mormons looked like, so always a lot of onlookers would come. I don't know whether there was a fence around. In my mind, there must have been a fence somewhere, because they said that the children would come and look to see if the Mormons really had horns. There was always a group standing there looking to see what they could see, what the Mormons looked like. . . .

While they were in the sheds or the lumberyard, when they wanted to have a bath they had to heat the water on the big restaurant-size stoves. Then they would get in their little partition and have somebody hold a blanket up around the little number-three tub that they heated water in, so that they could have a quick bath. It couldn't last very long, because people couldn't stand there and hold the blankets for a very long time. They had to spend time during the day preparing their meals. I'm sure they made simple meals, but it still takes time, and then there were children to tend. There were children who were in diapers, and the diapers had to be washed. The women had to hang them wherever they could hang them. They strung wires to hang the diapers on to dry. And they fought mosquitoes.

ANNA LUCILE ROMNEY

DAUGHTER OF COLONISTS
LAS CRUCES, NEW MEXICO, APRIL 12, 2012

MY FATHER, CLARENCE TURLEY, WENT WITH his parents to the northern part of Mexico, near Casas Grandes, Chihuahua, as we know it today. They lived there. It was a wonderful place to raise children. Everything was Church oriented—our schools were Church schools, our activities were plays and operettas. Then we had dances on Friday nights, and everyone went to the dances. We had a lot of activities, so there was no problem with going to the movies or finding something else to do; there was always something going on. It was a wonderful place for children to live and to grow up all those years—until things started happening The colonists had problems because of the other elements of people in the Mexican colonies who were against each other. The colonists had a lot of trouble until it got to the point where the stake president said, "We need to leave." And some of Church members locked their homes and went to the train that goes into Madera, Mexico and on into El Paso. Some of the people in the clan had forgotten something, but when they ran back home, already there were people in their homes pillaging things. So they tried to lock the doors and left on the train.

They went to El Paso, where the U.S. government was kind enough to give them tents to live in until they could find a home to rent. Some of them moved on to live in different places in Arizona and Utah, but some went into El Paso and rented homes. My father's father rented a home there, and the boys looked for work. I know that his oldest son, . . . Vernon Turley, got a good job . . . with the railroad. First he worked in the ticket office, then as a Red Cap, and he did very well. But it was hard to get work, so Grandfather Turley, my father's father, worked for the city police department, . . . helping the deputy. They got whatever work they could. My father . . . worked with four horses and scraper to help the family clear land for the farm. And it was not easy. It was difficult. But I remember one thing my father, Clarence, said: "We can remember how hot it was." It was in July and it was so hot in those tents. Then he said, "The only milk we could have was canned milk." He had been used to cow's milk, so that canned milk was awful. But they got along all right. They were faithful. . . .

Clarence Turley was twelve years old when colonists decided they needed to leave Mexico. He was living in Colonia Juárez and had go about eighteen miles away to catch the train in Casas Grandes. He went with the women and the children. Most of the men went on horseback, taking their cattle and whatever they had with them. Clarence had to come along with the women and the children. They got on the train and went to Ciudad Juárez, which is just out of El Paso. . . .

When I think of life in the Colonia Juárez area Mexico areas I think about how wonderful the Church was in our lives and how it meant a lot to us. Our parents loved the Church and loved what we doing; they taught us the basic cookbook of the gospel so that we could live right. It was a wonderful place to be raised, because we had our own Church schools, and we did so well. My father used to say, when he would come to El Paso to get supplies or something, "It sure is good to be back home." He was always happy to be home. It was a wonderful place to grow up. . . .

After they were in El Paso two years, my father and his father went down to the Colonies to see the situation. They decided it was safe to return, and so they did. They packed up and returned home. . . . There were a lot of bandits, . . . and some of them came to the house one day and said, "We want your team of horses." Clarence's father, Edward, always had very good cattle and horses and nice leather workings for them, and he always had every good wagon and stage to work with. So he said, "If you'll give us just two or three days, we are just getting our corn crop in. We have got to have these horses to get our corn crop in. So you can come back in three days and get the horses." The bandit said, "If the horses aren't here when we come back, we will burn your house down." So about eleven o'clock at night, father and mother came into Clarence's bedroom and said, "Clarence, could you go up to the field and bring those horses?" They finished their harvest and the horses were there at home for several days, but the bandits didn't come for them. So they took the horses to a special place up the riverM tied them up, and kept them there. At eleven o'clock at night my father (he was not quite sixteen) went by himself—he didn't have a horse, and he could only get the burro. He got on the burro, bareback, went to the field, and got his two horses. As he brought them back he heard another horse coming. It scared him. He stopped and simply turned to the man and said, "Who goes there?" It was Brother Wood, who owned the place that was keeping the horses. Clarence was so happy to find out that the other person coming was Brother Wood. Even though the war was over, there were still a lot of troublemakers in the area.

FLORENCE BLACK ROMNEY

DESCENDANT OF COLONISTS AND GREAT-GRAND-DAUGHTER OF WILLIAM MORLEY BLACK
SALT LAKE CITY, FEBRUARY 24, 2012

I'M A GREAT-GRANDDAUGHTER OF WILLIAM Morley Black, who was a great patriarch of a very large family that lived in the mountain colonies of Pacheco. Their exodus was very difficult, coming down the mountain, and many of my family have recalled experiences from that incident. My great-grandfather, who was eighty-six years old at the time, wrote about the experience: "I feel thankful to the good citizens of El Paso for the aid and sympathy they gave us." . . .

As a woman I can identify with the difficulties these members of my family and many other families had. Gathering their children, being frightened for the lives of their husbands, not knowing what to expect, being put on a train perhaps for the first time ever on a train, and in a cattle car, and then to be able to go for a distance and end up in El Paso in very difficult circumstances. How much it meant to me to know that there were wonderful, good-hearted people there who would accept them and care for them and make the best out of a very difficult situation. . . .

I grew up hearing stories about my legacy with my family in Mexico and coming out of the Mountain Colonies in Pacheco. William Morley Black was the father of my Grandfather David P. Black, who was very instrumental, being a sheriff in that community, and playing a very large role in helping get the women and children out of the mountain colony and down to where the train was. I've always felt proud of my pioneer heritage. At one time when I was ill, the doctor told me I was a strong pioneer woman, and I told him I knew why—because I know the stories of my grandma Black, . . . who had come down out of the mountains and found herself in El Paso with her large family, and being smitten with horrible pains of finding that she had appendicitis. She had to leave her children and be taken by these wonderful people of El Paso to the hospital through these trying times. Older children had to take care of the younger children. That was kind of the life they lived. I'm proud to be a part of that heritage. I'm proud that they were strong and that they could survive such a difficult time. Perhaps the good people of El Paso helped make it possible so that they could survive and have some good memories of a bad situation.

JOSEPH B. ROMNEY

EMERITUS FACULTY MEMBER OF THE RELIGION DEPARTMENT AT BYU–IDAHO
SALT LAKE CITY, FEBRUARY 24, 2012

THE MORMONS WENT TO MEXICO TO AVOID persecution from the federal government in the United States. The Church leaders said it was appropriate for them to go to either Mexico or Canada to avoid that persecution. Our family went to Mexico.

The advantage to the Mexicans for the Mormons to go down into Mexico in 1888 was that Porfirio Díaz, president at the time, was trying to build his presidency on a firm, economic structure. Americans in general went down there. . . . That economic base included other Americans who were mining and building railroads and so on. It also included immigrants who had come down to provide an economic base. The Mormons were able to provide that economic base, the ideal that President Díaz wanted. . . .

In 1885, when the Mormons went down under Porfirio Díaz, the political situation was very calm. That was unusual, because up until approximately 1875, when Díaz came to power, there had been a chaotic political situation, but in 1888 it was very calm, and the Mormons felt very comfortable as part of the Porfirian economic structure.

When the Mexican Revolution started in 1910, there had to be some decision what the Church and the United States would do relative to the competing parties. At the time of the Mormon exodus, the competing parties were the rebels, under a man named Pascual Orozco, against the president at the time, Francisco Madero. The Mormons had to decide how they could survive and how the United States could relate to that the situation. It was a difficult situation, because both Mexican parties alternately controlled the area in which the Mormon colonies were located, so it was a firsthand decision, it wasn't a theoretical decision. Question: "How can we accomplish what we're trying to do, stay alive, having the necessity of being able to placate both sides of the conflict?" . . .

Junius Romney, my grandfather, was a man of strong character and ideals. He had moved to Mexico at seven years of age, married there, had a family there, and then became stake president in 1908 when he was thirty years old, a very young age. He continued to have his family life. He was protecting his family, but his commitment was also strongly tied to his role as a stake president. He felt he had received a call from God, and so had a commitment to do a good job for the people over whom he presided. As the Revolution proceeded, he gave it his full attention, but then he found himself in the middle of what was happening with the Revolution. At the same time, he was trying to be the ecclesiastical leader of the Church in Mexico, which also meant he was the political leader of the Mormons in Mexico. He was not insensitive, but he was also determined to accomplish what he needed to do, whatever the difficulty might be. He was very careful to try to follow the guidance he received from the Church leaders in Salt Lake City and in counsel with the Church leaders in Mexico.

As the Mormons found themselves in the middle of the Revolution, they wanted to be prepared, which is a basic Mormon concept. They wanted to be neutral, but at the same time, they knew the time might come when they needed to prepare themselves. At one point in time the leaders of the colonies got together and said, "We need to have better rifles, because the rifles of the rebels are higher-powered and can reach a greater distance, and if they were to attack us they would be able to do that without us being able to respond."

The first attempt failed when the border guards were not informed that it was appropriate to let those weapons go into Mexico. The relationship between the United States government and those who were in the border didn't recognize that the government had given approval for the weapons to come in. A month or two later that got cleared up, so the rifles came over the border. The weapons then were taken by a couple of young men down into Mexico. They were purchased by the Church and then delivered to the bishops of each of the wards and hidden at a place where they could only be used for defensive purposes under the direction of the Church leader in the area. Eventually that was necessary and was very effective as the men were leaving the colonies. . . .

The Revolution impacted the colonies in all kinds of ways. It went on and on, and it touched their daily life—it touched how they earned a living, it touched about everything that they were doing. The rebels, in particular, needed supplies, so they would go to the stores owned by the colonists and requisition—which in effect was orderly looting—that is, collect those supplies, or go to the colonists and take their horses to ride on, or kill the cattle the colonists had in order to feed themselves. That created a general attitude of fear and uncertainty among the colonists, whereas in previous years they'd had a feeling of support and calm; they could go about their business, both ecclesiastically and economically, and build their houses, raise their families, and do other things that would build a good life. . . .

At one point during the revolutionary period, my grandfather had an occasion to meet with José Inés Salazar, the general in charge of Orozco's forces in Chihuahua. That particular time was a very unusual time. Grandpa felt a need to talk with Salazar.

He felt strongly enough that he and a couple of his friends, including one high councilor named Brother Bowman, went to the location in Casas Grandes where the general was sleeping and asked the guard to let them in. The guard said, "No, you can't go in," but President Romney persisted, and the guard let them in, at which time they had a rather heated discussion about the role relationship of the rebels and the colonists. Salazar said, "We intend to protect the Mormons, the colonists." Not long after that, that same General Salazar—Junius having known him not only on two occasions (the other time was when the general attended the Juárez Stake Academy)—requested a list of the weapons the colonists had. President Romney said, "I'll get the list," and he asked the leaders of the various colonies to give him a list, but he told the leaders not to be in a rush. He just wanted to be sure that he could honestly tell Salazar that he was getting a list.

About ten days later, a leader of the forces around Colonia Díaz, the colony closest to El Paso, made demand of the colonists there to have them give him their weapons. The leader of the rebels said, "You may give them to me voluntarily, or I'll take it from you forcefully." When that got to President Romney's ears, he approached Salazar, who said, "That is not what we're supposed to do at this time," which was chilling to Grandpa, who told Salazar that it was going to be sometime; he needed to prepare for that. But Salazar sent a message to the local commander which said, "Don't do it," which saved Díaz at that time. Two weeks later Salazar made a demand, and this time it was not to be refuted. Salazar had power behind that demand, as he had surrounded the colony of Colonia Dublán with a couple of thousand rebel soldiers, who were ready to take those weapons. . . .

The exodus of the women and children was a result of Salazar's demand for weapons. The leaders of the Church in Colonia Dublán, including President Romney, decided they needed to comply with that demand, so they sat down together and said, "We're going to give them our weapons, but we're going to give them our oldest weapons and retain these higher power rifles to protect ourselves." But they recognized at the time that their families no longer had any protection from the rebels. They said, "We've got to get our families out of here. We anticipate it will only be for a short time, but we've got to get them to the United States." So that very day, the afternoon of July 27, they made arrangements for their families to begin leaving the colonies for El Paso, which they began to do on the railroad that went up to El Paso, traveling on cattle cars and any way to get to El Paso. That continued then for several days until all the women and children were evacuated from the Chihuahua colonies. . . .

After the women and children were taken up to El Paso, there were still several hundred men down in the colonies in Chihuahua, and the rebels were going in and out of the various colonies. President Romney had made a determined effort to hold, to receive counsel from anybody who came from Salt Lake City, which included President Eyring, who'd been the first stake president, who was now an Apostle, and it included counsel with the ward leaders, not only the official leaders like the bishop, but also leading men in the colonies. . . .

Some plans were made for a meeting of the leaders of the colony at Colonia Juárez, but those plans went awry, and in the middle of the night, President Romney found himself in the desert, some of the men having already gone up into the mountains, and others still left in the colonies. He thought, "What's going to happen when the federals, or when the rebels, find this has happened? They will think the men have gone to join the federals." Up to that time, he'd had men with whom he could consult, but at that particular time, in the middle of the night when that came to his attention, it was only he. There was no one around that he could consult with. He had to make an on-the-spot decision. He turned to God, whom he could always talk to. Here's some of his language that described the situation: "I had with me a lantern and writing materials. Putting my trust in the Lord, I calmly proceeded to put into operation the only plan which seemed to me any sane man could regard as sound under the circumstances. It seemed to me with perfect clarity what was necessary to be done. It seemed perfectly clear to me that our only safety lay in gathering at the Stairs" (a rugged part of the Sierra Madre . . . about seven miles west of Colonia Juárez). That led Grandpa to write the order for the evacuation of the men to all the colonies in Chihuahua.

He said, "We need to go up now and join the men who are now in the mountains at a place called the Stairs." Even in the morning when that happened, he had the thought, "I made a horrible mistake." But he went forward, and the men moved up into the mountains, at which time they had the question "Now what are we going to do, now that we're all up in the mountains?" At least the men from Colonia Juárez and Dublán wondered that. That raised another question. At that particular time there was a division of opinion among the various leaders, some saying they ought to stay and wait the thing out, some saying they needed to go to the border. Grandpa felt they ought to go to the border.

The men had a meeting in which the various points of view were vigorously discussed, to decide what to do. There was a difference of opinion. They took a vote, and one of the participants in the meeting, a man named Joel Martineau, later wrote about that, because it was surprising to him, in spite of the differences of opinion that were made, the decision was unanimous in favor of going, which he thought was remarkable. They decided to go to the border en masse, but before they moved to the border, they deposited some of their documents and manuscripts in this area of the Stairs, and then some 235 of them, with horses and wagons, marched northward to cross the desert, trying to avoid the forces of the rebels who were in the area. In about . . . a week, they reached the border. . . .

As they approached the border they were carrying a white flag, but the cloud of the dust which they raised was such that it was difficult to see the flag or even who the people were. The detachment of American soldiers who were behind a rock wall defending the border looked at these people as Mexicans who were going to invade the United States. About the time that they were to fire on them, a man among the soldiers identified a man by the name of Tenney and said, "Those are the Mormons, don't shoot!" and that stopped them from attacking. The men then crossed the border, Grandpa being the last of them to cross, and as he did that, he wrote later that a great feeling of peace came over him, because he'd accomplished the goal of the exodus without losing the life of a single person. . . . What could have been a disaster became a miraculous salvation of the men. Every one of the men came out of alive.

Two days after the men crossed the border in Arizona, President Romney appeared before a Church committee called the Relief Committee. The first thing they wanted to talk about was "What justified you in giving the orders to move these three thousand people out of the state of Chihuahua?" For two days they discussed that matter. They didn't ever come to an official decision relative to that, but the discussion, which Grandpa called his court-martial, stayed with him throughout his life, and he was concerned to try to explain why he did what he did. He explained to them at that time, and later on, that it wasn't he who did it, he was led by God, and the process of the exodus was the hand of God, working through men on the earth, who, at that time, were not clearly aware that they were fulfilling the wishes of a just and all-powerful God. . . .

After the decision was made by the leaders for the women and children to go up to the United States, the women and children were asked immediately to pack a few of their things that would take them through a couple of days in the United States, after which they planned to return to their homes in Mexico. They then went to a nearby station on the railroad in a town called Pearson. Junius's family was under the control of his younger brother Park. Other families had experiences that can be presented by three other authors. One is by Anson B. Call, who is from Colonia Dublán. He said, "It was a very pitiable sight to see our loved ones loaded into boxcars and in many cases into cattle cars with hardly standing room. This on a hot July day under scorching semi-tropical sun. Should I stop and redo that? . . .

Anson B. Call, who was from Colonia Dublán, wrote this: The suffering that many of the weak and the aged people endured in these unventilated boxcars will never be known this side of eternity." Neil Hatch, whose family participated in this, and the author of a significant book about the colonists, said, "We're packed to leave up and leave immediately, . . ." He said this "through tight lips." . . .

When Nelle Hatch, a noted author of the Mormon colonies in Mexico, wrote this about a man who spoke to his family, the family responded this way: "'We're to pack up and leave immediately,' he said, through tight lips. 'That is, all of you women folks. So get ready and we'll take one of the first trains from Pearson.' 'But what shall we take?' 'Where shall we go?' 'What shall we do?' were all questions tumbling out at once." Another writer by the name of Alonzo Taylor wrote, "A sad procession." . . .

Another colonist, Alonzo Taylor, talked about the feeling of the men after they had taken their children and family members to the train. He said, "Those returning to Colonia Juárez from the train formed a sad procession. No one scarcely spoke a word on the return trip, except to occasionally remark that they were returning to a desolate and lonely spot that only a few days before had been the scene of happy and contented homes filled with women and children." . . .

After the refugees gathered together in El Paso, they had help from three sources. One of the sources was their church. The refugee committee was organized under the chairmanship of Anthony W. Ivins, who had previously been the first stake president, but was now a member of the Quorum of the Twelve and a member of the committee, which included the stake presidency, including grandpa and his two counselors, and about a dozen other leading men from the colonies. One of the things they talked about is what the colonists should do: should they return or not to their homes? Grandpa spent a week going down back to the colonies to determine what the conditions were, and what he found out is that the necessary federal troops to protect them would not be able to do that. He thought at this time that it was not appropriate for them to return. In due time, about 20 to 25 percent of the colonists returned to their homes. Help also came to the relief committee from the Church directly as they furnished money and advice on how to go about the business. Another source of help came from the United States, through the army, which furnished tents for their use, and money to move them other places away from El Paso. But a third source of help came from the good people of El Paso, who were confronted with a deluge of several hundred refugees. They provided places for them to stay, and food and other things that would help them get through these early days away from their homes without any other source of support. My family was able to find housing where one family was packed into a room in several houses. The help from the people of El Paso is particularly exemplified by the treatment that was given to the grandmother of my wife Florence, when she had appendicitis. She was taken into a hospital in El Paso, where that appendicitis was taken care of. Other things took place which I'm not aware of, but can be told by other people who were on the ground at the time in El Paso. . . .

One of the things I'd like to say for myself and my family, and for all of the colonists, as a matter of fact, is word of expression of gratitude to the citizens of El Paso who helped our ancestors at an exceptionally difficult time in their lives and blessed us as a result of what they did for them. . . .

The events of my grandfather's life in the colonies, including the exodus, was a focal point of his thought from that time on. It was an emotional subject, which he talked about, internally always and occasionally to other people.

The impact of the exodus and his stay in Mexico was always with Grandpa, and it came to mind particularly as I accompanied him and his son Eldon to the colonies in 1967 when Grandpa was eighty-nine years old. Grandpa talked to his friends and relatives and took with him a copy—a number of copies—that he had made of a talk in Salt Lake City that explained his interpretation of what had happened during that period of time. He also visited the home he had built there, a beautiful brick home that was of the highest quality of a home that size in Salt Lake City. He visited a brick home of his mother, which was next door to his. And more significantly to me, with about a dozen of us, he went to the orchard that he had planted just a month before he had left Mexico. He pulled from the trees apples and handed them to all of us, to recognize what he had done at that particular time to provide for his family. What he offered was delicious physically, but emotionally I felt that this was what Grandpa wanted to do. It was an important time for me, and I think it was an important time for Grandpa. At eighty-nine years of age he was able to find some closure in what he'd gone through fifty years early at that significant time, the most significant time in his life, as a matter of fact.

DAVID ROMO

DOCTORAL CANDIDATE AT UNIVERSITY OF TEXAS AT EL PASO, HISTORIAN ON THE MEXICAN REVOLUTION
UNIVERSITY OF TEXAS AT EL PASO, FEBRUARY 17, 2012

IN GENERAL THE MEXICAN REVOLUTION IS THE first major revolution of the twentieth century. There was tremendous upheaval in Mexico. In 1911, it was relatively bloodless, let's say. Francisco Madero, leader of the revolution, with the help of some of the more famous generals, like Pancho Villa, defeated the dictatorship of Porfirio Díaz. Very few casualties took place during this period. Later, it became a civil war. Different generals, different leaders of the Mexican Revolution, turned against each other. The civil war went on for about ten years. About three million Mexican people were either displaced or killed as a result of the Mexican Revolution. What happened was that some of the revolutionary leaders that originally belonged to the Madero movement, such as General Orozco, General José Inés Salazar, and others, rose up against President Francisco Madero. This was when the Revolution began to become a lot more bloody. I'd say this is where the civil war started, and it started on the border with the United States.

Just as a background, the border played a huge role in the Mexican Revolution. It was unlike other revolutions—the Russian Revolution or the French Revolution—which usually take place in the central areas.

The border was the seat where most of the early stages of the Mexican Revolution were sparked. Most of the big names, the leaders that came from the Revolution—who included Madero, Pancho Villa, General Orozco, and General Salazar—were from the border. So that's where major events took place. The year 1912 was the time when General Orozco declared a counter-revolutionary movement against the central government of Mexico, which was a liberal, progressive government that now was opening up, including more democratic reforms.

The United States preferred stability in Mexico in 1912, so it cut off freight and arms . . . and created an arms embargo against the counter-revolutionaries led by General Orozco and General Salazar. And this created . . . more anti-American feelings among those counter-revolutionary leaders. So they began to pressure different American businesses and communities. From their point of view, there was resentment that some of these American communities had been given favorable treatment, not only by the previous dictator, General Díaz, but now by the government of Francisco Madero, including Pancho Villa. The early stages of the movement were very, very pro-American. Villa would go into . . . the Mormon colonies, and not only provide them protection, he befriended many of the Mormon settlers along the northern part of Mexico.

General Orozco seized the arms embargo by the United States as a kind of intervention against this movement. He was extremely angered by the embargo. In fact, the embargo that took place along the US-Mexico border, especially in regions like El Paso, had a direct impact on what took place in the military battles in the interior of Mexico. What happened here in the streets of El Paso on the U.S. side of the border played a huge role in the revolution; in fact, Ciudad Juárez, the town immediately across from El Paso, was the provisional capital of the counter-revolutionary movement of Generals Salazar and Orozco. . . .

The Revolution was a very, very complicated era of Mexican history. There was . . . myriad of factions, and it is very difficult for the normal person to understand what really went on. Most Mexicans, not to mention foreign communities, outside communities, or non-indigenous communities in Mexico, were going to find it very difficult to remain neutral. The Mormon community was caught between a rock and a hard place, in the sense that if the Madero government supported them, then the counter-revolutionary movement of Orozco, Salazar, and Antonio Rojas was going to go after them. This is something that every faction of the Revolution had to decide—whether they were going to take a pro-American stance, and in that way avoid intervention, or, at times, purposefully provoke intervention. The reason they wanted to provoke intervention is because they felt that the Mexican people would rise up on their side.

Then Salazar and Orozco went in to pressure the Mormon community to take their arms, arms that the Mormons had had to smuggle in from the United States against the wishes of both the Madero government and the United States. The . . . counter-revolutionaries knew that the Mormon community had these weapons, so they used this as part of their very complicated international political maneuvering. They used the Mormon community in order to carry out their greater aims. . . .

The counter-revolutionaries led by Orozco and Salazar wanted the Mormon community to hand over their weapons, as part of their broader geopolitical maneuvering going on at this time. Most Mexicans didn't have good feelings towards the counter-revolutionary movement of Orozco, Salazar, and Antonio Rojas. . . . It was really the counter-revolutionaries who added the element of ruthlessness that both Madero and even Pancho Villa would show in some of the counter-revolutionary acts of violence against American communities, because it wasn't in Villa's interest either to have American public opinion against the revolution. So all of these things made it very, very complicated. Usually people that don't know much about Mexican history see the Revolution as one big monolith—well, … they probably know of Frito Bandito, the savage, brutal concept of Pancho Villa. It's this vision of the Revolution that usually goes out to a wider audience. But it was very, very complicated. The geopolitics were simple. What the Mormon community experienced in northern Mexico was exactly what most Mexicanos experienced. They too were caught between a rock and a hard place. And that's why hundreds of thousands of Mexicanos migrated to the United States in that period. . . .

When the counter-revolutionaries led by Orozco and Salazar and Rojas went to the Mormons and forced them to hand over their weapons in exchange for protection, Mormons were of course going to be in a very difficult position. They were not going to have the protection of the central government, and now they were probably going to be even more vulnerable to this counter-revolutionary movement, yet that was the same experience of most Mexicans and American businesses and other communities that had been brought in during the . . . government of Porfirio Díaz. . . . There were going to be some sectors of Mexico happy that American and other foreigners had come into the country under the government of Porfirio Díaz, but there were also going to be others who were resentful that Porfirio Díaz was bringing in people in order to purify the indigenous blood of the majority of poor Mexicans by bringing in "superior European bloodstock." So there was going to be a lot of pressure, both from the governments, from the counter-revolutionaries, and also from the popular sectors of the community.

BERNIE SARGENT

CHAIRMAN OF THE EL PASO COUNTY HISTORY COMMISSION
EL PASO, FEBRUARY 19, 2012

EL PASO OVER MANY GENERATIONS HAS BEEN A pass, hence the name *El Paso*. You had the natives traveling north and south, east and west, following the valley between the two mountain ranges, the beginning of the Sierra Madres and the beginning of the Sierras. You also had the Rio Grande going north-south, so it provided a source of water. Where there's water there's livestock or wildlife, and there's also vegetation. It provided a natural food supply for these folks that were traveling long before the Anglos or the Caucasians even thought about coming to this part of the world.

Then a number of explorers came out of Mexico looking for gold, silver, minerals, and land, and looking to proselytize the natives—looking to expand the Spanish realm, so to speak. They followed the Rio Grande through the pass. Ultimately the railroads came into this area; from 1881 till 1883 seven railroads constructed lines through El Paso. The wagon trains came through El Paso, for example, the Butterfield Trail, a natural route you could follow virtually 365 days a year. It was a natural route—accessible, easy to find, and easy to protect if you needed to protect it from bad people or other folks, folks with nefarious things in mind. In 1881 the population was virtually under a thousand people, most of whom are Caucasians, and by 1912 when the exodus occurred out of Mexico, over thirty thousand people lived in El Paso. It exploded in growth, and it came to be considered the focal point of the Southwest for many, many years. . . .

So El Paso in 1912 was . . . an exploding area; very large stores were being built here to service not only the people on the border of the United State but also those folks who lived across the border in present day Ciudad Juárez and south of Chihuahua City. Large refineries were refining metals from all over the Southwest as far south as Chihuahua, Mexico and beyond, and also all over the Southwestern United States. Schools were being built, businesses constructed, and the military was building up because of the obvious situation in Mexico, where the Revolution was beginning to swell up.

The incursion of the refugees from Mexico included Mexicans themselves, who were trying to get away from the violence that was taking place in Mexico. The buildup in arms on the U.S. border corresponded with what was going on in Mexico. Then there was the fear of what was going on in Europe; Fort Bliss in El Paso could be used as a training ground for what might happen in Europe as well as in other parts of the world.

With all this taking place—the railroads bringing more and more people into El Paso and the concerns that come along with growth, as well as the kind of people moving in—that kind of growth might deeply concern the people in this particular area. John Phillip Sousa came to El Paso to perform, his second time in the area. The first time, he wasn't very impressed, but the second time he was overwhelmed by the support he got. Virtually all of the "Who's Who" of stage life in the world came to El Paso to perform. It was a wonderful place to be in, vibrant with growth. . . .

El Paso at that time could be considered a city of refuge because of the many job opportunities. There was work not only in the business establishments, such as the stores downtown, but also the manufacturing facilities being constructed, support facilities for the refineries, and highways being built. Not only were folks moving in from Mexico to escape the revolution, a huge migration of Chinese immigrants came up through the border, up from South America through Mexico. A melting pot was forming—all these cultures, all these religions, the result of an open-door policy. People from all over the world were coming to settle in the Southwest, given the uncertainty that followed the waning of the Spanish American War.

There was lots of military opportunity, following buildup of Fort Bliss, along with job and support opportunities for the military. The more G.I.'s in the area, the more people needed to support them. Automobiles could take you from the East Coast to the West Coast on the major thoroughfares being constructed, although they were dirt in most areas. The first concrete roads in the state of Texas were right in El Paso. El Paso was a place for opportunity. . . .

It goes without saying that we have today the same growth patterns as a hundred years ago. With the situations across the border, areas economically tainted, so to speak, there is again an influx of Mexicans coming to the safety of El Paso and the Southwest, and elsewhere in the United States. El Paso again continues to be a political refuge. We have opportunity here, we have jobs here, and so we have growth here. Fort Bliss continues to grow. . . .

El Paso has an open-door policy for all kinds of people, especially the downtrodden, folks that are being abused, whether politically or religiously. We've welcomed them all, and that was the situation in 1912 when the exodus came up from Mexico. If you are willing to work, we have been willing to have you here. Traditionally, the Mormons did a wonderful job in establishing their colonies in Mexico, and we figured they would do the same here, because they would see this as their home. If we opened our arms and welcomed them, they would do the same here.

MELISSA SARGENT

CO-PRODUCER OF THE EL PASO HISTORY RADIO SHOW
EL PASO, FEBRUARY 19, 2012

BEING A WOMAN, AND HAVING THE THOUGHT of having to pick up everything—my family, my children—and leaving my home, my husband, my friends, my animals, my livestock, everything I had worked so hard for all these years, and having to run north to escape Colonel Salazar and his troops, who were telling us we had less than twenty-four hours to get out of town, and we couldn't take anything with us. Putting the children on a train, going to some place we didn't know, . . . having grown up in Colonia Juárez or Dublán, wherever it was that they were coming from. And then to travel this distance in fear of being . . . robbed . . .—all that was a very frightening thought.

Once you got to the border and El Paso, what were you going to? You knew you were going to be back in the United States, but what would be waiting there for you? Well, what was waiting for you was a community that opened their arms to those refugees from Mexico, much to their surprise. I would imagine more than anything else, there wasn't a lot that could be offered them. Homes were opened and some families went to those homes, but as a rule, about five hundred of them lived in the lumberyards in El Paso for a time, not the best of conditions but better than the alternatives. . . .

You traveled that long trip north, and when you were there, people were waiting to greet you, including the mayor. Fort Bliss brought out tents, food, sanitary supplies and such to help you. I can imagine the refugees were probably more astounded than anything else, yet grateful that the people had opened their arms to them. They also had the fear of what was happening behind them—the husbands left behind, and what was happening with them. They knew, at least, that they were safe, their children were safe, and they would be there until the men arrived.

The community . . . opened its arms to these people. A gentleman came with a buggy, took children for rides around the city of El Paso, and took them to see the alligators in San Jacinto Plaza—an example of kind of outpouring of love to people. They had not the greatest facilities that we would all like to have for our families, but it was summertime, and it was safe, a place where they could relax and their children could play and be with other children. They could pump water from the Rio Grande for cooking and cleaning. They also had one communal cook-stove area, where all the families could do their cooking. Perhaps many of the older refugees could remember their experiences when they first left Utah and went to Mexico.

The refugees had to start from scratch all over again. Many of them thought they would only be there only a few weeks, but nobody knew for sure. They were frightened, they wanted to go home. El Paso was great, but we always want to be back in our own homes. I don't know how I would have dealt with the thought of never going back to their homes. . . . . But they were strong women.

The mayor . . . offered up many services to the families: movies and other entertainment. Some families took children into their homes. Some children attended some of the local schools. When it all ended, many of them, . . . when they knew they weren't going back, stayed in El Paso. They found it nice, so close to their own culture, the young ones having grown up on the border in Mexico—and here they were on the border, where they could enjoy same wonderful cultural feeling they had perhaps had in the Colonias; a little bit of that was here in El Paso.

I know that many dispersed and went back to Utah. I have read letters from lovers that met in El Paso. . . . They came north from Mexico, married in El Paso, then went north to Utah and were remarried in the temple. They wrote about being here for this time, but they wanted to go back to Utah, where they felt there home was. There were some large, large families, because of polygamy, and that had to cause some uncertainties; they had left the United States because polygamy was illegal there. . . . So many things weighed on these women's minds, I'm sure. They had to be the strongest of women to be able to go through all that. . . .

Being a woman, I'm thinking again about having left everything behind: homes, family, livestock; and to be put into a lumberyard as the only place of refuge. Some women were pregnant. Some women had just had new children. Conditions were not sanitary, and it was difficult being a new mother in those days. Many things affected your children. There was dysentery; being close to the Rio Grande, you had to deal with mosquitoes. There were many different issues to deal with, not to mention bugs and rodents. But the women persevered in what they did. Local cab drivers gave people rides around town to get them out of the lumberyard, or brought them from one area to the next. The mayor brought more sanitary supplies in.

One family let the women come and do laundry and bathe in their home. In 1912, you did not have the sanitary conditions we enjoy today. These women, having the Mormon Church, . . . and being so involved in their faith, they really believed that faith would carry them on. . . . They turned to that faith. . . . Their faith was important to them, and it carried them on.

Many women stayed in El Paso. Many went on to other parts of the country. . . . They had to be very, very strong women. And women were much stronger back them, because they didn't have the luxuries we have today. . . .

Another thing that perhaps surprised many of the Mormons was the fact that El Paso really didn't know who the Mormon community was, what their faith was, what their beliefs were. Maybe some did not share the Mormon beliefs, thinking that the Mormons were not Christian. . . . It was a unique faith, . . . polygamy, of course. I've heard one story: my step-grandmother used to say she thought the Mormons were Arabs, because of the simple fact that they had several wives, a natural error. People just didn't know. They jumped to conclusions, which happens many times. But I think the Mormons found that El Paso had many faiths. We had the Jewish here, the Arabs, the Chinese, the Japanese, the Greeks. The Christian churches here helped build the first Jewish synagogue, something you probably wouldn't have seen in the rest of the country. . . . So this is the city of refuge; in this sense, we all are our own little refugees. We came from all over the country. So I think that once the Mormons got here, they found they were just like you and me. They'd had situations, they had families, they had children. They were fighting to survive in this rough country that we live in. . . . Living down in Mexico had been very difficult, and I think people's whole attitude changed, and perhaps that's why many Mormons stayed here.

JARED TAMEZ

DOCTORAL CANDIDATE IN HISTORY AT THE UNIVERSITY OF TEXAS AT EL PASO
EL PASO, FEBRUARY 17, 2012

BEGINNING IN 1875, BRIGHAM YOUNG BEGAN TO send missionaries into Mexico. Part of the reason is the Church has a theological compulsion to preach to indigenous peoples, which they believe Mexican people to be. Part of it also is because Brigham Young was trying to get these missionaries to search for a place of refuge. In the United States at this time, the Mormon Church was practicing polygamy, and the federal government was beginning to take notice and pass laws to curtail that practice. So Brigham Young was sending missionaries to find a place where the Mormons might be able to practice polygamy outside of the confines of the United States, hopefully to practice their religion in peace without being molested.

In 1875, a small company that left Salt Lake City and went through Northern Mexico identified a few locations that might be suitable for settlement. But it was not till 1879 that the Church sent missionaries to Mexico City; Apostle Moses Thatcher headed that mission. He began negotiating with European land holders. He began speaking with government officials like Porfirio Díaz and other national leaders about Mormon intentions to settle in Mexico. At the time, LDS leaders were not ready to approve settlements, but once further legislation was passed by the United States government, the need to colonize became increasingly urgent. So in 1885, Church President John Taylor decided that it was time to create colonies in Mexico for the purpose of sheltering Mormon polygamists. When Mormons arrived, they were not greeted with open arms by people in the area. They were seen as an invasive force, an arm of American imperialism, and because they had arms, they were viewed as threatening. The Mexican people remembered very clearly other attempts by Americans with guns who came into Mexican territory and settled, Texans being one of those examples. Fresh in their minds was the loss of Texas and other filibustering expeditions. . . . The Mormon presence in Mexico, for many, was a clear and present threat to the territorial integrity of the Mexican nation. . . .

Although many Mexicans viewed Mormon colonization as a threat, Mormon leaders negotiated directly with President Porfirio Díaz and other government leaders. And Díaz, at this time, sought to emulate many of the qualities, economic and social, of the United States. He wanted to pursue a course of modernization for Mexico. And part of his vision in doing that was to invite foreigners to come and settle to Mexico in the hopes that their entrepreneurial nature would help elevate the Mexican nation economically, even socially. When Mormon leaders meet with Porfirio Díaz, he welcomed them with open arms and arranged that many choice lands in northern Mexico be made available for sale. This, of course, again alienated many Mexicans who had previously owned these lands, who saw these lands as their ancestral heritage. Within three or four years, Mormons had bought up a significant amount, up to fifty percent, of the lands around Casas Grandes. In doing this, Mormons were now competing very rigorously with local Mexicans for resources: water, timber. And all of this continued to breed some amount of resentment. . . .

From the beginning of their settlement, Mormons had tried to present themselves as a neutral force, . . . in Mexican political affairs as well as American. They didn't want to put themselves between the two nations. Increasingly, that position became untenable, when the United States placed an embargo on arms. This angered revolutionary forces, and they began to eye Mormon weapons as something that they wanted to acquire. This came to a head on July 26 when General

Salazar summoned Junius Romney, the Mormon ecclesiastical leader, to Casas Grandes. He ordered Romney to issue an order demanding that all colonists turn in their arms. Romney refused outright. Salazar, incensed, demanded further and sent some of his guard with Romney back to the colonies to assure that his order was carried out. There, Romney and other leaders devised a strategy, whereby they would collect the oldest guns in the colonies, some non-functioning by that time, and hide away their best arms. They did that; they turned in some of their older guns and made preparations immediately to transport their wives and children outside of the colonies. On July 28, just a few days later, those women and children were boarding trains on their way to El Paso. . . .

The reason the Mormons had gone to Mexico in the first place was to escape a great deal of political persecution, as well as prosecution, in the United States. They'd had enough of American politics; and coming to Mexico, they similarly just wanted to be left alone, to mind their own business and pursue their lives and their religion in peace. They took a fairly strong view that they did not want to get involved in political matters; they wanted to remain neutral. Particularly, as conflict brewed within the nation among warring factions, and particularly once the United States began to get involved as well, one thing to remember is that the colonists had a great deal invested in these colonies. They had built the colonies from the ground up, and they had invested not only money, but time and faith. They saw themselves as the vanguard of saving the Church, in a sense. So they did not want to leave. This was their home and they had formed many friendships and relationships, not only of business nature but of a personal nature. They loved the lands, and many of them had great love for the people around them. Leaving was a very difficult thing, and they wanted to return as quickly as they could. . . .

Mormons came to Mexico in large measure because they did not fit the mainstream idea of what it was to be an American in the United States at that time. Somewhat ironically, almost thirty years later, they were leaving Mexico because they were seen as American. There was a tension among this people of nationalities struggling to find a place in the larger societies. . . .

Today, Mexico actually has the next highest population of

Mormons outside of the United States. It has the highest concentration of LDS temples and stakes outside of the United States, and so the fruits of Mormonism in Mexico have grown in the last hundred years. . . . The seeds that these colonists and missionaries planted a hundred years ago have germinated. . . .

In many ways, the question of Mormon Americanness is still a question hotly debated today. We've seen in the presidential candidacy of Mitt Romney questions about whether or not he and Mormons in general are true Americans; and whether Romney will be able to give his allegiance to the Constitution or if his allegiance lies with Church authorities in Salt Lake City. That question has been around for well over a century. Romney's father, George Romney, was actually born in the Mormon colonies. At age five years, he was one of those children that got off of the train at El Paso.

RICHARD E. TURLEY JR.

ASSISTANT CHURCH HISTORIAN FOR THE CHURCH OF JESUS CHRIST OF LATTER-DAY SAINTS
SALT LAKE CITY, FEBRUARY 23, 2012

THERE WAS BOTH A GENERAL AND SPECIFIC reason why the Latter-day Saints moved south across the Mexican border into Chihuahua and Sonora. The general purpose was settlement. From the very early days of the Church, the Saints sought to move out and settle various locations to build religious communities, cities of Zion. The Latter-day Saints who moved into Mexico were moving in as settlers; they were forming colonies. The specific purpose that prompted them to go south into Mexico was the prosecution of the people who were engaged in plural marriage, the Mormon marriage system, commonly called "polygamy." . . .

There were of course advantages both to the Latter-day Saint immigrants and to the local Mexican governments by having the Saints settle in northern Mexico. The advantage to the Latter-day Saints of course was asylum and the opportunity to acquire some property on which they could build homes and farms. The advantage to the government was an area it wanted to be settled, and you had people who could come in and establish an economic base. Particularly as time went on and the Mormons developed, for example, production of fruit, it came to bless the entire country as that fruit was distributed. . . .

By the time the Latter-day Saints moved into northern Mexico they were accustomed to moving from place to place and building settlements. I myself have two sets of great-great-grandparents who moved into northern Mexico. My Great-great-grandfather Isaac Turley had moved repeatedly over the course of his life. He was born in Churchville, Upper Canada, in 1837, and very shortly after that moved with his family into northwestern Missouri. He and his family were driven from northwestern Missouri into Illinois; they left Illinois and crossed Iowa to the Missouri river. They later traveled across the plains to what became Utah, and there they settled for a time. They then moved with Latter-day Saint settlers from there into San Bernardino, California. They then left San Bernardino and came up to Washington, a small settlement in Utah, then to Minersville, and then to Beaver, and from Beaver to the Little Colorado area of Arizona. By the time Isaac Turley arrived into northern Mexico, he was accustomed to moving from place to place and building a new community, a new settlement, and a new business. In his case, he was both a farmer, as all people were in those days, and also a blacksmith. He did a lot of blacksmith work for the people in the colonies.

My great-great-grandfather on the other side was Henry Eyring. Born in Europe, he was German speaking. He moved to St. Louis, Missouri and was working in an apothecary shop when he had his first encounter with Latter-day Saints. He later was baptized into the faith and was sent on a mission to the Indian mission, which is today's Oklahoma. He moved from there up to the plains, where he met Mary Bommeli, a young Swiss woman who was crossing the plains at the same time. When they arrived in Utah, they married and ended up going down to St. George. Ultimately they went from St. George into northern Mexico. They too were accustomed to moving from place to place, as were most people in that part of the country. In fact, in the northern hemisphere of the western hemisphere at that time, people were largely agrarian, but other things kept them busy as well. People had occupations like blacksmithing, or weaving, and other skills. In my family's case the Turleys did smithing as well as some agricultural work and odd jobs here and there. Henry Eyring ran a cooperative store that was an important economic contribution to the community. He was also an ecclesiastical leader in the area, and his wife Mary developed the best vineyard in the colonies at the time. Her grapes were quite famous. . . .

My ancestors who went into northern Mexico, both the men and women, were actively engaged in Church activities. Mary Bommeli Eyring had an important responsibility with the Relief Society. She'd had that responsibility in St. George, and as the Church became better organized in northern Mexico, she had that responsibility as well. My Turley female ancestors had a role in what was then the Young Ladies Mutual Improvement Association. They were active not only in their normal roles of providing for their families, preparing and growing food, but also in the women's organizations of northern Mexico. . . .

The exodus of 1912 was a very frightening experience for my family members. As the women and children left on the train, the men went up into the mountains and tried to negotiate some type of settlement. At that point, no one knew what their future would be. There was much uncertainty—concern about personal safety, about the safety of the property they had left behind: homes, vineyards, farms, shops, and all the things for which they had been working, many of them for two or two and a half decades. There was considerable fear, concern, and uncertainty associated with that. In the case of my Great-great-grandmother Mary Bommeli Eyring, her husband had died and so she was widowed. Just before she left she packed her suitcase, in which money that was going to be her support. A bandit came in and robbed her, leaving her without the money intended for her own support. . . .

It's fascinating to me that these Latter-day-Saints were willing to move to Mexico and learn Spanish, a new language. I think of my Great-great-grandfather Henry Eyring, who came into this world as Heinrich Eyring, a German. When he came to the United States he became Henry Eyring; then he moved to Mexico, where according to the stationery he made (and that I have), he became Enrique Eyring. That ability to transition from German to English to Spanish showed the faith of these people and also their tenacity. The Latter-day Saints who moved into northern Mexico and learned Spanish became the leaders of the Church in many Spanish-speaking nations of the world. I think of my own family, who came out in the exodus in 1912; most of the family went back into Colonia Juárez in September of 1914. But my grandfather, who was fifteen at the time of the exodus, got a good job in El Paso and, except for going back to graduate from the academy in 1916, spent most the rest of his life in El Paso. His descendants have for the most part been in the United States since that time.

I look at just what has happened with our family. My father became a mission president in the Hermosillo Mission in Mexico. All of the prior mission presidents for that mission except one have been my relatives. That shows how much the contribution of Spanish-speaking members of the Church has made to leadership of the Church in various parts of the world. I've heard it said that it would be very difficult to find a small population that has contributed so much to leadership positions of the Church in Spanish speaking areas particularly as have the people who grew up in the colonies in Northern Mexico. . . .

In Latter-day Saint history we talk often of the inhabitants of Quincy, Illinois, who accepted the Latter-day Saints as refugees when the Saints were driven from Missouri. I think there's an equally compelling story to tell about the citizens of El Paso. When my family members left northern Mexico in 1912 and crossed over the border into the United States, they were full of uncertainty; they did not know how they were going to survive in the United States. They didn't know if they would be returning to Mexico. The people of El Paso welcomed them; they made it possible for them to live and to thrive. The reason my Grandfather Edward Vernon Turley remained in El Paso for virtually the rest of his life was because he'd a warm welcome there and was himself able to find employment and contribute to the economy. My father subsequently was born and raised in El Paso, and I spent time in El Paso as a child. So we have fond feelings towards the people of El Paso and the way they greeted the Latter-day Saints when they were driven from northern Mexico. . . .

Like many refugees who find themselves in a new country, these Latter-day Saint refugees from Mexico had experienced a sudden change in their economic circumstances. My ancestors who lived in Northern Mexico had prospered considerably: they had homes, they had farms, they had shops, and they had risen to a point of cooperative prosperity. When they crossed over the United States border into El Paso they suddenly found themselves evicted from their property, uncertain about whether they would ever be able to occupy their farms, homes, and shops again, and uncertain about what their economic future would be. They suddenly found themselves at the mercy of those who were willing to be charitable to them. That was a new experience; they were used to being the ones who gave out charity, not the ones who received it.

JOHN RAY WALL

SON OF JOHN EDWARD WALL, LDS PHOTOGRAPHER OF THE MORMON EXODUS
NORTH SALT LAKE CITY, FEBRUARY 23, 2012

MY FATHER, JOHN EDWARD WALL, WAS BORN in Manti, Utah, 13 February 1890. His mother was Susie Bench, second wife of Francis George Wall. . . . John Edward Wall was in Mexico by himself; his family had left by a train, and he was over by Junius Romney's home. . . . Brother Romney asked my dad to stand guard in the house there, while he went in the house. This was nighttime, because they were getting ready to leave and go up to Stair Canyon, so Dad stood guard while Brother Romney went in and got the stake records (Junius Romney was president of the stake). He saw Junius Romney put them on his saddle, and they went up to Stair Canyon, just above Juárez, about a few miles uphill, into a narrow canyon. They waited about two days for other colonists to come there with people, and eventually about 250 men gathered there, with maybe four hundred head of horses. Stair Canyon was a small canyon, and while they were there they organized themselves in a little army; they had a general, General Thurber, and they chose my father to be the photographer of the outfit, because his father had just bought him a lot of film in El Paso. He developed his own films and actually wrote on some of the films what they were, before he developed them.

He knew that Junius Romney had the records. He saw Junius Romney get on a horse, with his two other people, and leave the group. There were a lot of people there, so Dad just figured they were going to hide the stake records. Anyway, they had to leave the area, so they rode through the group of people, went up through a gate, and found a place where they were starting to bury the records. They found my father following, and nobody was supposed to know they were doing it, but they caught him and said, "Okay, come and take our picture." So he stood in front of them and took two or three pictures of them holding those stake records. The picture shows the records, and you also see a tin can. My father said the records were buried in tin cans, on the right side, under some flat rocks, where they sat. . . .

This is the camera my father had when he took the pictures. . . . As far as I know, the records are still buried there. We've tried to find them, but so far we haven't been able to locate them.

APPENDIX A

RECORD OF THE EXODUS

OF THE MORMON COLONIES FROM MEXICO IN 1912

This document reproduces an original typescript of a report written by Alonzo Taylor, chronicling the Exodus and aftermath. Taylor was the official clerk of the Juárez Stake when he composed the report, which he presented to Bishop Joseph C. Bentley shortly after the exodus. The report is reproduced here in its entirety for the first time. (Extracts from the original handwritten report were extracted in Harold W. Taylor, Memories of Militants and Mormon Colonists in Mexico, 245–60.)

(THIS ACCOUNT OF THE EXODUS OF THE COLONists from their homes in Mexico, in 1912, on account of the Revolution of 1912, was written by Elder Alonzo L. Taylor, who was at that time the official Stake Clerk of the Juarez Stake. The report was delivered to Bishop Joseph C. Bentley by Alonzo L. Taylor, as none of the Stake Presidency or other Stake Authorities returned, as officers of the Stake, and Bishop Bentley was the only Bishop of the Stake who returned. So this report was given to Bishop Joseph C. Bentley soon after the Exodus.)

From the beginning of the Orozco revolution in Mexico assurances have been given the colonists that their lives and property would be respected and that owing to their neutral position even their firearms would be left in their possession. These promises were kept for several months and whenever an occasional violation occurred the matter was always remedied when reported to the authorities or leaders of the revolution. As conditions became more serious with the revolutionary party and they began to suffer one defeat after another at the hands of the federals they were forced from their position in the southern part of the State of Chihuahua and the headquarters or stronghold of the rebel army was finally transferred to Casas Grandes. The U. S. government kept a close vigilance on the border and the obtaining of ammunition soon became very difficult for the rebels. As the Federal forces under Generals Jose de la Luz Blanco and Sangines were moving from Sonora through the Pulpit Canon and Las Varas country to make an attack on the rebels at Casas Grandes a desperate effort was made by the rebels to obtain arms, ammunition and other munitions of war in order to be able to check this advance. [page 1]

On the 24th of July 1912 General Ines Salazar told Bro. H. E. Bowman that all his promises to foreigners were now void, that he needed arms and ammunition and supplies, that the Mormons and other foreigners possessed these things and that they proposed to get them at any cost. On July 25 in the morning Prest. Junius Romney, H. S. Harris, Guy C. Wilson and H. E. Bowman went to Casas Grandes to interview Salazar. Prest. Romney and Bro. Bowman were admitted to Salazars office while Bros. Wilson, Harris and some of the other brethren waited on the outside. Salazar flatly informed the brethren of his intention to take the arms of the colonists. A demand was made by Salazar for Prest. Romney to issue an order to the Colonists to surrender their arms and ammunition and received the answer that the arms were the personal property of the men, and they were under no obligation to surrender their property on this order even if he were disposed to issue such an order which he could not and would not do. Salazar informed them that they would be held until the order was given and was told that he would have to hold them a long time. Finally Salazar issued an order for the Dublan people to surrender their arms and sent 50 men to enforce the order, the rebels also had six cannons at the stock yards below Dublan and threatened to use these on the town in case of resistance. Pres. Romney and Harris and Bros. Bowmen and Thurber went to Dublan with the guard and Bro. Wilson returned to Juarez. As soon as the party arrived at Dublan the demand for funs [*sic*] was again made and the leader proposed that the Colonists would bring their arms and ammunition to one place [page 2] that the houses would not be searched. Consequently the arms and ammunition were brought to the school house and 87 rifles a few pistols and several thousand rounds of ammunition were delivered. As Salazar had told the brethren that all his former guarantees and promises were withdrawn and as the people were now disarmed many of the brethren did not deem it safe for women and children to remain in the Colony. Consequently steps were immediately taken in Dublan to remove the families to the U. S. and that same night several hundred people left for El Paso.

Prest. Romney returned to Juarez that evening and the men of the town were in meeting considering the question of whether to move the women and children from Juarez or not. The majority of those present were of the opinion that it would not be necessary but a vote was not taken as it was desired to know what Prest. Romney would have to report and he was expected to arrive before the meeting closed. Prest. Romney arrived and reported that it was absolutely necessary the the [*sic*] Dublan people to surrender their arms or to fight and that against tremendous odds as there were approximately 2,000 rebels in our section of the country, well armed and possessing severl [*sic*] pieces of artillery. Said also that he did not consider it safe for women and children to remain in the country after men are disarmed. Said Salazar threatened to bring on intervention and stated that the following day a body of men would be sent to Juarez to collect the arms of the people of this place. Prest. Romney said that he noticed that a good many present including some of the leading men of the town opposed the sending out of the women and children. Said that he would not urge anyone to do so if they were not disposed to but so far as he is concerned expected to send his [page 3] family out on the first train and felt that what was safety for his family was the only safety for others. A vote was then taken and it was the unanimous sentiment to prepare to move out our families at once.

Sunday July 26--About half of the women and children of Colonia Juarez left for Pearson to take train to the U. S. On the road to Pearson a bandit belonging to the command of Felipe A. Cavada of Col. Maximo Castillos Command held up several of the wagons and robbed Bryan Macdonald of $25.00 cash, Geo. E. Redd of $20.00 Alma Walser of about $5.00, Edmund A. Richardson of a watch. About nnon [*sic*] Col. Luis Ponce, Melquiades Alvarez, and about 25 men came to Juarez for the purpose of receiving the arms of the people. The men brought their arms and ammunition to the band stand and there delivered to Col. Ponce, 34 rifles, several pistols, and several thousand rounds of cartridges. These arms and ammunition were listed by Bishop J. C. Bentley. During the disarming of the men, the same bandit who had robbed the people on the road to Pearson entered the home of Sister Mary B. Eyring and robbed her of $40.00 and later stole a hat from Juan Treviso the local police officer of Col. Juarez. Col. Ponce ordered the man arrested on the charge of stealing the hat not knowing of the other robberies. Alma Walser appeared and complained of having been bobbed [*sic*] and Ponce sent for the man to be brought to the band stand and searched. The watch fob was found in his socks and part of [page 4] the stolen money was found concealed in the clothing. Col. Ponce stated to the crowd that he would have the man executed as soon as he could communicate with Gen Salazar. Lieutenant Melquiades Alvarez insisted that to hold the man would mean his probable escape during the night and he urged that he be executed at once. Just after sundown Juan Bautista and two others took the prisoner to the old grave yard on the hill east of Juarez and executed him, slightly covering the body with earth by caving of a bank of earth, in the wash below the grave yard over the body. Next morning Junius Romney, E. A. Clayson and Ernest Hatch buried the body. A guard of ten men and a captain named Miguel Castillo (of Galeana) were left to maintain order in Col. Juarez and they took every precaution to see that no robbing or other disorders should exist.

Monday July 27--All the remaining women and children of Colonia Juarez left for Pearson and about 6 P. M. took train for the U. S. This train carried about 400 women and children and aged men together with a few able bodied men who went along to care for the helpless and to assist Apostle Ivins in caring for them when they should arrive in El Paso. About 6:30 the men of Col. Juarez returned with 37 wagons and other vehicles which had been used to move the families to Pearson.

It was a sad procession, scarcely no one spoke a word on the return trip except to occasionally remark that they were returning to a desolate and lonely spot that only a few days before had been the scene of happy and contented homes filled with women and children. For several days the men seemed unable to settle down to work. The business of doing their [page 5] own cooking and other house work was new to the majority and almost all the men and boys could be seen in small groups on the streets discussing the conditions and speculating as to how long these conditions would last. These scenes were going on in Dublan except that the local guard left in that place was not as faithful as the one left in Juarez and instead of enjoying the peace and quiet enjoyed in Juarez homes were being entered and property stolen. The homes of Alex Jameson and Ammon Tenney in Dublan were looted and Bro. Jameson was poked in the side with a gun when he protested. Bro. Tenney was threatened with death if he persisted on interfering. The local guard seemed unwilling to attempt to stop this looting and the people of Dublan felt that the limit of endurance had been about reached and it was decided to stack their arms in one place and if the abuses were carried much further to resent [*sic*] them with arms. Horses were driven off. Stables and barns searched for saddles and horses and work teams worth several hundred dollars were taken and used by the rebels as cavalry horses. The stores of Union Merc. Co. and Farnsworth and Romney were thoroughly stripped of thousands of dollars of merchandise.

In Juarez the local guard faithfully did its duty and when rebels from Pearson came to Juarez with orders drom [*sic*] their captain to take horses, saddles and merchandise, Capt. Castillo informed them that he was stationed there under orders of Gen. Salazar and that if any one attempted any looting or disorder there would be some more executions. This had the effect of ridding the town of small bands of rebels for several days and the town was left in absolute quiet. [page 6]

On July 29 a number of the brethren from Dublan went to Juarez to consult with the brethren there as to the advisibility of abandoning the Colony. After considerable discussion it was decided that as long as life was not in absolute danger to not abandon our homes.

In the afternoon of August 1st Major Calcido and Capt. Cavada of the command of Col. Maximo Castillo came to Juarez with about 50 men and stationed their soldiers in the yeard [*sic*] of E. L. Taylors home. The local guard under Capt. Miguel Castillo were of the opinion that they had not come for any good purpose as they had asked to see their order and were informed by the lieutenant of Major Salcido that they had none written but were dispatched to watch the passes north of Col. Juarez to see that Gen. Blanco did not come in and surprise the rebel army now concentrating at San Diego.

Soon Capt. Cavada rode up to the guard and asked if they had executed any more of his men. He was told that they had not executed anyone, that Ponce had ordered the execution. Cavada remarked that they had better not execute another and added that whenever the "Cabrones Mormons" made any complaint against a man the guard was ready to execute him. Cavada said further that he knew who urged the execution, that it was Lt. Melquiades Alvarez and he would fix him if he got the chance.

The Capt. of the guard also told Eugene Romney that Cavada and his men were angry about the execution and had made some threats.

These expressions together with other quotations and misquotations which came to Prest. Romneys ears convinced him that [page 7] Cavada and his men had come for no good purpose and that they were seeking to avenge the death of their comrade and he thought they would choose him as their victim as he was the man in charge of the Colonies and did not object to the execution but according to their belief approved of it and urged it. Prest. Romney hurriedly called anumber [*sic*] of the men together to consult and it was decided that the only safe policy was to leave town owing to the fact that no one seemed to know the real purpose of the presence of the soldiers, the threats that had been reported made by them and the inability of the local guard to cope with so large a number. Prest. Romney arranged for E. C. Eyring to arrange and notify all on the west side of the river to gather at a certain point and for Miles A. Romney to notify all on the East side. It was arranged by these two for those on the west side to meet at Ed Eyrings barn in the hollow above the pipe line and those on the East side to meet at M. A. Romney's place at the lane above town, and that those from the East side would go over to the Ed Eyring barn and then a council meeting would be held. About the time Prest. Romney called the men together to discuss the proposition of going out of town that night the Capt. of the guard, Castillo, called A. L. Taylor to go with him to the telephone central office and stated that he desired to get in communication with Col. Demetrio Ponce at N. Casas Grandes, Ponce could not be reached but Col. Alanis happened to be in Farnsworths store and he told Capt. Miguel Castillo of the local guard that Cavado's men were there under proper orders for the purpose of watching the passes north of Juarez to prevent Blanco from surprising them at San Diego as the rebel forces had been whipped by Blanco at Ojitos and [page 8] were concentrating at San Diego.

Alanis told Castillo to watch Cavado's men and see that they did not do any looting also to tell them positively to take nothing from the Colonists except some good saddle horses, saddles and necessary provisions, that if this order is violated to advise him and he would send men to assist in putting down any disorder.

Bro. Taylor hurried out to inform Prest. Romney of this information as all had supposed the soldiers were there of their own accord and for no good purpose. As Bro. Romney could not be found Bro. Taylor hunted through the town which seemed to be almost deserted, and not knowing of the decision to move out finally met Bp. Bentley and told him of the conversation between Castillo and Alanis.

Bp. Bentley said, "Prest. Romney will be glad to learn this and after we meet in council at Bro. Eyring's barn I believe we will all go back to our homes to sleep but in the meantime we must proceed to carry out the program as arranged. About 10 P. M. about 40 men mostly armed and with some provisions and bedding met at Frances Romneys place. Bp. Bentley and M. A. Romney got on a horse and rode across the river, which was rather high, and went to Ed Eyrings barn to meet Prest. Romney and the brethren from the West side of river. Not finding them at the barn they searched the hills and washes in the vicinity and returned at a little after midnight to the Romney place and reported that Pres. Romney and men could not be found. However they decided to try again and after searching until about two o'clock in the morning heard some one call from the Macdonald springs but decided it was some of the guard herding the horses. They returned [page 9] at 3:15 A. M. to where the men were stationed and reported their failure to locate the men. Several of the men stationed at the Romney place has [*sic*] already gone home but most of them waited for Bp. Bentley's return. It was then decided to leave the guns in a cache and return home. About 4:20 A. M. one of the party who had been searching for Prest. Romney and party reported that he had located them at Macdonald springs and that Prest. Romney desired all to join him at once as he had sent couriers with orders to Dublan, Garcia, and Pacheco to move out and join him at the "Stairs" in the mountains. Most of Bp. Bentleys party were at Bro. A. L. Taylors place and had just prepared to sleep, but several of the men were at their own homes and scattered as far as the mill of D. Skousen. As the rebel guards were stationed on the hills watching for Gen. Blanco's forces it was decided almost impossible to leave town armed in daylight so it was decided to send word to Prest. Romney that they would join him the next night.

About sunup Aug. 2 Bp. Bentley and A. L. Taylor interviewed Major Salcido and Capt. Cavada who received them very courteously and assured them they would do all possible to maintain order and that no looting would be permitted which promise they faithfully kept. About noon a meeting was called at the home of Geo. S. Romney for the purpose of discussing means of joining Prest. Romney and party that night. While in meeting some one reported that another bunch of rebels had entered town and were looting Bro. Hatch's house. Bp. Bentley, E. A. Clayson, Jno. Wilson and A. L. Taylor went to Tithing office and found Col. Escobosa and Capt. Gutierrez, who were in charge of the [page 10] recently arrived rebels. They stated that the Mormons of Dublan had risen in arms against the Liberals, that those of Pacheco were also leaving and there was a plan for the Juarez Mormons to join them in the mountains and for all to go and join Gen. Blanco. They said that Capt. Gutierrez command had tried to intercept the Dublan people but that they could not overtake them so had fired on them several times and the Dublan men returned the fire. They said the Mormons were well armed with short Mausers 30-40 and 30-30-rifles they had been close enough to see well with glasses and could dtermine [*sic*] from the shells the caliber of guns used. They said they had been sent by Gen. Salazar to Col. Juarez to stop the Mormons of that place joining those who had already gone out and if they had already gone to join those from Dublan they were to burn the town leave it in ashes and follow the Mormons into the mountains and if possible to not leave a man alive, but if they found that the Col. Juarez Mormons had not gone out to take them all prisoners as a preventative. They said that owing to the excellent report given by Capt. Castillo and Capt. Cavada's men they did not feel like carrying out the order at present but warned the men to not attempt to leave town. In the evening a meeting was held at E. A. Clayson's place to determine what to do about joining Prest. Romney and the men in the mountains. At conclusion of the meeting A. L. Taylor and Eli Abegg were going to the house of the former when Col. Escobosa accosted them and wanted to know why the Mormons had been in meeting and asked what their plans were. He also accused them of having taken a package of dynamite to the meeting which was intended for use against [page 11] them. It happened that Eli Abegg was the person who brought the supposed pkg. of dynamite and he happened to have it under his arm at the time so he untied the package and showed Escobosa a shirt and some other articles of clothing in the package. Escobosa then demanded saddles from A. L. Taylor, E. F. Turley and Frank Lewis and promised that on delivery of these they would be permitted to go to their homes in peace and their homes would not be searched or looted. The saddles were delivered and Escobosa's promise was kept for the next morning an attempt was made to loot two of the houses of these men but immediately restraining orders were given by Escobosa. After the saddles were delivered Escobosa placed E. A. Clayson and others under arrest stating that he suspicioned they intended leaving town that night. Bro. Clayson explained that the meeting held at E. A. Claysons was simply for the consideration of our own welfare and no plotting against the Liberals was thought of, that among other things they discussed where the men would sleep tonight. Escobosa answered saying that they need not worry about where they would sleep as he had already decided to have them all sleep in the school house with the soldiers. Later Bp. Bentley talked with Col. Maximo Castillo who said to pay no attention to the order and gave the brethren permission to go to their own homes or to go to the home of A. L. Taylor and sleep instead of the school house where the soldiers were quartered.

Saturday Aug. 3/12. About 9 o'clock in the morning the rebels stationed on the mesa north of Colonia Juarez sighted a scouting party from the Federal army about the mouth of the Topiecitas arroyo. They (Liberals) hurriedly gathered up every [page 12] available horse including work horses, gentle colts, and stallions, even taking "Distingue" the registered French Coach horse which the Colonists purchased for $8,000. Capt. Felipe Cavada remained a little longer than Escobosos men and Bp. Bentley and A. L. Taylor succeeded in getting back a number of the work horses and colts by exchanging ponies for them and in some cases paying a few dollars. However the Coach Stallion had been taken out of town and twelve good saddle horses demanded immediately for his return which was an impossible request to fulfill.

During the day Bp. Bentley visited the houses of the town to ascertain the extent of the looting and found about fifteen houses had been broken into.

In the evening the brethren in Juarez met at the house of A. L. Taylor to discuss the best thing to be done now that the rebels had left town and were preparing to retreat to Sonora through the mountain colonies. While in this meeting Bros. S. E. McClellan and Ernest Hatch came in. They had just come from the "Stairs" in the mountains where Prest. Romney and a number of the brethren from Juarez also the Dublan men were stationed. These two brethren said that they had come on an important mission with a message from Prest. Romney stating that he desired the brethren who were in Juarez to come out into the mountains, that the Ja. [Juarez] Stake of Zion was there and that night would be their last opportunity to join them as they expected to leave in a body for the U. S. if the brethren in Juarez did not come at once. Bp. Bentley immediately said that even though the rebels had gone and there was now apparently no reason for leaving so far as he was concerned he was going out that [— —] Prests. Romney and Harris were and he counselled [*sic*] [page 13] all present to do the same. It was already 10:30 P. M. when the meeting adjourned and all began preparing to leave before daylight. Bp. Bentley and A. L. Taylor awoke Felipe Chavez the local president also a number of other Mexicans and explained to them that owing to the repeated abuses of the Liberals and the insecurity of remaining with the Federal Army and the Liberals on the other we had decided to go into the mountains for a few days and that they desired to put the Mexicans of the town on their honor to look after the property of the people the best they possibly could. They placed Felipe Chavez the president in direct charge of the town giving him two letters, one to Gen. Blanco of the Federals in case they occupied the town and another to the Liberals in case they should return. Jno. W. Wilson placed Encarnacion Martinez in charge of the store and Mexicans were placed in charge of the shoe and saddle shops and other public and all private property and all were to look after it until the return of the owners which they were told would be in a very few days as soon as the Federals came in, as at that time none of the brethren had any idea of going to the states but expected to only remain in the mountains until the Federals came in and then return.

At 3 A. M. the party consisting of the following men left town: J. C. Bentley, E. A. Clayson, Jno. W. Wilson, Alonzo L. Taylor, E. C. Eyring, John Hatch, Ernest Hatch, Ed Black, Fred Humphrey, Dayl Humphrey, Edw. F. Turley, Eugene Romney, John Allan, Frank Lewis, R. L. Scott, Danl Skousen, Wm. Walser, Alma Walser, Ed Clayson, and S. E. McClellan. A. P. Spilsbury and Byron Macdonald remaining behind not wishing to go. [page 14]

The party traveled to the stairs reaching there about 9 o'clock Sunday morning Aug. 4. In the afternoon the company of men present were organized. The Stake Presidency was in a general way in charge. Bp. A. D. Thurber Commander of the expedition, A. E. Call in charge of home guards, M. A. Romney in chg. of scouts, Gaskell Romney Quartermaster, S. E. McClellan Asst. Quartermaster, Geo S. Romeny [*sic*] in chg. of camp discipline and moral conduct.

A. L. Taylor, Capt. Co. No. 1
E. E. Eyring " " " 2
Martin L. Harris " " " 3
Wm. Jones, Jr. " " " 4
John Bingham " " " 5
F. M. Stocks " " " 6
Scouts:
Nephi W. Thayne, Capt. #1
Loren Taylor " " 2
N. C. Tenney, Capt. #3
Saul Hawkins " #4
Ira Pratt " #5
Egerton Lunt " #6

Omni Porter " #7
Jno. Beecroft " " #8
John A. Whetten " #9

At 4 P. M. a Council meeting of the Stake Presidency, Eprics and High Councilors also all general officers was held and it was unanimously decided for the Company to stay together until it could be decided whether it would be best to go to the United States or to return to the Colonies in a few days after conditions should become more settled. In the evening the brethren of the Pacheco Ward arrived in camp.

Monday Aug. 5th. The Company laid over in the forenoon in camp in Stiars [*sic*] waiting for the Garcia and Chuichupa brethren to arrive as word had been sent to these colonies to join the other wards as soon as possible in the stairs. In the afternoon the company moved from the stairs to the Park in Left hand [page 15] Fork and in the evening held a council meeting in which it was decided to go to the United States unless some condition should arise immediately favorable to a safe return and peaceable possession of our homes. Just before dark the García Ward arrived and stated that it was very uncertain whether Chuichupa would arrive soon as the men had left the ward and gone out into the mountains and the Company may have to wait several days if they waited for that ward.

Tuesday Aug. 6th. The Company left the Park about noon and traveled to the Tapiecitas arroyo reaching there about 9 P. M. Camp was pitched and the usual pickets placed on guard around the camp and the scouts doing duty further away. The heat and excitement had the effect of unbalancing the mind of Bro. John Allan of Col. Juarez and during the night he was watched to see that no harm came to him.

Wed. 7th. It was decided by the Council to lay over all day at Topiocitas [*sic*] and wait for the Chuichupa brethren in case they should be near enough to overtake the Company. Bro. Allan seemed somewhat improved. Several of the boys were given permission to go to Juarez and Dublan and bring some provisions, look after some of their own interests, and find out the general conditions. These returned during the night bringing from Juarez a six passenger coach and wagon belonging to James Haws and loaded with provisions and fruit. They reported everything quiet in Juarez and so far as could be ascertained the Mexicans who were left in charge of affairs were taking care of things but reported them as living in some of our houses. The brethren from Dublan also brought some provisions and horses and reported things quiet in Dublan but said the local Mexicans did not show a very [page 16] friendly spirit. During the night Bro. Allan quietly left the camp barefoot and without hat, coat or shoes leaving also his gun, dog and other effects. In the morning (Thurs. Aug. 8) a searching party of about 100 men scouted the hills and brush in search of the lost man. About 9 A. M. all returned without having found him. Volunteers were called for to stay and continue the search and when Bro. Allan was found to overtake the Company. Bros. Adelbert Taylor, Harvey Taylor, Jesse Smith, David Black, and David Haws returned and went to Col. Juarez where they found Bro. Allan who had walked about 12 miles barefoot. He was being cared for by the local Mexicans. The brethren decided best to leave him in the care of the Mexicans as they seemed to be taking good care of him. The Co. left camp at 9 A. M. and just as they reached the top of the hill going out of wash Bro. A. M. Tenney broke the tire on his wagon and had to leave it using one of his work horses and a quilt for a mount. The Scouting Companies protected the front, rear and flanks of the Main Company keeping a sharp look out for rebels and federals as it was deemed best to avoid an encounter with either especially the rebels. A white flag was carried by the company in order to avoid being mistaken for 'dgers and fired upon by the federals also to demonstrate to the rebels that the movement was a peaceable one. The Company consisted of men all of whom were mounted and 269 loose horses were driven along. There was also a six passenger carriage and provision wagon with four horses besides a large number of pack animals. The Company had 221 rifles, 19 shot guns and 78 pistols with approximately 2,600 rounds of ammunition. The Column marched in companies, [page 17] guarded the front, rear and sides, the rest of the scout companies occupied the front of the main column. Then came the provision wagon and carriage which carried Bros. R. L. Scott, Hillstrom, Masten, Stout, Tenney and others of the aged brethren who could not endure long horseback riding changed. Then came the ammunition packs then Companies 1, 2, 3, 4, 5, and 6 and finally the loose horses and horse wranglers. The Column usually extended from a mile to a mile and one half in length and as the weather had been dry for a few days the dust was terrific. The Company reached the "Big Tank" on the Corralitos ranch for noon, camping about an hour and a half. Just after breaking camp a Mexican (Aurelio Hernandez) and a companion came to the Company carrying a white handerchief [*sic*] and stated that he was the captain of 10 men who were on their way to Ojitos to join the Federals under Blanco who had recently repulsed the rebels at that place, stating that his men were a short distance back.

A company of Scouts were dispatched to capture them and bring them to the column as Prest. Romney and those in charge of the expedition were inclined to doubt the story that they were on their way to join the federals but thought they may be rebel spies. The rest of the Mexicans were soon brought in and the whole eleven taken along as prisoners until danger of their returning to any rebel comrades was passed. They were given into the custody of Co. No. 1 as A. L. Taylor personally knew 5 of the 11 men. The Company camped that night on the Janos river near Agua Fria ranch, where the Mexicans were kept under guard. Their arms consisted of 1 mauser, 1 30-30, and 5 pistols.

Friday August 9th the Co. left camp at 7 A. M. passing just east of Colonia "Seca," taking the 11 Mexican prisoners along [page 18] until the Palotada Creek was reached where their arms were returned to them, some provisions given them, and they were released. As their horses were given out they rested at the head of Palotada until the next morning then proceeded to the headquarters of General Blanco at Ojitos where they entered the service of the Gov. as volunteers thus proving the truth of their statements when captured. The Column watered at Palotada then moved on about 15 miles north and camped for noon at three windmills on the Palomas Land and Cattle Co. ranch and were informed here that 60 rebels had camped at Palotado the preceeding [*sic*] night and 400 more were reported at Ascencion about 20 miles east, this number, however, proved to be greatly exaggerated.

At this camp Adelbert and Harvey Taylor, David Black, Jesse Smith, and David Haws overtook the Company and reported that they had found Bro. Allan in Col. Juarez, that he seemed improved mentally and was in charge of Mexicans who had found him and seeing his condition had fed and cared for him. They engaged a Mexican, under the general supervision of Bro. A. P. Spilsbury to continue to look after

Bro. Allan. These brethren reported conditions quiet in Juarez and said that no rebels had been in town, or any disorder had occurred since the people left.

At 2:30 P. M. the camp moved and traveled north crossing the U. S. Line at 6:20 P. M (Friday 9th) about 3 miles east of Dog Springs where 20 U. S. soldiers were stationed and fortified behind rock walls ready to fire on us thinking we were a band of rebels, but on finding out their mistake they gave the Company the best of treatment and all assistance possible. Camp was [page 19] made here for the night.

Aug. 10th Sat. at 10 A. M. the column traveled to "Alamo Hueco" and camped for night at the ranch when a heavy rain came up in the night and nearly every one with their outfits were soaked by the rain. Left "Alamo Hueco" at 8:30 A. M. (Sunday Aug. 11) and traveled all day through the Playas Valley and camped for night at the "Old Hatch Ranch" about 15 miles from "Hachita". At this camp a very heavy rain came up in the night and continued nearly all night and with the exception of a few who got quarters in the ranchers house, everybody and their complete outfits were drench with rain and the camp ground which was a low place under about 4 inches of water.

Monday Aug. 12 we left camp at 7:30 and traveled through the mud reaching Hachita at 11:30 A. M. where arrangements were made for the horses (about 500) to be herded until arrangements for band could be made. Arrangements were also made for a place to store saddles, guns and equipment.

The Stake Presidency notified all ward and Stake officers to prepare to go to El Paso on the night train which was due to leave Hachita 12:55 midnight. About 60 men slept on the floor of the waiting room without bedding (as all bedding had been stored away) until 3 A. M. when the belated train arrived and departed for El Paso with those who had been waiting aboard, arriving at El Paso about 9 A. M. Aug. 13.

At 2 P. M. Aug. 13 a meeting was called at the American National Bank building for the Stake Prescy, Bprics, High Council and other Stake authorities. Prayer was offered by Bro A. W. Ivins. Apostle Ivins stated that there had been [. . .] [page 20] move out of Mexico and whether or not it was necessary. The fact is we are all now here and must decide as to our future policy. Said he considered that the whole body of men of the Juarez Stake would not move out unless there were reasons for so doing; protested against the further discussion of this matter on the streets and in improper places. Said if Bro. Junius Romney feels that his policy and administration is not ap reciated [*sic*] and is criticized by him (Bro. Ivins) said he was not aware of the fact and did not know what had called forth such remarks on the part of some people. Protested vigorously against the publishing of heated remarks and unchristianlike names against the Mexicans such as was breathed out in the published statements of Orson P. Brown in this mornings paper. A copy of a letter from Apostle Ivins to 1st Prescy was read setting forth conditions surrounding colonists at the time of disarming of the men and relating in detail the incidents of the exodus of the women and children. Said that was the only report he had made so far to the 1st Prescy, and called attention to the fact that no criticism had been made. Read copy of letter addressed to Consul Llorente stating that hundreds of refugee American citizens had now reached the border referred to the property left behind and nothing but a few horses and saddles etc. of each person could be brought out. Referred to the incendiary speech of Salazar against Amer. citizens and the intolerable conditions following and wit drawal [*sic*] of guarantees by Salazar. Read extracts of a letter he had written to 1st Prescy as to whether the Colonies should be abandoned or whether all be left to use their own judgement about returning or whether all be advised to go back. Suggested that he could not see [page 21] how the abandonment of the Colonies could be possible and as the collections of claims is so uncertain felt that it would mean the rendering of hundreds of prosperous people homeless and penniless, that he had only had one thought in mind and that was for all to return to their homes as soon as possible and it was at all safe to do so.

Prest. Romney stated that when he returned to Colonies recently from El Paso, that he was very much dissatisfied with the results of his visit with Bro. Ivins and felt that Bro. Ivins had later realized that fact and that he had gone down to the Colonies later and given much encouragement. Said that the 1st Prescy. had placed the responsibility on Bros Ivins, Brown and himself and in turn that Bro. Ivins had placed the responsibility on Pres. Romney. The Bishops and leading brethren of the Colonies also placed the responsibility on on Pres. Romney. The Bishops and leading brethren of the Colonies also placed the responsibility on him and as some of the staunch and strong men of the Colonies differed in their opinions refused to move except on his counsel. Stated that his instructions had always been to avoid conflict with the natives. When the women and children were ordered out he gave this advice acting on his impressions and according to his best judgment. Referred to his order to move men out of Colonies and said it was because of the absolute statement of Salazar that he intended to force intervention, the disarming of our men, and their defenselessness, the robbing of stores and shops, the looting of houses, the ordering of our men around and other indignities perpetrated until it seemed the next step would be the taking of lives. The rebels even robbed [page 22] refugees as they were on their way to Pearson. The leading robber was arrested by Lino Ponce and executed in Colohia [*sic*] Juarez. Prest. Romney stated that as he had urged the execution himself of the bandit, that some of the robbers friends, he believed, had felt revengeful against him. Two days later Capt. Felipe A. Cavada of command of Maximo Castillo in command of the company to which the executed man belonged came to town and it was reported that he threatened to avenge the execution of his man* upon Prest. Romney. Castillo and Cavada asked for quarters in the upper end of town but the T. O. was offered instead, this offer was ignored but instead the men took up quarters in the yeard [*sic*] and buildings of the Juarez Tanning and Mfg. Co. Prest. Romney asked the men in charge if they came as friends or foes, he answered that they came as friends and intended no harm. Referred to the conversation between the 2nd Capt. of the local guard (also a Liberal) and Bro. A. L. Taylor and which conversation, according to the way the report came to him, inferred that Cavadas bunch considered Prest. Romney most responsible for the execution of the bandit referred to. A. L. Taylor here interrupted with the statement that no such inference had been made in the conversation and that the report of same as carried to Prest. Romney was incorrect; that Melquiades Alvarez one of Lino Ponces men was the man held to be responsible by Cavadas men and Prest Romneys name was not mentioned nor any reference made to him.

Prest Romney continued, saying that he had gone out and prayed humbly and according to his impressions and judgment the ordering of a general move or the men was the only thing to be done. He decided himself to move out and together with (Note: This report was denied by Cavada and never proven.) [page 23] the brethren residing on the West side of the river in Colonia Juarez left town with the intention of moving out but most of those on the East side got a different understanding and thought all were to meet at the barn of E. C. Eyring above town and decide but after hunting all night for those who had gone out from the West side the other brethren returned to Colonia Juarez. Said he had already issued orders to Dublan, Garcia and Pacheco to evacuate their towns and join the party who had left Juarez and were then in the "Stairs". As part of the men had stayed in Juarez and it appeared that the move was now unnecessary he sent a courrier to countermand the order sent to Dublan but the people had acted so promptly they had already moved out about sunrise, consequently there was nothing left to do but move out of the country in a body. The people mived [*sic*] on his advice, he siad [*sic*], and not because they were afraid. Some of them did not want to leave and only left on his urgent advice, especially the ones who left Colonia Juarez last.

Bro. Ivins asked if Salazar had ever threatened violence or death if people did not give up their arms and asked how the statement that after disarming the men they were left defenseless yet when they came out they brought to the U. S. hundreds of guns and thousands of cartridges.

Prest. Romney said Salazar had not said so in words but his actions suggested it. That at the time of disarming men they only gave up part of their arms keeping most of the best weapons. Bro. Ivins stated that he had not replied to Bro. Romneys [page 24] questions, during visit in El Paso, referred to, in a spirit of anger or indifference and thought he had always treated Bro. Romney in his calling with as much or more respectful consideration than Bro. Romney had treated him in his calling. Denied vigorously the statement made by Prest Romney that he Bro, Ivins, had said that the "Mormons were in Mexico as any other Americans and because they had no better sense". Said he did tell Bro. Romney that neither Government troops nor Bro. Brown with his proposed volunteers could set with any degree of promptness in ease of violence, and that if a crisis should arise we would have to act as Booker and Bayd and other American companies would act and that is to handle the situation according to their best judgment and impressions.

Prest. Romeny [*sic*] stated that he had always tried to give the Bishops advice when perplexing questions arose and felt that Bro. Ivins had left him alone and did not try to help him with advice as to what he should do.

Bro. Ivins said that when Prest Romney had asked what to do in case funs [*sic*] were demanded it was an impossible thing to answer definitely what would be the wisest thing to do until the condition should arise then there was only one thing to do and that would be to handle the situation according to our best judgment and as our wisdom should dictate. Bro. Ivins asked if all rebels had left Juarez and Dublan when the last body of our men had left Juarez. Prest. Romney answered that they had all left and gone to the mountains. Bro. Ivins asked [page 25] as to the attitude of local Mexicans. Answered that some were sorrowful and others pleased to see us go.

Bro. Harris was asked as to his opinion of the move. Answered that the Mexicans had used vile language and assumed a menacing attitude against the Mormons and thought bloodshed would have resulted had our men not moved out. Bro. E. C. Eyring said that in his opinion had one of our men struck a rebel with his first he would have been answered by a shot. B. Stowell also thought that in order to avoid bloodshed the leaving of the Colonies was necessary. Danl Skousen thought all could have remained in Juarez but thought the mountain colonists would have been safter [*sic*] out of towns during Salazars presence but thought they could have safely come to Juarez then return later to homes. D. V. Farnsworth said Col. Demetrio Ponce had said that there must and would be intervention and with this in view he thought move necessary. Willard Call thought it was time to leave owing to conditions and was in sympathy with move. Jno. W. Wilson thought the move unnecessary and thought if we had stayed in the mountains for a few days and sent a commission to see Federals and ascertain their intentions that many of us might now be in peaceable possession of our homes. S. E. McClellan thought the move prudent and necessary but thought if all could have acted wisely the whole thing could have been avoided. Alex Jameson thought it necessary to leave and felt that otherwise there would have been bloodshed. Bro. James Skousen said he thought the move could have been avoided. P. H. Hurst thought from reports move was necessary but was not in

Colonies so could not say. Bro. J. J. Walser thought that [page 26] after guns were delivered it was not safe to remain although he thought that if all had used wisdom move could have been avoided. Guy C. Wilson thought that if the men had used judgment and could have controlled their tempers move would have been unnecessary. H. M. Payne was of same opinion. A. L. Taylor thought that if we had not imported any firearms and had remained strictly neutral in our expressions we could have remained in our homes unmolested and that even after we had vacated the settlements that we could have remained a few days in mts. and then have returned unmolested and occupied our homes. Thought move unnecessary. R. E. Bowman was of the opinion that owing to the fact that men cannot always keep their tempers that the move out of the townm [*sic*] might have been necessary but thought they could have remained a few days in the mountains then returned as Federals were expected in soon. Bp. Thurber and A. M. Tenney were of opinion that move was necessary. Bp. Bentley said he felt different from some of the Brethren regarding the Mexican people. Said he sent his family out in obedience to counsel of Stake Prescy. Related in detail conditions leading up to vacating of Colonies by men and felt that the rebels had not treated the people of Col. Juarez nearly so badly as treatment reported by brethren from Dublan. Was consequently of the opinion that our lives were safte [*sic*] when we left but was also conscientious in following the counsel of Prest Romney and that was the sole reason either he or his family had left their homes. Felt that time would determine the wisdom of the move which he did not presume to say was either right or wrong but his personal judgment and opinion was that we might have all [page 27] remained at home.

Prest Romney differed with Bp. Bentley in most of his ideas and said he had grown old in the last five years carrying the burdens of the Juarez Stake and thought unless the leading authorities of the Church changed in their attitude toward his administration and the Mexican Colonies that he would never return there to preside unless called to. Prest Ivins said he would never be called to return nor to preside unless he wished to that the policy of the 1st Prescy was to give every one their free agency about returning. Thought Prest. Romney was assuming a wrong attitude the way he felt regarding the attitude of the leading authorities of the Church and that he was mistaken in this assumption.

Bro. Ivins stated that after tomorrow any refugee can go to any part of the U. S. free of charge and it will either be necessary to return to Mexico or go to other parts in U. S. as it will not be possible for so many to remain in El Paso. Adjourned.

Minutes of meeting held in Am Natl Bank Bldg Aug 14, 1912 at 8 A. M. Apostle Ivins presided prayer by A. D. Thurber. Present all of Stake Presidency and St. Clerk, Apostle A. W. Ivins, Bp. C. P. Miller, Prest. Jos. E. Robinson, Prest. Rey L. Pratt, H. E. Bowman, A. M. Tenney, Martin L. Harris, Hish [*sic*] Councilors: J. J. Walser, B. Stowell, D. Skousen, F. H. Hurst, E. C. Eyring, Guy C. Wilson, W. Call, H. M. Payne, Alex Jameson, F. W. Jones Jr., Jno. W. Wilson, S. E. McClellan, Geo S. Romney, A. B. Call of Dublan, J. W. Skousen Jr. --Bprics. J. C. Bentley, T. C. Romney, and B. A. Clayson, Juarez; A. D. Thurber, Gaskell [page 28] Romney, A. B. Call of Dublan; J. T. Whetten, L. B. Farnsworth, Hyrum Cluff, Garcia; J. E. Stemer, D. P. Black, Jas. Carroll, Pacheco; James Mortensen, Cd. Juarez Branch; Alma Fredericksen of Col. Diaz.

Bro. Alma Frederickson was asked as to his opinion of the move and abandonment of Colonies. Said conditions in Diaz were different from those reported in the other Colonies as the few rebels at Asencion were peaceful at time of evacuation, however thought the move must have been necessary or all would not have left.

Bp. J. E. Stemer was in sympathy with move as we had never had redress of murders committed in the past and had no confidence in the government. In Pacheco up to the time of leaving no threats bad been made but as rebels were now in Mountains thought it best for all to be out. Thought the majority of people approved of move but some murmured and thought we acted too hastily.

Bp. Whetten said they had not been troubled in Garcia as in the other colonies, in fact no trouble was apparent until the time order came for men to move out at which time rebels came to disarm them. The order to move had not impressed him favorably but after talking with his brethren decided to follow counsel as he desired to act harmoniously and now thought move all right.

D. A. Brown of Chuichupa said when order to leave came it was very much of a surprise and disappointment and many did not wish to obey but after much consideration decided it the only thing to do owing to the fact that the other Colonists had gone out. After hearing the remarks of all representatives present who had not previously expressed [page 29] views, Apostle Ivins suggested that a resolution be adopted regarding our leaving and return.

Bro. Ivins suggested that where anyone personally knows of instances of violence, vandalism or threats of intervention that affidavits be sworn to. This should be first handed and not hearsay. Stated that the question of our future policy was now to be considered and in the consideration of this question we assume that all we have left behind us is lost and chances of indemnity very remote in case we decide to abandon the Colonies. Said he had but one thought from the beginning and that was to get back as soon as possible and repossess our homes and property. Bro. Bowman said he had been appointed to talk with Mr. Grockett and Thede of the Pearson Co. Mr. Thede came up from Pearson yesterday on a hand car to Guzman and from there by train. Reported about 4,000 federals in and around Casas Grandes, all apparently orderly and well disciplined troops. The Pearson Co. are desirous that we return and offer work and good wages to all who will go back; their policy is to push their work more vigorously than ever. Bro. Bowman said that he had but one thought personally and that was to bet [*sic*] back and that we go at once and not wait for the RR. to be repaired. Moved that we take steps to return immediately. Seconded by J. J. Walser and S. E. McClellan. Bro. Ivins suggested that on voting on this question with for or against it we were not bound to act as we had voted if later we feel otherwise. The greatest liberty is extended to all in this matter.

[page 30] Bp. Bentley said he first went to Mexico under the sanction of First Presidency he had always felt it was right for him to be in Mexico and desired to return immediately.

O. P. Brown said he feared for those who were yet in Mexico and thought there was great danger in returning. Said he had no love for those despoilers of whom he had said harsh things and that he had not yet repented of his attitude. There is no stability to the government and for himself and family he would rather live on a rock than to return to live among those black devils who had driven us from our homes. Was against the resolution proposed by Bro. Bowman. Thought we had better go in a body to Morelos and assist in the defense of homes, lives and property. Bro. Jameson had a great desire to return but had no confidence in the government. Thought a committee should first go and investigate. Guy C. Wilson thought all wished to return but that the conditions under which we return was the point at issue. He had never felt afraid and did not look at things with so much alarm as some others. Had no occupation to return to as school will probably not be held this year but he wanted to go back and favored the resolution.

Bro. E. C. Eyring said that if resolution meant to return under present condtions [*sic*] he opposed it but if it meant to return when a great change had come and the federals had driven rebels out of state then he favored it. Bro. Frederickson said the people of Diaz did not want to return unless something more stable than Federal Soldiers was [page 31] present. J. J. Walser favored heartily the resolution and thought a company of men could return at once with comparative safety to look after our property.

H. S. Harris thought we could not safely return at present but thought some one should be sent to investigate the existing conditions and if found favorable that we return in a body. S. E. McClellan felt as Bro. Harris. After considerable discussion the resolution was unanimously passed.

Prest Romney said he did not favor resolution but would not oppose it. Thought that if it was right to go back now it was wrong to have left and if it was right that we should leave it was wrong to go back now as conditions had not changed. Said his troubles did not begin with the Revolution but had its beginning at the time of reorganization of Juarez Stake and as before stated he had grown old in five years. Thought that the condition of the Juarez Stake was not understood by the general church authorities. Our educational institutions had been restricted our appropriations cut down and apparently but little interest or sympathy manifested for us. Unless the attitude of the authorities of the Church changes he does not want to return to Mexico and will not do so unless called to go. Thought that unless move [*sic*] than passing interest is manifested on the part of church authorities there should be no general move back to Mexico but only a few return to dispose of what we might have left.

Apostle Ivins was sorry that the inference had been thrown out by Prest. Romney that the Church authorities [— — —] in the [—]

colonies. Said he could not [page 32] recall a single instance when the authorities had ever denied the colonists anything that could be granted in reason. More interest has been manifested in their welfare than in any of the Colonies in Canada, California or other places. Regarding the appropriations for educational purposes said an unusually large sum was appropriated one year and after due investigation it was decided to be out of proportion to other stakes and was consequently cut down. Did not like the arraignment of the general authorities and it was not prompted by a proper spirit. Did not want this body of men to get the idea that the authorities had lost interest.

Bp. Miller said he felt very much grieved that Prest Romney should take the view he had taken and hoped he would soon be able to look upon the matter differently. Was sure that interest in Juarez Stake had not abated since its reorganization. This stake has received back 90% of tithes paid in appropriations. Bro. Bowman suggested that hose [*sic*] who wished to return meet together and discuss details and plans of return. Bp. Bentley moved that the question of those going back who wished to go be left for the Relief Committee and Stake Prescy to decide as to the policy of return and submit to a later meeting.

Reconvened Aug. 14, 2 P. M. The question of abody [*sic*] of men returning to Colonies to look after our property was brought up and whether they should return with or without firearms. Bro. H. E. Bowman introduced the following resolution: "We recommend that all the male refugees from [page 33] from [*sic*] the Chih Colonies who can leave their families and who so desire shall return to said colonies for the purpose of protecting our property do so at the earliest possible date that it can be done so with a reasonable degree of safety and in so doing that we ask for the protection of the military and civil authorities of the Mexican Gov. and that we exert every effort possible to work in harmony with them also that we go unarmed and continue our policy of strict neutrality." The resolution was unanimously adopted.

Guy C. Wilson moved that the Sonora Colonists be advised to move all persons and articles that can be conveniently moved to the G. S. line at once if they feel that conditions so warrant. Also that H. S. Harris leave for Sonora tonight to carry the word to them. Adjourned.

Reconvened 8 P. M. Aug. 14. Apostle Ivins presided. Said that a resolution had been adopted this afternoon that all male refugees who so desire return at once to Chih Colonies and thought same should be carried out as soon as possible. O. P. Brown moved that Junius Romney be appointed to look after the making of affidavits and depositions regarding the threats of violence to our people by the Mexican rebels, of the threats to bring intervention, of the looting of homes etc. Unanimously carried.

Bro. Bowman was assigned to take charge of arrangements for the return move of those who will return to Mexico in the near future. BP. O. P. Miller suggested that young men be warned not to go to Gd. Juarez out of curiosity as three of our boys were failed this afternoon as suspicious characters. [page 34]

APPENDIX B

"JUAREZ STAKE RELIEF COMMITTEE MINUTES"

This document reproduces the original transcript of minutes kept from August 1 to October 20, 1912, during meetings that were held by the committee at the American National Bank Building and Buckler Building in El Paso, Texas. As noted in minutes of the inaugural meeting, the committee's purpose was to organize "various committees, etc., for the care and succor of the Latter-day Saint refugees expatriated from the Republic of Mexico by the so-called rebels under Pascual Orozco and his subordinates."

This document is reproduced exactly from an original bound typescript that was preserved and later donated by Joseph B. Romney, grandson of Juarez Stake president Junius Romney, to the Church History Library in 2011. These minutes are being published for the first time, shedding light on the Mormon relief efforts that until now have not been well understood.

The original bound typescript has one page of the August 16 notes incorrectly placed at the end of the manuscript. The page has been restored to its original position in this document.

Minutes of meeting held August 1st in 408 American National Bank Building, called by Elder A. W. Ivins for the purpose of organizing, various committees, etc., for the care and succor of the Latter Day Saint Refugees expatriated from the Republic of Mexico by the so-called Rebels under Pascual Orozco and his subordinates.

There were present at this meeting Elder A. W. Ivins of the Quorum of Apostles, Jos. E. Robinson of the Californian Mission, Henry E. Bowman of Dublan, O. P. Brown special Church Agent at El Paso, and Guy C. Wilson Principal of the Juarez Academy of Colonia Juarez, Mex.

Elder Ivins, whose health was much impaired, reviewed the situation and the efforts put forth by himself and Bros. Bowman and Brown to receive and shelter the Colonists and of their present condition. Elder Robinson had been sent by Pres. Smith to assist Elder Ivins and Elder Wilson had been sent out for the same purpose by the Stake Presidency of the Juarez Stake.

After discussing various matters, the Latter Day Saint Relief Committee was appointed and sustained as follows: Henry E. Bowman, Chairman, A. W. Ivins, O. P. Brown, Guy C. Wilson, and J. E. Robinson as members, Elder Ivins, by virtue of his appointment, having general supervision over all.

It was the sense of the Board that all those who were indigent, aged and in ill health, or those who desire to go to Utah or other remote points, to be sent away at once; whilst those who desire to return to the Colonies should be encouraged to remain here or in the immediate vicinity and not get too far away.

The following committees were appointed, each chairman or committee priviledged [*sic*] to call for aid as conditions would warrant:

Transporation:-- Jos. E. Robinson and O. P. Brown; Information:- Guy C. Wilson; Finance:-- Henry E. Bowman. Bro. Bowman had secured, free of charge, two fine office rooms with two desks and several chairs at the American National Bank Building, Numbers 408--9.

Telephone and other necessary equipment was ordered.

A card of appreciation for the help so generously tendered by the Auto Club, Transfer Companies and people of El Paso was drafted and ordered printed in two daily news-papers.

It was determined, the most important thing for the present, was transportation and steps were taken to follow up what had already been done to secure rates over the various railroads entering this City.

After some further discussion, the meeting was adjourned subject to call.

E. C. Done, Sec. pro tem.
[Miss Ethel C. Done, stenographer and typist]

Minutes of the relief committee meeting held August 12th.

Present A. W. Ivins, Bishop O. P. Miller, O. P. Brown, Guy C. Wilson, Chas. E. McClellan, and Jos. E. Robinson.

The expense incurred in the burial of Elder Byron H. Allred, the first martyr to the Mexican exodus, was discussed and on motion, the sum of $50.00 was allowed the family to help liquidate said account. Elder A. W. Ivins reported having received a check from Hon. Ed Loose of Provo, sent to help the Refugees, and suggested this check be turned to this account, remaining amount of $25.00 be drawn from the general funds.

J. E. Robinson, Sec. Pro tempore.

Minutes of a meeting of the Relief Committee with the Juarez Stake Presidency, Members of the High Council and Bishops of the Wards and leading Brethren numbering about 35 in all, at L. D. S. Relief Headquarters, 408-9 American National Bank Building, El Paso, Texas, August 13th, 1912. Elder A. W. Ivins presiding.

After offering prayer, Elder Ivins stated the purpose of the meeting to be to get from the leading brethren their feelings towards the evacuating of the L. D. S Colonies in the State of Chihuahua, Mexico. He regretted the fact that the matter had been discussed in the papers, pro and con, as well as on the street corners by our own people and strangers and that the action of the leading Brethren in the Stake in bringing the people out had been questioned and designated by many, as unwise. He stated the fact that we must determine for ourselves the course to be pursued under conditions of this kind. He also read a telegram from the First Presidency, stating that the Brethren who were upon the ground and familiar with the situation must take the responsibility of determining the policy to be followed. He felt that some of the Brethren were too bitter, in their denunciation of the Mexican people and that kindness, consideration and the spirit of conciliation would have prevented many overt acts upon the part of that people. That the spirit of hate to fight and anger brings words and deeds of violence. That he could not feel in his heart that the Mexican people have said as many hard things of us as we have of them. He said, "They are more to be pitied than blamed. If they felt as we have reported them, they would have killed us all."

He then read a copy of the letter to President Smith dated July 30th 1912. Also letter of committee to the Mexican Consul of August 6th, a copy of which was filed with Mr. Edwards, the American Consul. Then asked the Brethren to clear up all points as to the past and their exodus from Mexico, then we would discuss the future. Said he had confidence in the ability, integrity and judgment of the Presiding authorities of the Juarez Stake and felt therefore that they had done the right thing and no man should question it.

President Junius Romney said he had felt that the gravity of the situation in Mexico had not been realized and the dangers thereof minimized. Had felt that it was for more than ordinary reasons that we went to Mexico and if it were not so, there is no reason for us to remain. When he had asked for advice, the responsibility of advising the people had been put upon his shoulders by those in authority over him, and when he appealed to the people, they had "rolled it back" upon him. So he "assumed absolutely the responsibility of moving out the women and children." Said that Brothers Bowman, Thurber and Harris had stood with him. He had tried to live worthy to receive inspiration from the Lord. Had advised the people not to resist indignities put upon them and to avoid blood-shed. When Salazar demanded arms, recognized the fact to refuse them would mean to fight, and remembered that the lives of the women and children were of paramount importance, and when the crisis came, had no other inspiration, than to do as he did. Conditions grew steadily worse after the women and children were sent out. Salazar told him they would have intervention at any cost, that the Unites [*sic*] States in helping Madero was killing the followers of Orozco. Now he proposed to kill some of the American citizens and make the United States fight. Told of his interview with Salazar at which Elder H. E. Bowman was present. How every pledge and guarantee of protection, both spoken and written, was recalled, and that he and his men proposed to take anything and everything they wanted from the homes and elsewhere, and would take out guns at any cost. Said we were a menace to them because we were neutral, and they were foolish to allow us to remain so. Told of incidents [*sic*] prior to the evacuation of Colonia Juarez and of their trip into the mountains, and of his sending word to the other Colonies for all the men to get out. They came in obedience to his council and not because of fear, and added "If the Lord did not want us out he had no business to let conditions come about that would make us get out." Said the Colonies of Pacheco and Garcia could not have stayed longer and Dublan, to a man, declared they had to get out.

Brother Ivins asked "Did Salazar say anything that would indicate that they would molest you if you gave up your arms?" and Bro. Romney answered, "He said if we complied with his demands he would protect us, but would have intervention at any cost." Bro. Ivins asked, "At the time the Juarez people left were the rebels still there?" "Yes when three-fifths of the people left, but some remained until later and there were no rebels there when they (the last Colonists) left." Bro. Ivins asked, "What was the attitude of the local people when you left?" Bro. Romney answered, "It was mixed, some showed bitterness, others were sad. The attitude was not uniform."

Pres. H. S. Harris told of the vicious things done and of the gross indignities and the vile epithets heaped upon inocent [*sic*] people, until it became intolerable. He told how Mexicans had said they were going to drive us out and had even designated the homes that they intended to occupy when we were driven out. Witnessed the looting of homes when men protested. Saw them take the clothes of the dead Tenney baby, while the father stood by and pleaded for them not to do so. Told of the shots exchanged between the rebels and Dublan men as the latter left the Colony, amounting to between fifty to a hundred shots. Said when we fired in return they ran. Now, they declared, we were their enemies and the only thing was to fight or give up. Elder Ivins asked, "Was it necessary for men to leave the Colony to save the shedding of blood?" Answer, "Yes sir!" Question: "Was looting done in private homes before the men left?" (Junius Romney) Answer, "Yes Sir!" Pres. Romney stated that the men sent to intercept the Dublan Brethren thought that they were unarmed, and when they found differently, fled to Juarez and became very indignant because our brethren went away armed, and were instructed to sack and burn Juarez if the men had left, as they had done at Dublan. He added this, "We were probably justified in concluding the enemy would massacre us in order to bring intervention." They said too, it would take ten lives of our men to attone [*sic*] for the life of the bandit that had been executed. This threat, coupled with the many indignities perpetrated upon us, was sufficient to justify us in leaving the Colony. Brigham Stowell, Dan Skousen, F. W. Jones, Sr., Deronda Farnsworth, Willard Call, John W. Wilson, Ed McClellan Alexander Jameson, James Skousen, P. H. Hurst, George Romney, J. J. Walser, Sr., Guy C. Wilson, E. H. Payne, H. E. Bowman, A. M. Tenney, Bishop Thurber, and Bishop Bentley, each gave some incidents of their experience, approved of the exodus and expressed their confidence in the Stake Presidency. Bro. Alexander Jameson said, "It was highly necessary for the people to leave when they did, and I do positively know, blood would have been shed, if we had remained." Bro. Deronda Farnsworth said that Demetrio Ponce told him and Bro. Spencer over a year ago that the rebels were determined to have intervention. Bro. A. M. Tenney said they exhibited the same spirit the Apaches had done in the past, that is of murder.

Bishop Thurber stated, "This movement was the only thing and was done in the nick of time to prevent a massacre."

Bishop Bentley always loved the Mexican people, and never felt in fear of life being taken. Said he expected robbery and loot, for one of the rebel captains ("the Little Captain") had remarked of one band of rebels left in Juarez, "These men are here for no good purpose. I believe we will have to scrap them to-night." Said when treating directly with the leading officers in command, we were well treated, but of course had to give up our horses and arms. He felt that the guns had been a menace to us all the way through and they were uneasy until they had been buried. Personally, he felt that he might have remained with his family at Juarez without trouble, but bore testimony to the fact that the only thing for the Colonists as a whole to do was to come out and upheld the Stake Presidency in this movement. Said the local natives felt kindly towards them, and many wept when we left, and the rebel officers shock [*sic*] hands when they left with kindly expressions.

Bishop Bentley made a present of a very valuable horse to one of the officers and he seemed to appreciate it deeply. He also paid in advance a month's salary to the local presidente and reports this man as doing good service and conserving the interest of our people.

Adjourned until 8 P. M. Tomorrow,

J. E. Robinson, Sec. Pro Tem.

Minutes of meeting held in continuation of yesterday's session of the Relief Committee, Stake Presidency, High Councillors, [*sic*] Bishops and leading Brethren, 32 present.

Prayer was offered by Bishop Thurber.

Bro. Alma Fredricksen of Diaz reported conditions that had obtained there. Said he knew the evacuation was the result of inspiration, and the proper thing to do." [*sic*]

Bishop Steiner of Colonia Pacheco, Bishop Whetton of Garcia, David Brown of Chuichupa, each told of conditions in their respective wards and testified the exodus to be the proper thing.

At this point the following resolution was unanimously adopted; "RESOLVED: - That it is the sense of this meeting of representative from the Mormon Colonies in the State of Chihuahua, Mexico, that the abandonment of the Colonies from which we come was the only course that could have been pursued to have avoided open war with the rebel forces, which are in full control of the section of country where the colonies are located."

"That it was the manifest intention of General Inez Salazar and other rebel officers to force intervention by the United States, by attacking the "Mormon Colonies" and that, in our opinion, there was no means by which a conflict could have been avoided except that adopted."

"We, therefore, endorse the policy which has been pursued in the abandonment of the colonies and in bringing the people to the United States for safety."

Elder Ivins advised the brethren to make affidavits as to voilence [*sic*] done and threats made by Mexican officers, rebels and natives in order to bring on intervention. He said, "Shall we abandon what we have there and take chances in getting something out of it, or shall we return and regain possession? What shall we do? How shall we proceed? I do not expect peace or that it is safe now to go back, but is it worth while taking chances for?"

Bro. H. E. Bowman quoted an interview with the Pearson Company, who said a fine body of Federal soldiers now occupied the Casas Grandes valley, and the Pearson Company were going to push more vigorously than ever their various projects in that land. They desire our people to return, will give them special rates in so doing and employment. Bro. Bowman suggested that if the Representatives of the Government would not make an inventory of our properties as they remain, that we appeal to the Military power to do so, and if they will not, then to do it ourselves in an organized way so there shall be witnesses to said inventory. Advised going back as quickly as possible.

The minutes of the Relief Committee meeting held August 4th was then read by Elder Ivins, showing it was the sense of that body that we should return to the Colonies.

On motion of H. E. Bowman, seconded by J. J. Walser, the following resolution was passed; "It is the sense of this meeting that the Colonists return to their homes in the Colonies as soon as possible under proper conditions."

Bro. A. M. Tenney asked if the action of this meeting would bind those present to go and those who were not present, if they did not care so to do. Pres. Ivins answered, "Men will be left to choose for themselves. That it was not the policy of the Church Presidency to hold men to the Mexican mission."

Bishop Bentley said he wanted to go back, for despite their degradation he loved the Mexican people, but he wanted to go without arms, and when he does go will not expect to protect himself with a gun. Felt we must cultivate a kinder feeling towards the Mexican people.

Bishop O. P. Brown stated that he felt that the conditions of our people in Sonora most grave. Said, "I do not love the "bunch" who despoiled my Brethren, and cannot see how we can return and live under such undesirable conditions to be 'spat upon and have it rubbed in'," Recited how we had enriched them with schools, roads, buildings, bridges, and so forth without aid or assistance at their hands, and how the very men who had been trained in our schools were now preying upon us. Has no more faith in Federals than in Rebels, and proposed going to Morelos "to protect our people there, let come what will". Whilst in this meeting Bro. Brown received a dispatch from Douglas, announcing the death of his son Galbraith by accident yesterday, as the family were fleeing to the United States for safety. The wagon had tipped over, crushing the boy under one of the wheels and twisting the foot of his older son, so that he had to walk with crutches. Despite all this, Bro. Brown felt that "there are times when a man's duty to his fellows is greater than to his family," hence he was here.

Bro. Alexander Jameson, Guy C. Wilson, E. C. Eyring, Brigham Stowell, J. J. Walser, H. S. Harris, S. E. McClellan, George Romney, stated that they all felt like going back as soon as conditions would warrant it. Alma Fredricksen said that the people at Diaz were somewhat divided in sentiment; some were ready to return if assured of a stable Government, while others did not care to return at all.

Pres. H. S. Harris suggested a committee of investigation should be sent to the Colonies to ascertain conditions and report on same before the people returned.

Bro. A. M. Tenney said, "I don't want to go back." Bro. Ivins you know how I loved that people, I was pregnant with love for them, but there has been an abortion performed, and it looks like suicide to me to go back."

Vote on the motion and the resolution passed unanimously.

Pres. Junius Romney said, "I have grown old in five years since the time Pres. Ivins left Mexico and I was given the responsibility of the Juares [*sic*] Stake of Zion. I do not feel the Presiding authorities have understood conditions there. I do not want to go back restricted to what we can do within ourselves,-- educational interests curtailed-- appropriations cut down-- no academy-- unless the Presiding Brethren tell me to sacrifice my family to that end. If the Lord says so, I will do it, but I do not want my family to grow up among those heathens because of force of circumstances-- just because we are there as an incident of passing interest. If the Lord wants us to return, it is up to Him to make the way clear."

He said, "I think our interests require some one to go in and look after them, that our families need not go, and we can preach the Gospel from American soil as well as from Mexican. Let us sell out to Mexico and start afresh elsewhere.["]

Reported prospects the best they had ever had and the Stake would have been a help instead of a burden to the Church, but to go back now--poverty stricken-- between Rebs and Federals and intervention hanging over us would mean only another exodus. "I have neither phisycal[*sic*] nor spiritual strength to go through again what I have endured the last eighteen months." Added, "Unless the Church can give us cognizance as in other sections, I do not care to return." Stated he appreciated to the full how the brethren had stood by him through it all.

(At this juncture, word was brought to Pres. Rey L. Pratt, who met with us, that his brothers Leon and Ira with Oscar Bluth were being held for ransom by the rebels at Ciudad Juarez. A demand that one hundred dollars each should be paid for their freedom before sundown, or the rebels would not be responsible for their lives.)

(Later they were released by order of Orozco without ransom).

Elder Ivins said, "There had never been among the Presiding Brethren the same interest shown in any other Colony that has been in the Mexican Colonies. I know they are fully in sympathy with them and with and have felt to do and have done everything consistent for them, and there has been no change in their attitude regarding this people since I left Mexico." Told of history of Academy and schools and interest taken in the same.

Bishop O. P. Miller bore testimony to what Elder Ivins had said.

H. E. Bowman said, "This people can not walk off and leave their property in the Colonies and retain their self respect among men." Said we should list our properties, return prepared to bear again some of the indignities we have borne, if necessary, "and for those who want to go now to meet and formulate plans, recognizing the Government Officials, relying upon them and then do things lawfully."

Bishop Bentley endorsed Bro. Bowman's talk and made a motion that "the Relief Committee and the Stake Presidency formulate a policy to present to the body of the Priesthood at the succeeding meeting." Carried.

Bishop Thurber in seconding this motion, said, "I want to go back to Mexico, but I want a guarantee from Pres. Madero that a garrison will be maintained at Casas Grandes for some time to come." Said he regarded it suicidal to return to the Colonies by the way they came without arms.

Adjourned. Sine Die.

J. E. Robinson, Sec. pro tem.

Minutes of meeting of Relief Committee and Stake Presidency August 14th, 1912. A. W. Ivins present-- stated the question was, the discussion of plans and means to re-occupy our homes and lands in Mexico

H. E. Bowman submitted the following motion. Seconded by Bro. Guy C. Wilson; that we recommend that all of the male refugees from our Chihuahua Colonies, who can leave their families and who desire to return to said Colonies for the purpose of regaining possession of our properties and protecting same, do so at the earliest possible date that it can be done in safety. That in so doing, the assistance and protection of the Civil and Military authorities of the Mexican Government be asked and every effort possible made to work in harmony with them. Also that we go unarmed and continue our policy of strict neutrality. Carried unanimously.

Guy C. Wilson made a motion that the Colonies of Sonora be advised to get all the Colonists to the line, who are not prepared for quick flight, and that Hyrum S. Harris carry the word and visit the Colonies there, leaving at once. Carried unanimously.

Adjourned sine die.

Minutes of meeting of Relief Committee, Stake Presidency, Junius Romney, Guy C. Wilson, High Council and leading Priesthood. The resolution carried in afternoon meeting was read and upon consideration of S. E. McClellan moved adoption of the Resolution. Seconded by Thomas C. Romney. Carried unanimously.

On motion of O. P. Brown, seconded by President Junius Romney was appointed to secure and collate depositions of depredations, assaults, acts of violence made, inflamatory [*sic*] and treasonable, speeches, and lootings made and anything inimical to the peace and safety of the citizens and against law and order. Carried unanimously.

On motion, H. E. Bowman was chosen to list the names and advise those of the Colonists as to returning to the Colonies.

Matters of arms, transportations, horses, etc. were discussed and advice given.

Benediction by Bro. Jameson.
Adjourned sine die.

Minutes of Committee meeting held August 15th, 1912. Present the Committee and Pres. Junius Romney.

Bro. Ivins spoke of the many brethren and sisters, who are without funds and in absolute need of clothing and other necessities-- which was discussed and the sense of the meeting was that Bro. Ivins draw on the Presidency the sum of $5,000.00 for the purpose of relieving these needs--- making small loans to deserving men and take their notes for same, payable to the Trust-in-Trust.

On motion, H. E. Bowman, Guy C. Wilson and Jos. E. Robinson were appointed to draft communication to Mexican Consul, setting forth the fact the men folks from all our Colonies are here and anxious to return and ask for protection, etc., and safe conduct to and peaceful occupation of our homes.

Adjourned sine die.

Minutes of meeting of the Relief Committee and the Stake Presidency held August 16th, 1912.

Pres. Ivins said he had visited the camps this morning and found some despondent women , who wanted to know what they could do and where their husbands were, etc. Some sick, etc. Asked the Bishops and leading brethren to go to the camps and cheer and comfort the sisters and their children. Encourage them with the hope they may soon return to their homes in Mexico, if they chose. That those who have visits to make elsewhere, or business, now is a good time to go, otherwise we feel it best to return.

Discussion as to when we may go, how, conditions, elsewhere, etc. Guy C. Wilson says he expects to go back and hold the Academy.

H. E. Bowman said he had had assurances from the Mexican Government, that it would maintain a garrison at Pearson to protect their interests there. Said Railroad would be built immediately and there would be employment for men and teams. Those who do not want to go to Mexico, ought not to go, but those who want to go, should be encourage to go.

Bishop Thurber is ready to go back, wants to go with the first company of me, [*sic*] who go. Would like to say to our people, "Be patient and we will be able to go back in a little while".

O. P. Brown feels that it would be unsafe for Colonists to go back to the mountain settlements until peace is established, etc.

Bros. Jameson, Whetton, Wilson, Robinson, McClellan (Charles), Bishop Bentley, gave their views on various matters of interest.

Bishop Bentley feels as long as he is a member of the Juarez Stake and an officer of it, that he sould [*sic*] go back whether others go or not. Is willing, with his family, to return as soon as his brethren say they feel it can be done.

Bro. Ivins said he felt that after the first train run over the line and the rebels are gone, some one should go down. Full of hope that conditions are not so bad as we have thought they were. Said he will say what he thinks and what he would do,--- but he would not impose his views upon anyone that does not want to go back---to have them do so. Thinks we should say to old people, women, who have parents in Stakes, etc. to go there now--- but those able to take chances should be encouraged to go back. Encourage the down-hearted.

Bishop Miller said he had encouraged the Saints to keep close to the border so that they can readily return. Thinks those going to remote places will meet hard conditions.

Conditions of Diaz Colony discussed and it was suggested that as soon as the rebels are out of the District, they return and take the horses with them.

Pres. Bennion of the Central States Mission spoke of his feelings and of the good the Government has done for us.

Adjourned until 5 P. M. Saturday the 17th

Minutes of meeting of Relief Committee held August 17th, 1912.

Bishop Thurber reported that the boys who were left with the horses at Hachita need more help-- so many have left, the boys are too few for the labors.

Bro. Beecroft reported conditions. Bishop Brown suggested a man from each Colony take charge of each Colony's horses, as Chairman. On motion of Bro. Brown, the Bishops of the different Wards were appointed a Committee to supervise the herding, selling, bonding, etc. of the horses held at Hachita.

Bro. McClellan was appointed to take charge of the meetings at the Camps at 2 P. M. tomorrow.

H. E. Bowman reported the Managers of the Mexico North Western Railway, saying they would furnish all the Colonists work if they desired it at Pearson, etc. and on the road, building, lumbering, etc. All anxious. Will do all they can to facilitate business for the Brethren.

A. W. Ivins instructed the Brethren to encouraged the people at Church tomorrow and not to discourage them. Tell them good news. Wherever there is a person who wants to go back to Mexico, encourage them.

Bro. Brown feels we have much better prospects in Mexico, than can be found for us in the United States.

Letters from those who have gone away, show dissatisfaction with conditions found there, and an anxiety to return.

Jos. E. Robinson corrected the impression that no more good can come from the Federals that the Rebel government, for should the Federal Government oppress the Colonists, then the United States would of a certainty intervene.

On motion adjourned sine die.

Minutes of meeting of Relief Committee and Stake Presidency held August 19th, 1912.

Elder Hyrum S. Harris reported his trip to Sonora. Reported reaching San Jose Colony at one o'clock A. M., found people loading up to leave for United States, told them not to hurry, but to cache, hide, etc. matters, and leave in companies of 5 or 6 wagons at a time to afford protection, but it was the "instruction of the Committee to get out". Went to Morelos and got Priesthood together at 2 P. M. and told them of our condition and for them to get out, but do so leisurely-- taking corn, fruits, food, etc. and to get out to the line. Bishop and Counsellors [*sic*] not there, but men voted to come. Next day Bishop arrived and felt it was a mistake and wired Elder Ivins, who told him by telephone and were not to stampede, but to use their own judgement. [*sic*] That Bro. Harris had misapprehended his mission and set the people in a panic, etc. Felt badly if he had misrepresented the Committee.

Bro. Ivins explained what he had said and read telegram he had sent to Bishop Lillywhite. Reported visit of himself, Bishop Miller, Pres. S. O. Bennion and Jos. E. Robinson to Hachita, that people there, except about a dozen, voted to return to the Colonies, desiring to do so as soon as it is safe. Reported condition of Colonia Diaz not badly looted, except food and clothing -- the town was as the Colonists had left it. Pleaded for wisdom and prudence in advising the people to move and to return to Mexico. Many running away and no place to go to and nothing to do with.

Bro. Harris reported Brethren from Colonies coming out to camp near Douglas.

On motion Miles A. Romney was appointed as an assistant to transportation committee.

On motion it was determined that Lester Farnsworth and Adelbert Taylor care for baggage in place of Ed Payne. A. B. Call to care for commissary at Camps in place of Willard Call. Bros. Payne has a trip to make to Tucson and Bro. Call has left for Utah.

Recent reports of condition of troops in Mexico given. Suggested that a copy of all Colony brands be furnished the Patrol Department -- they having suggested it as helpful to "line riders' in detecting stolen animals, etc.

Matter of employment discussed and on motion, Bishop Bentley was appointed Chariman [*sic*] of Bishops Committee on Labor to list applications for help and those seeking employment.

Adjourned sine die.

Minutes of meeting held August 20th, 1912. A communication from Andrew Kimball was read in relation to conditions in Arizona, St. Joseph Stake, asking about transportation, sustenance, etc.

Bro. A. W. Ivins read communication to Elder Heber J. Grant, delegate to Trans-Mississippi Congress, suggesting the condition of our people and their need for help here and protection in Mexico, and this body of men to use their influence to assist us and bring the necessary pressure on Mexico to give us our rights, etc. and return us to our homes there.

H. E. Bowman spoke upon matter of inventorying property found by those returning to Colonies to have witness, if not done by State or Government authorities—this to form a basis of their future claims against the Mexican Government.

A telegram from General Blanco to Alonzo Taylor was received to-day. "Conditions quiet, and protection ample if the Colonists want to return". Sent from Pearson.

A telegram from Senator Smoot was read, stating that General Steever would be authorized by the War Department to furnish tents for our people coming from Sonora to Douglas and vicinity.

Adjourned until 5 P. M. Aug. 21st.

Minutes of Relief Committee held August 21st, 1912.

Pres. Romney reported his interview with Consul Llorente, the Mexican Consul, who said it would be necessary for us to take up our case with the Governor of Chihuahua, claimed the Governor must look after ourtransportation [*sic*] back, securing permission to return over railroad in the near future, said he would take up horse proposition at once and arrange for return of our horses to Colonies. Llorente said the Government would maintain garrisons in the country and maintain peace and would protect us, and we could return within three or four days, said we should not take our guns back without consent of Government, but he would take up the matter at once, and suggested that we list our guns, etc.

H. E. Bowman reported meeting with the Railroad officials of the Mexico North Western, who would give one-half fare railroad rates to our people desiring to return to Colonies. Thinks we should go organized with part of Stake Presidency and Ward Bishops at the head. Feels we should not go unorganized and should have some one in charge in each Colony to look after the interests of the Colonists, to lay proper foundations for our future, claims, etc.

A. W. Ivins spoke for a committee to be appointed.

After much discussion pro and con, a motion was made by Chas. E. McClellan that a committee of four men be appointed to go to the Colonies on Special train tomorrow, if arrangements can be made, ascertain situation and condition there and report same to this Committee. Miles A. Romney volunteered going and Dan Skousen and Alonzo Taylor, H. S. Harris and D. V. Farnsworth were sustained as said committee.

On motion Chas. E. McClellan and Guy C. Wilson were appointed as the Office Force at Headquarters to attend to the transportation of Refugees, answer questions and attend to labors, etc. of office. On motion it was determined to retain on salary, Miss Ethel Done as office Stenographer and typist.

A. W. Ivins read telegram from Pres. Smith, stating a subscription list was published in the *Deseret News*, that Colonists are to determine for themselves whether they return to Mexico or not, and that Mexico Government should assure protection. Suggested that Pres. Junius Romney be made Committeeman and be general supervisor and chairman of all Committees.

Bishop Whetton was appointed, on motion, as "Camp Supervisor" to look after the comfort, health and sanitation of the Refugee Camps, etc.

Adjourned until 5 P. M. tomorrow.

Minutes of meeting of Relief Committee held August 22nd, 1912.

Bishop Thurber reported the condition of the horses at the Hachita as not in best condition, because of corraling [*sic*] them each night. Had obtained some barb-wire, fenced up some "corners" where the horses could be held over night on feed. The band of horses was segregated and herded under different Colony Bands. Reported the coming of Salazar via Marco Soto, and Ascencion (?) to Palomas. Said 400 of his men had camped in the Tapiacitas the night before. Salazar made a speech at Marco Soto, in which he declared they were going to have intervention at any cost. Got permission to hold the horses at Hachita indefinitely, if they were properly herded. Said Mr. James H. Robinson, line-rider, was most considerate in this matter.

Transportation matters and probable movement of rebels, etc. were discussed.

H. E. Bowman presented the bill of the Mexico North Western Railway for $14,519.02 fares of Refugees from the Colonies to El Paso from Dublan, and Pearson and intermediate points. They evidently have charged full fare for adults and half fares for babies in arms, and yet our people rode out in freight cars, box cars, and without water or other comforts necessary.

On motion of Bishop O. P. Miller, Bro. H. E. Bowman was requested to present the matter to the leading officials of the road to ask for a reduction or consideration of terms.

Adjourned sine die.

Minutes of meeting of Relief Committee held August 23rd, 1912.

Pres. A. W. Ivins read telegrams from members of committee sent into Colonies. One from Pres. H. S. Harris, dated Dublan, Mexico, August 23rd, , [*sic*] said, "Most wheat secure. Political situation insecure. Will return tonight". Telegram from Alonzo Taylor of the same date said, "Agreeably surprised conditions Juarez. Foodstuff. Will arrive train today".

A letter from O. P. Brown telling of conditions at Douglas and in Sonora was read. Bro. Brown wanted to know whether he should return to El Paso or remain at Douglas and help our people from the Sonora Colonies, who are coming to Douglas,--- some 25 families having already arrived there.

Elder A. W. Ivins read a telegram from the Presidency, saying prudence should characterize the movement of our people to reoccupy the Colonies, and that Elder Ivins, Bishop Miller and Elder Robinson should use their own judgment as to when they should return. He asked the Brethren how they felt about these brethren going home, reviewed the situation as nearly as we understand it.

Bishop Miller expressed his appreciation of the courtesies shown him by the brethren and with Bro. Robinson felt there was no more need for them to remain and that Pres. Ivins should return on account of his ill health.

Bro. Ivins said he was so much better he did not want his health considered as a reason for going home.

Bishop Bentley moved we express our appreciation to the Relief Committee for their labors. This was ammended [*sic*] by Pres. Romney, by adding that we also release them to return home, as they see fit.

Carried unanimously.

On motion of Pres. Romney, Bro. O. P. Brown was continued as an associate member of the Central or Relief Committee---- the personnel now being Junius Romney, Hyrum S. Harris, Charles E. McClellan, (Stake Presidency) Guy C. Wilson and O. P. Brown.

Bishop Miller admonished the brethren to be careful to keep vouchers for all disbursements, etc.

H. E. Bowman again called attention to the laying of a proper foundation for future claims for indemnity and claims should be made as a whole, not individual.

Pres. Romney concurred in what Bro. Bowman had said. H. E. Bowman said, "Let the word go out for the people to prepare their evidence and keep in touch with the Committee."

On motion of H. E. Bowman, the Committee was instructed to prepare blanks for the people to list what properties they find upon their return. Carried unanimously. Cautioned to be careful in getting up blank forms by Bro. Ivins.

Adjourned until 8 A. M. tomorrow.

Minutes of Committee meeting held 8 A. M. August 24th, 1912. There were also present Elder A. W. Ivins, Bishop O. P. Miller, and Pres. Jos. E. Robinson. Elder A. W. Ivins presided.

Pres. H. S. Harris told of his visit to Dublan. Said the Spencer family had "put in their time" trying to keep places locked up and matters intact so far as possible. Said the homes had been looted and clothes, dishes and bedding had been carried off. Mr. Spencer had "run" the looters out of Bro. Bowman's home and had been threatened by the mob with guns, knives, etc., but he and his son Josiah had their head-quarters there.

After the Rebels left, local Mexicans began to rob, but Josiah Spencer secured the services of one-hundred soldiers, which patroled [*sic*] the town for two or three days. He had hired men to herd cows and horses and had done much to conserve the interests of the Colonists. The furniture was pretty well retained; Jackson's home was rifled; all graineries [*sic*] with grain were intact, with one exception. Pres. Harris said that he did not know of one place the Mexicans had taken possession of--- of their own volition. Mr. Spencer had put tenants in many homes;-- some of the tenants had proven true to the trust, while others had not.

Bro. D. V. Farnsworth reported almost the same as Bro. Harris. Said that they called on Sanjinez, who said it would not be wise for us to take our families there as yet, as the country is full of rebels and Sanjinez said, "we may be called away at a moment's notice." Also said that they would afford protection to all of the Colonists while they were there, and that looters would be made to return many things that had been stolen. The people from El Valle and Galeana had been there looting and carried many effects to their homes,-- especially from the stores.

Bro. Harris also said the Mexicans reported that the Mountain settlements were gutted -- furniture wantonly destroyed, and the crops were destroyed by the horses of the rebels being turned on same.

Bro. Alonzo Taylor reported on conditions at Juarez. Said that he called on General Blanco first, at Pearson; that he acted as interpreter for an American line man, who reported that there were ninety rebels up along the Railroad. Blanco sent seventy men up to rout them, and the Federals killed five rebels, captured thirty, and captured sixty head of horses, about half of which were saddled and equipped. These rebels were of Lino Ponce's men, who took arms from the Juarez Colonists. The Federals had a lot of local 'dgers in the thirty that were captured.

The eleven men that were captured by our brethren when they came out, were in the vanguard of the Federals, who had captured them.

Bro. Taylor said that Blanco had wondered why we left with arms and evaded the Federals and had left the country; that Blanco said had he met the brethren, would have disarmed and sent them back. Blanco says that if we return, he will give us all assistance possible, returning of property through searching party---- repairing of the telephone lines, and acting as guards and couriers.

Bro. Taylor reported that they arrived at Juarez late at night in a rainstorm, that the natives came out to meet them and expressed much gratification at their return. Next morning he called on the Presidente and with him made a tour of the town. Bro. Taylor said, "We found three additional houses that had been entered since we left, but most of the homes were in good shape and our interests conserved. Part of the merchandise at Croft's had been taken, but the rest had been returned to the store. Pres. Romney's house was open, but everything seemed intact. The Presidente had been to the house and had carried the typewriter to the Shoe Shop, and had hid two sacks of flour up in the attic, and destroyed the ladder so that others could not climb to the loft." Bro. Ivins house and Bro. Walls' store were found intact.

In Bro. Taylor's report, he said that the Presidente had organized natives to care for the homes,-- locking them, etc.,-- that the store was in good shape, that not much had been lost, possibly $7,000.00 Mex.; that a Mexican was in the store and had sold about $1,000.00 worth of merchandise, and some few accounts to keep from insubordination and loot. That local natives had been organized, who were prepared to resist looters--- on signal, and had turned back proposed looters from Casas Grandes and also from Pearson. The Pearson natives said it was of no use to go to Juarez, because the Mexicans there were "Muy Bravo". That $30.00 had been collected from looters of orchard and garden for the melons and fruit taken.

Reported that Bro. Wilson was going to open the store, that Bro. Spilsbury [*sic*] was well and said that he had been well treated, and that the Mexicans had formed a company and had assessed themselves of two days work to repair ditches, etc. That they visited Bro. Allen, who is well, and, the Mexicans said, much improved mentally; that a man had been detailed to look after him, and had stayed with him day and night; that he was not yet fully balanced mentally, but that he was in his own home, and a Mexican was taking good care of him.

General Blanco reported to our brethren that Salazar and men were coming to Pearson to fight, but that the men refused to do so equipped as they were. Salazar said, "You loot a town thoroughly when ordered, but won't fight, etc. 2; [*sic*] That Salazar had taken his leading men and had left for Palomas-- leaving his men in broken bands or marauders. General Blanco said, "My command will give protection and maintain a garrison at Pearson until the rebels are entirely overcome and driven out of the country. The rebels are presenting themselves for amnesty." He said that amnesty was only for the political offenders.

There are plenty of foodstuff in the store, houses and also flour at Casas Grandes. There was fruit in abundance, which is ready to pick and market, and the alfalfa is ready to cut. The country is like a meadow; the young horses were left, and other horses were returning. Blanco says that until the 30th of August, men may recover their horses by claiming same with witnesses.

There is a Banner at Pearson. The letters on same were three feet in length and said, "Welcome back Brave Boys!" The sign on the hospital was "Sure cure for Cold Feet see Dr. ----", but the welcome was genuine.

Letter from M. A. Romney as follows was read,

Colonia Juarez, Chih., 8--23--12.

"Bro. Ivins or Junius Romney,

We arrived at Colony all O. K. late last night and found conditions of property much better than we were lead to expect. Natives here have taken excellent care of all property, using every precaution to prevent local stealing. Every home we have entered, (with but one exception, B. L. Croft's) has the appearance of the occupants just having left, throwing a coat here, a hat there.

The natives welcomed us with much pleasure and expressed a great desire for us to return and I believe their expressions to be sincere.

Everything looks favorable to me for the immediate return of all our people so far as this Colonia is concerned. If the men return without families they can do nothing with putting up fruit, cheese-making and providing for the winter. A little later and it will be too late, as fruit to be bottled and dried is just right now. Corn is in roasting ear, and potatoes ready to dig.

I can not bring myself to believe that the people of this land will take our lives and I feel that if we are going to return to our homes in this land, now is the time.

I am your Bro.
(Signed) M. A. Romney."

Pres. Ivins read copy of the telegram to Senator Smooth, [*sic*] asking for pressure to be brought to bear on Mexican Government to maintain a garrison at Casas Grandes to protect out [*sic*] people.

Bishop Miller asked Bro. Alonzo Taylor if he felt it the proper thing to go back. Bro. Taylor replied, "Yes! I think we should go to care for our crops at once. I think the men would be safe."" [*sic*] and said that Sanjinez was of the same opinion.

The local Mexicans are under a stress at Juarez and very anxious for us to return to protect their lives and property -- as they feared invades from lawless citizens from other sections.

The President at Juarez was granted amnesty by Blanco and upon our request, was retained as our Presidente, which had a good effect.

Bishop Bentley felt we should not change our policy about going back, and that families might be taken back with due propriety, even now, and that men were of not much avail without their families.

Bro. Harris thinks we should wait a little while before we take our families, and give the Yaquis a free hand for a week or two to break up the bands marauding there.

Proposition of returning discussed pro and con by various brethren.

On motion "Representatives of this Committee be authorized to call upon General Tellez and request a permanent garrison in Casas Grandes Valley and ascertain his attitude on this question", Pres. Junius Romney was appointed to wait upon Gen. Tellez and take with him whomsoever he desires.

On motion of Bro. Guy C. Wilson, it was agreed that a limited number of brethren, desiring to go to the Colonies tomorrow, be allowed to do so; and any others who desire to go Monday be allowed also.

The men were to consult their Bishop about going tomorrow, and those that felt safe in taking their families in Monday night also consult the Bishop,-- the responsibility being put upon him; the Committee, of course, advising as to conditions and if danger threatens, restrain them.

Discussed some points that were to be guarded and conditions required.

Bro. Lester B. Farnsworth was released from service on Baggage Committee.

Adjourned until 4 P. M. to-day.
J. E. Robinson, Secy. Pro Tempore.

Minutes of meeting held August 24th, 1912 at 4 P. M. Present the General Committee and the leading Brethren.

Elder Ivins read two communications from Mexican Consul, E. C. Llorente, referring us to the Governor and Custom's House Official for some matters we had referred to him.

Pres. Romney reported his visit with Bro. McClellan to General Tellez, who was most accessible and courteous. He assured the brethren that he was anxious to have the Colonists return, as he could possibly be, and the Government would retain a garrison in the Casas Grandes Valley,--- that his Government would never leave it again, but would hold it with a strong garrison in the future. Said it would be absolutely safe to take our families at once to Dublan and Juarez, but not to go to the Mountain Colonies yet,--- until the Rebs were cleared out of the mountains. Will send an escort to conduct horses at Hachita into the Colonies, but does not want us to go to Diaz to stay until Sanjinez has driven out the "Bandidos". Said we could retain our arms and carry them back with us—having no objection whatever to us so doing, and seemed to appreciate the fact that we had not surrendered them to the "Bandidos". Said he would have the Diaz district pacified as soon as possible. Said he would help us in every way consistent with his office, and that the Government is under obligations to protect us, Americans particularly, and if we found any of our property in the hands of others, to apply to an officer and he would see that it was returned to us. Said he might issue a general edict to cover this question.

Reported Conzul [*sic*] Edwards as saying he had had no instructions from the Government, and therefore had no instructions to give us, but thought we should go back, in fact should have gone back before now, but he would give us no instructions in writing.

Bishops Bentley and Thurber invited the Colonists from the Mountain Settlements to come to their respective wards and occupy the vacant homes, and ample employment would be given them until they were ready to go on into the mountains to their own homes.

Adjourned sine die.
Jos. E. Robinson, Secy. pro tem.

Minutes of meeting held at 9 A. M., August 27th, 1912, at Room 408 American National Bank Building. Present Office Committee and Pres. H. S. Harris. Committee consisted of Bros. C. E. McClellan, Guy C. Wilson and O. P. Brown.

Bro. Wilson presented a number of request for loans from different brethren. Geo. Davis"[*sic*] request for $50.00 was not granted, but his family will be given transportation from Arizona to El Paso according to his wishes.

A. Camphouse, who has assisted considerably at the Tent City, was given $5.00 to aid him. Two dollars ($2.00) was given H. S. Harris in rebate for money spent by him as train fare from Chico to Dublan, when he went up to assist the Chuichupa Saints.

Elmer Johnson, a Mexican citizen, unable to take advantage of the free transportation offered by the Government, has asked for a loan of $50.00 to assist him to get to his family who have gone to Idaho. It was decided to loan him this amount, and to take his note for same.

The question of transporting men to Hachita was discussed. It was decided to ask all those who desired to go to Hachita for the purpose of returning with the horses to the Colonies, to wait until we get permission to return the horses, then we will endeavor to get free transportation to all who desire to go for that purpose.

It was decided to send a telegram to Senator Reed Smoot, requesting him to get permission from the War Department to return to Mexico the guns and ammunition that our men had brought out. The telegram follows:

Aug. 27, 1912.

"Senator Reed Smoot, Washington, D. C.
Mexican Federal, General Tellez, willing our men should return with arms brought out. Can you get permission from our Government? 326 promiscuous rifles, fifty pistols, 75,000 rounds of ammunition.

(signed) Guy C. Wilson."

C. E. McClellan reported that having been informed that our people at Hachita were yesterday expecting to send twenty-five armed men to Diaz as an investigating committee, but that in view of the fact that General Tellez had advised us not to return to Diaz without permission, and because of the proximity of rebels in that district and the complications likely to arise, he, Bro. McClellan, had telegraphed for the Committee to Bishop E. V. Romney not to make any movement into Diaz until further instructed.

Bishop Geo T. Sevey of Colonia Chuichupa, who had just returned from Thatcher, Arizona, where we had gone to look after the refugees there, reported that he had found the people quite comfortably fixed. The most of them were living in houses, but some were in Government tents. Provisions were being supplied them through the Committees arranged for that purpose. There is little sickness and the people are generally quite cheerful, and most of them are desirous of returning to Mexico. Pres. Kimball says many more could be provided for. Little information is obtained by them about conditions in El Paso, except through the newspapers. The Committee decided to formulate and send them an official letter. Bishop Sevey was given permission to go where he might choose in search of employment, as there is little prospects of his being able to do much work.

Alexander Jameson was appointed to look after the baggage instead of Bros. Lester B. Farnsworth and Adelbert Taylor, who have left the City.

H. S. Harris and C. E. McClellan were asked to communicate with General Tellez with reference to whether the time had arrived for taking in our horses.

In view of the fact that it is reported that bridges have been burned between here and San Pedro on the Mexico North Western, and that the train carrying about a hundred of our people to the Colonies had been turned back, it was thought by the Committee that no other women and children should attempt to go down till we feel conditions to be safer.

Adjourned till 5 P. M.

C. E. McClellan Sec. pro tem.

Minutes of meeting held at 5 P. M. August 27th, 1912.

Present Office Committee, a number of High Counselors, Bishop Whetton, Bros. Thomas Romney and Edmund Richardson, the latter had just returned from Colonia Diaz. Prayer was offered by Bro. Thomas Romney.

Bro. Richardson reported that he had recently made two visits to Diaz to get, among other things, some ward records. He saw last Friday at Diaz Inez Salazar, who said he was going south or west, he had not decided which. Had about a hundred men with him and 300 in advance. He went toward Nogales Ranch, taking all the horses he could find in the vicinity of La Ascencion. Bro. Richardson said, also, that he talked with a deserter from Salazar at Nogales, who said Durango is their desired destination. Balderamo R. Rodriguez is this man's name, and he has come on to El Paso to report to Consul Llorente.

Every house in Diaz, except Alma Frederickson's has been thoroughly looted of everything valuable that could be carried of, [*sic*] but there has been little wanton destruction. Some dishes have been left, but no bedding, clothing or provisions.

Bro. Richardson said that he had arranged with a reliable Mexican to prevent looting in the night as much as possible. A non-Mormon by the name of Wilson does what he can during the day to prevent thieving. The reported fight at La Ascencion on Sunday, Bro. Richardson says did not occur, but he reported a little fight which occurred between Loren Adams and a Mexican rebel at Diaz some days ago, in which several shots were exchanged but no one struck. No wheat has been taken from Diaz to speak of. Loose hogs are doing considerable damage, and if the people could return now, they could save considerable property from destruction. He also reported that there are no rebels in the Boca Grande country. Thinks a dozen men might with safety and profit return quietly to Diaz. All the recent bands in that vicinity have passed by Diaz, presumably because there was nothing more to loot from the Colony.

O. P. Brown reported a communication from the Mexico North Western R. R. Officials saying that nine bridges had been burned this side of San Pedro, and that there would be no train to-morrow.

Benediction by N. K. Young.

C. E. McClellan, Secretary.

Minutes of Committee meeting held at 5 P. M. August 28th, 1912 at Room 408 American National Bank Building. Present H. S. Harris, C. E. McClellan, Guy C. Wilson, O. P. Brown, also High Counsellors [*sic*] P. H. Hurst and E. C. Eyring.

Bro. O. P. Brown, at the request of Pres. Harris, reported his recent visit to Sonora. At Douglas he met with Bishop Martineau and others who were anxious to talk with him. There was considerable interest among them relative to Pres. Harris' visit and the idea that he had given instructions not in harmony with the ideas of the Central Committee. Bro. Brown disabused their minds of this idea and said Bro. Harris had done only what he had been authorized to do. All of these brethren testified that Bro. Harris had not created a panic, not said anything likely to create a panic. Some of the families were already to come out when Bro. Harris reached San José and Morelos. Bishop Lillywhite had discouraged the idea of the people coming out.

Bro. Brown said he regarded the conditions such that he felt the people ought to move out. Told of the arrangements he had made with the Douglas Civil and Military authorities for the care of the people who were coming out of the Sonora colonies,---- securing tents, locating, etc. He had then left matters in charge of Bros. Mitchell Lillywhite and John Butler. Also told of having telegraphed on Sunday night last to Mitchell Lillywhite of the reported presence of Salazar at the Nogales Ranch with 800 men, and the fear that they were removing west toward the Sonora settlements, and urging him to send a courier to the Mormon Settlements with this information and with instructions to move over the line.

Bro. Wilson read a newspaper article from the El Paso Times, through its Douglas reporter, reflecting upon our honor in the matter of transportation, and his reply thereto, vindicating our conduct.

Pres. McClellan reported that the reason Prs. [*sic*] Harris and he had not visited General Tellez yet, was that they were waiting developments in the La Ascencion district that would justify urging again upon the General immediate action.

A telegram from Pres. Smith urging the necessity of maintaining, especially at this time, a strict neutrality, was read.

Bro. Brown referred to a team which had been stolen from one of our sisters on the Gila, and now in the city here. It was decided to assist in recovering team with help and money.

Benediction by Bro. E. C. Eyring.

C. E. McClellan, Secretary.

Minutes of meeting held August 29th, 1912, at room 408 American National Bank Building. Present Committee, and members of Bishoprics and High Counsellors. [*sic*] Prayer by Bro. Alexander Jameson.

A letter from Mitchell Lillywhite at Douglas was read in which he said the people from Colonia San José were in Douglas, but mostly in rooming houses and paying their own expenses. The tents were ready to be put up by the Government at any time, if the Morelos people moved out and need them.

Bro. Brown said the people from Morelos were not yet coming out from the Colony, but have scouts out to give warning in case of approaching danger, in which case the Colonists are ready to move out. Said today's reports are that El Tigre mines have been asked to-day to surrender, and threatened in case of a refusal.

Bro. Wilson reported receipt of a telegram from Senator Smoot, saying that General Steever had been instructed regarding our arms now at Hachita.

Pres. Harris reported a telegram received from Pres. Romney saying all was well, and that the Steven's family are in Colonia Juarez. Also that General Sanjinez is repairing the R. R. and expects to open it Saturday

Brother Wilson reported that it is necessary to abandon the rooms now occupied by us in this building before the first of next month, rooms have been rented in the Buckler building, to which we shall move probably to-morrow or Saturday.

Benediction by Bishop J. T. Whetton.

C. E. McClellan, Secretary.

Minutes of special meeting of Office Committee, held at 12 M. August 30th, 1912, in room 408 American National Bank Building.

A loan of $75.00 was made to John Robinson, as he has devoted much time, and given most efficient service and is greatly in need of this assistance.

Bro. O. P. Brown read a letter written by him to Bishop E. V.

Romney, in which he told him of receiving a communication from General Steever containing positive instructions that none of our people must connect themselves in any way with armed bodies crossing into Mexico, or attempt to carry arms over the line without full permission from the War Department. This permission may be obtained by complying with certain requirements specified in the letter, such as giving caliber of gun, number, etc.

The Committee decided that, in view of the disquieting reports from El Tigre mines, and elsewhere, we feel to caution against families returning to the Colonies until we deem it safer. Men may go if they wish.

C. E. McClellan, Secretary

Minutes of Committee meeting held August 30th, 1912, in rooms 408 American National Bank Building. Present H. S. Harris, C. E. McGlellan, [*sic*] Guy C. Wilson, and O. P. Brown. Prayer by Pres. H. S. Harris.

O. P. Brown reported a visit to Consul Llorente this afternoon, made at the invitation of the Consul, when Bro. Brown had asked for a "salva conducta" for E. G. Taylor.

The Consul accused Bro. Brown, among others, of trying to bring about intervention. Bro. Brown presented to the Consul written documents, showing his attitude on the question of intervention--that he was trying to prevent it. The Consul said the conditions between the two governments are now very much strained, and irresponsible men may precipitate trouble. He appeared very much worried over general conditions. He said that in case we did anything to provoke intervention, that all guarantees given in the concessions made to us would be revoked. Bro. Brown assured him that it would have been possible for our people to bring on intervention, but we had carefully avoided it.

After much discussion, the following resolution was unanimously passed:

"Notwithstanding the development during the past few days of threatening conditions, we do not feel justified in over-ruling the former decision of the Central Committee, which permitted men who felt it safe to take their families back to the Colonies with them, to do so."

At this point, at the suggestion of Bro. McClellan, the Committee called in, from the adjoining room, about twenty of the brethren who were waiting there, including some Bishops and High Councillors. [*sic*] And at the request of the Committee, Bro. Wilson acted as their spokesman in explaining the reasons why we have been forced to differ at times in our opinions, and have been less definite in our decisions that we should have liked to be. And also gave the reasons why we have hesitated in regard to advising families to return to the Colonies. He also explained that the Committee were united on the above resolution, and on the general policy, and are resolved that in the future we shall strive to have our views as a committee, more united, and would try to prevent any individual opinions be circulated that might tend to counteract the ideas given out by the Committee.

Pres. McClellan gave a few definite reasons why the situation had seemed to justify the question being raised as to whether we should at this point advise against returning families to the Colonies. He also pleaded for harmoney [*sic*] among the brethren.

Pres. Harris spoke along the same line.

Bishop Bentley reviewed some of the experiences of those who were trying to return to the Colonies, and said while it would be considerable expense and disappointment not to go now when the train runs, still if the brethren really feel that is is [*sic*] not safe to have families go, he did not desire to go contrary to their feelings. H thought he voiced the sentiments of others who were expecting to go.

Bro. Brown stated that he proposed to act in harmony with the committee.

Benediction by Geo. M. Haws.

C. E. McClellan, Secretary.

Minutes of Committee meeting held in Room 8, Bucklef [*sic*] Building, August 31st, 1912.

Prayer by Bro. Guy C. Wilson.

Bro. Brown reported receiving a telegram from the Hachita people, saying they were out of provisions, and that he had taken up the matter with Fort Bliss Commissary, and supplies would be sent as soon as possible, which might not be before Tuesday. Also reported an interview with Senator A. B. Fall held to-day. The Senator expressed the idea that intervention soon is not a probability. That monied interests of the U. S. control the revolutions both in Mexico and Nicaragua, and intervention or revolutions will come only as it suits certain monied interests. When their control of Mexico is sufficiently absolute, intervention will undoubtedly come. Said Pres. Taft's proclamation for Americans to get out of Mexico was a great diplomatic blunder. Said the chances of American citizens for getting damages from Mexico are good. Said Democrats had blocked intervention through fear of political consequences.

Benediction by O. P. Brown.

C. E. McClellan, Secretary

Minutes of Committee meeting, held September 2d, 1912, in rooms 8 and 9 of Buckler Building. Present Bros. H. S. Harris, C. E. McClellan, Guy C. Wilson, and O. P. Brown. Prayer by Bro. C. E. Mcclellan.

Bro. Brown said he had learned from N. C. Tenney some things that explain why there had been talk of a filibustering expedition, as referred to in Pres. Smith's telegram. Feared there was still danger of some of our hot-headed men or boys creating trouble; and suggested that we ask our brethren at Hachita to look the guns over and oil them well, and then turn them over with proper receipts to the U. S. Military authorities at Hachita, to remove any possibility of their being made us of unwisely. The committee decided to present the matter to General Steever through O. P. Brown and if the General approves of the idea, it will be carried out at once.

Two letters from M. W. Lillywhite at Douglas were read. He reports that thirty families are on their way out from Morelos to Douglas, and that about ten families were remaining. Also that the rebels were reported to be withint [*sic*] fifteen miles of Morelos.

Bro. C. E. McClellan brought up the question of a few men who are doing constant duty out at the Commissary, who are in need of a little help financially. It was decided to assist them with necessities.

Pres. Romney's and Bishop Thurber's letters, which were received yesterday and were read at the Sabbath meeting, in which the latter advised against taking families down to the Colonies, were read. The Committee felt to leave the matter of returning just where it has been, optioned with the heads of families, all of whom, perhaps, have heard Bishop Thurber's letter and know the feeling of caution that the presiding brethren feel should be exercised.

Benediction by Pres. H. S. Harris.

C. E. McClellan, Secretary.

Minutes of Committee meeting held September 3rd, 1912, in room 9 of Buckler Building. All members present. Prayer by Pres. H. S. Harris.

Bro. O. P. Brown reported that he had referred the matter of turning over the guns at Hachita to the Government to General Steever, but the General said he did not care to assume the responsibility with the forces the government now has there. It was desided, [*sic*] therefore, to leave the guns where they are for the present.

A letter from Mitchell Lillywhite said all the people were on the way out from Morelos except about fifteen men, and that the rebels were within six miles of Morelos when the people left.

Benediction by Bro. Guy C. Wilson

C. E. McClellan, Secretary.

Minutes of Committee meeting held in room 8 Buckler Building, September 4th, 1912. Besides the committee, there were present President Romney, who had just returned from the colonies, and also Bishop Thurber and his counsellor , [*sic*] A. B. Call, and High Councillor, [*sic*] P. H. Hurst. Prayer by Bishop A. D. Thurber.

The secretary of the Committee read a copy of a long communication which Pres. Romney had written to the First Presidency, also the affidavits of the Steven's girls, giving an account of the killing of their father, and also a letter written on September 1st, to the committee here at El Paso. The last and first of these, res- [text missing]

Sept. 1st, 1912.
Presidents Harris and McClellan,
Bros. Orson P. Brown and Guy C. Wilson and associates,
El Paso, Texas.

Dear Brethren: -

I shall enclose herewith a copy of a letter which I have today written to the First Presidency and this will serve to put you in possession of what facts I have of interest and of my views so far as I feel called upon to express them.

I will simply say in addition that if you find it necessary in order to prevent my family from coming in just now, kindly tell them that I prefer not to have them here at present.

I do not know what turn things are going to take now that Huerta is entering this section of the country, but if he continues the same tactics as have been followed since I have been here, we need look for nothing in the near future that will make me feel justified in bringing my family back into such conditions, since I am now permitted to exercise my own judgement [*sic*] with regard to my own family affairs.

I shall permit all others to do as was decided in the committee meeting which we held, viz. use their own judgement [*sic*] as to when it is proper for them to bring their family here, but I have felt it my duty to put you in possession of the facts as I see them, in some detail, and I presume that some of the brethren will class me as among the timid ones, but the thing does not look good to me for my family.

I wired you the other day ahd [*sic*] have also written you once since I cam [*sic*] down, and I was considerably surprised today to neither receive any letter from any of you or even a paper and also to have received no wire from you while the railroad was cut off.

Hoping that the Lord will soon clear things up in some way for the people of the Stake and make know [*sic*] His will concerning us for the future, through some one whose right it is to know, I remain,

Yours sincerely,

(signed) Junius Romney."

Colonia Juarez, Chihuahua, Mexico.

Sept. 1, 1912.

"Pres. Joseph F. Smith and Couns.,

Salt Lake City,

Dear Brethren: - I can scarcely realize that today is Sunday, but it is and I shall spend the time in writing reports to you and in making various formal demands or requests on the military and civil authorities, all of which requests, if I am to judge the future by the past, will receive favorable promises or replies, never to be fulfilled.

One week ago today, after having interviewed General Joaquin Tellez in Ciudad Juarez the day before and received from from [*sic*] him every assurance that we would be perfectly safe in returning with out [*sic*] families to Colonies Juarez and Dublan, I left El Paso for this section in company with a number of the brethren from Dublan and Juarez.

The presiding brethren in El Paso, and I, myself, thought it proper that I should come down with the first to return, with a view to stay, so that I might be in a position to make whatever arrangements should be made with the military authorities in the way of laying the foundation for acquiring whatever of our horses might have fallen into the hands of the Federals, and for getting them to take some official acknowledgement of the conditions of our homes and property at the time of our return.

General Tellez told me that the day before he had ordered General Sanjinez into the mountain country to clear out the rebels in the neighborhood of our Colonies, and that in order that he might take his force up there without exposing Casas Grandes country, Tellez had sent five hundred soldiers down to Nueva Casas Grandes to remain there as a garrison till the return of Sanjinez, which he thought would only be a question of a very few days, and that as soon as Sanjinez should return he would receive orders to march at once to Colonia Diaz and to furnish an escort to meet our people at Dog Springs on the line with our horses and to escort them to Colonias Juarez and Dublan. The General added, however, that we must not expect to remain at Diaz till he could leave a strong garrison there, and that he would not be able to do that till the arrival of some additional troops which he had ordered from Chihuahua. He told me that he was just as interested in our return as we could possibly be and that he would arrange it so that we might bring back our fire arms and horses and would give us every assistance within his power. His talk was very encouraging, and I believe that if the army were made up of such men, or even if the officers under him were all in sympathy with such sentiments, some effort would be made to make this beautiful dream a reality.

As we approached Dublan, we discussed the best method of proceedure [*sic*] and concluded that I had best go on to Nueva Casas Grandes and there, while the train was stopped, endeavor to ascertain whether Sajinez [*sic*] had really gone, and if he had, see if there was any ranking officer over Blanco there, with a view of going on to Pearson to interview Blanco, providing he were the ranking officer in the District. On arrival at the station, I met Porfirio Talamantes, whom I knew to be an officer in the army, and I inquired of him and found that both Sajinez [*sic*] and Blanco were at Pearson.

I went on up to Pearson, arriving there early in the afternoon, and after considerable delay, I managed to find them both together, and being acquainted with Blanco, I addressed myself to him and told him what my business was in the interest of the Mormon Colonies. He told me that Sanjinez was the man to talk to and introduced me to the General and then he, Blanco, arose and left.

I told General Sanjinez that I had come in the interests of the Mormon Colonies to see what the conditions were, and to ask some help from for them. He at once told me that he did not think it proper for us to return at present, as the country was not pacified, and at least he thought it unsafe for the families to return.

I asked him what had been done in the way of clearing the mountains of rebels, and he said nothing, except along the railroad and that there were many rebels in the neighborhood of the mountain Colonies. I explained to him the urgent necessity of our returning with our families on account of their being without food for winter while our crops are perishing and must either be prepared at once for winter use, or they would be lost. He said things were entirely uncertain and he could not tell how long it would be before we could return with our families. I then told him of my conversation with General Tellez, and what he had told me. He simply smiled and said he respected the General's opinion and sentiments, but that these things were not governed by our feelings, but by circumstances. I must confess, with due respect to General Sanjinez , that the result of this conversation, as every subsequent one and my observation of his conduct of affairs, was to impress me that circumstances, either great or small, would govern instead of his governing the circumstances. I appealed to him to appoint some one to visit our Colonies and make an official report before we should take possession and interfere with the condition of things. He referred me to Porfirio Talamantes, who he said, had been appointed Presidente at Casas Grandes. I also suggested that he issue an edict or order that all persons having in their possession any property belonging to the Mormon Colonies, return it within a certain length of time with the understanding that if they complied, they would escape punishment, but failing to do so, they would be punished severely according to the law. He also referred me to the civil authority for this, telling me that a very great deal of our property from Dublan had been hauled over to Galeana and El Valle. I asked him to make the acquirement of our horses simple, because of the scattered condition of the owners, and their papers and suggested that if we could prove with two competent witnesses, that a horse belonged to the Colonies, it ought to be sufficient to justify his being turned over to us, as we were without horses to cultivate our crops. This he promised to do.

I came on over to Colonia Juarez, expecting to be able to telephone to Dublan, since our committee, who had come down and reported that Blanco had repaired the telephone lines between the two places. In this, however, I was disappointed, so I hunted around and located s [*sic*] [a] team and vehicle and induced the local Presidente to accompany me to Casas Grandes, so that we might talk matters over with the Presidente there. We left here Monday Morning and conferred with Talamantes on reaching Casas Grandes. He told me that he had been appointed by the Governor to act till the Legislature of the State could decide either on the appointment of some one to complete the term for which Portillo had been elected or a new election by the people. Talamantes acquiesed [*sic*] in each of the propositions which I suggested and said that if I could go and arrange with Mendiola, who was the rebel judge, and who is in charge of the Juzgado now for the present, it would be all right for him to go over to Dublan with me. Mendiola said he would go if the Presidente would give him a written commission. Talamantes told Mendiola that if he knew how to write the necessary paper, he would sign it. This was done and we arrived in Dublan soon after noon.

We inspected the two stoes [*sic*] and four residences which had been looted, and returned to Colonia Juarez that same night.

There was practically nothing left in either store and especially in the Union Mercantil. There must have been taken from these two stores alone anywhere from one hundred thousand dollars of merchandise.

No effort seemed to have been made to force the Union Mercantil vault.

At the home of Joseph Jackson, we found nothing left except the house, but we could not tell Mendiola much about how the house had been furnished.

We found that the home of Annie M. Romney had been ransacked and much of the clothing taken and all provisions as well as some other things, but the furniture had pretty much all been left and had not been destroyed. This home was said by the brethren to have suffered least of any they had visited, which had been entered.

The home of Orin N. Romney was found to be in very much worse condition, practically everything having either been taken or destroyed.

The worst sight of all, though, was the large brick home of Sister Mary Farnsworth from the eight or ten rooms of which practically every article of worth had either been taken or entirely destroyed. This large home had been well furnished throughout and a plentiful supply of provisions had been left there, as also some boxes of merchandise, which the boys had brought there from the store when the rebels had been making such sweeping demands before they left. The only article of worth which I remember to have seen in that home after the wreck, was a china cupboard with glass front from which all dishes had been taken and it had apparently been left because it would be impossible to haul it away without crating it or breaking it, and why it was not destroyed, as some other articles which they did not wish to take, is a mystery to me, unless they intended to return and take it later. A large portrait of 4hung on the wall and against this a two quart bottle of blackberries had been thrown, ruining the picture and besmearing the wall and floor. The carpets had been torn from the floors and the window blinds and curtains from the windows. Literally the only thing left, was the house with the exception of the article mentioned.

Mr. Mendiola told the merchants to take a careful inventory of what is left in their stores, and send a copy to him, and he will certify to it and attach to his "acta". He said he would return and visit the rest of the houses when the owners come, if we desire and we can settle for his work all at once, and I have no doubt that the Government will permit him to make whatever charge he sees fit for this inspection, and us to pay the bill.

After reaching Dublan, I received from one of the brethren who came in on the train, a telegram in answer to one I had sent to Governor Gonzalez two days before leaving El Paso. The telegram reads as follows:

Chih. Aug. 24.

"Received your telegram of this date. I will, in the near future, name a Judge who will investigate the losses suffered by you in your properties, and I now transcribe your telegram to the Ministro de Gobernacion, that it may be decided by the proper party regarding your request for transportation from the Government."

(signed) Abraham Gonzalez.

I showed this telegram to Mendiola, but he went ahead with the investigation. Have received no farther word yet from the Governor, as the trains have not been running.

On Tuesday morning Bros. S. H. Johnson and Edward Lunt came up from Pearson with the news that Bro. Joshua W. Stevens had been murdered about noon the day before, and that the family was still at Pacheco with the unburied body. They said that Bros. Omni and Joseph Porter had gone over from the top of the mountain the night before to prepare the coffin, but that they would need more help to attend to the burial and get the family out. These brethren proferred [*sic*] to go if we could get some kind of animals to ride and after several hours of hunting, we managed to get three mounts and sent these two brethren and Joel H. Martineau up to Pacheco. A. P. Spilsbury [*sic*] also went up.

Bros. Lester B. Farnsworth, John Beecroft, Chas. Whetton, Jas. B. Darton and Ernest Nielson of Colonia Garcia were here and deSireous [*sic*] of going home to investigate conditions. We finally decided that they had better make the trip. They were only able to find one poor little Mexican horse to carry their bedding and a little food, and started out on foot a distance of 35 miles, with the prospects of swimming the streams which are all swollen or ferrying across one at a time on the horse.

By way of a report of the death of Bro. Stevens, I enclose herewith a copy of my journal of the 30th. ult., which gives in detail the testimony of his girls who were eye witnesses to the tragedy. I made carbon copies of this day's entry in my journal, so as to lessen the work of reporting.

After these brethren had gone to the mountain settlements, I decided to go down to Pearson Tuesday, and see what I could do in the way of procuring some of our horses that Bro. Stowell had seen there on Monday, and had been unable to get, and also to investigate a report that the troops were all going to leave this section and go to Madera, because they were threatened by the Red-flaggers on the North.

I found on my arrival that the troops were loading hundreds of horses, and that among those already loaded were some of our Colony horses. The troops were also embarking, but when I got an interview with Sanjinez, I found that he was taking most of the troops with him to the North to repair the road and see if there were any of the enemy there, according to his statement. I talked things over with him at length again, and he told me that he would leave the matter of the delivery of horses, which were still left at Pearson with Blanco, but that he could do nothing about those loaded till they should return either there or to Casas Grandes. That means that the horses will be of little use then, as they will be ruined with sore backs and will be so poor that they will be of no use this season, if we should succeed in getting them back at all. He told me that he was leaving Blanco at Pearson, and 250 men with him, but I learned from other sources that Blanco had 160 men so the General may have meant to include those left at Casas Grandes also.

I hunted Blanco up and asked if I could get the horses belonging to the Colonies, and he asked if the owners were there with the proofs of ownership, and after I explained that they were not, but that I could prove up on them, he wanted to know what horses I knew to be there in their possession, and I told him of a mare belonging to P. S. Williams of Dubland, [*sic*] and a horse belonging to Miel C. Pierce of Colonia Diaz. I told him that there was a member of each family there who would claim the horses. He then said that if I could find the horses and would have two good witnesses sign a certificate as to the ownership of the horses, with a clause in it, providing that if they did not present the proper papers within a specified time, that the horses would be returned to him, and if I would sign this as the agent of the Colonization Company, then he would permit the horses to be delivered to us. I decided to make a test case of this so I started out to hunt up the horses among the bands which were being herded on the hills. I found the two I was after and a number of others, but I decided to only take the two and test whether they would give them up or not. The man herding the horses at first refused to take the horses up to town, and said that the sorrel horse was one that Blanco had picked out for his own use. Finally he said that he would take them up and find his captain Candelario Cervantes, but that he would not take them to Blanco without the previous consent of Cervantes. When we found Cervantes, I showed him the papers which I had prepared, according to the instructions of Blanco who refused to let his secretary make them because he said he had other things to do. Cervantes demurred and said that he needed the horses to mount his men, but after I had explained the conditions in which we had been left, he said he would let me have these horses but wanted me to bring in Terrazas or other horses, which had been left around our towns by red-flaggers to take the place of these. It took me all afternoon to get these two horses, so I told him that I would be back in a few days to get some more, but I have not yet been back to try it over again for lack of time, and means of travel.

Edward Lunt had gone from here to Pearson on Monday for the purpose of making inquiries regarding the conditions in the mountain settlements and when he came back on Tuesday morning, he made the following report of his findings: When he reached Pearson, he talked to Blanco and asked him if there were any rebels in the mountain settlements, of ir [*sic*] it would be safe for some of them to go there. Blanco told him there were no rebels up there to amount to anything, but said he might go and talk to a man by the name of McKenzie who had been in charge of Booker's affairs upon the mountain. When Lunt told Mc. what Blanco had said, he began to curse Blanco, and said that a few days previous when he, Mc., had returned from a trip to Pacheco, he had reported to Blanco that he had discovered some rapid fire guns, a cannon and a lot of ammunition, which the rebels had left hid in a cellar at Pacheco. He said that instead of appreciating it, Blanco had placed him under arrest and forced him to go back with 60 soldiers to get the artillery and that while up there he had informed the captain of the soldiers that there was a group of red-flaggers over in Hop Valley, a distance of three of [*sic*] four miles from Pacheco, but that the officer refused to believe it. They loaded up what they could of the stuff he had found, and on the return journey the wagon mired down till they could not extricate it, so they took the rapid fire guns and a part of the cannon, and went on to Pearson. When they got down there, Blanco forced Mc. to go back with three men and get the rest of the material, and bring it to Pearson. Mc. told Blanco that there were about sixty rebels in Hop Valley, but Blanco refused to believe it and said no there were none there, so Mc. told him that they were a bunch of cowards, and if he would send sixty men with him, he would volunteer to take them up there and put them where they would have to either fight for their lives or be killed. Blanco admitted that they were afraid to go up, and refused to do so. Mc. told this also in the presence of two of the other boys, and offered to go with Lunt to Blanco and tell him that he was a d--- liar. Another American standing there testified to having heard Mc. tell Blanco what he claimed to have done. I cannot vouch for the truth of what Mc. says, only to say that so far as developements [*sic*] have gone, they show his story to be true. He also told the boys just what conditions they would find to exist in the mountain settlements, and said that in the San Diego Cañon, they would find men stationed, who would pretend to be working there, who were nothing more nor less than rebel spies and that they would make it their business to know just who went up the mountain, especially if they were Americans. This was all verified in every detail.

Wednesday we rounded up some bronco horses, which we have since been trying to break, sold some fruit for the Academy and others, and Thursday, among other things, I got the Presidente to call all of the local Mexicans together, so that I might express our appreciation for the interest they had taken in looking after the town and see if by explaining to them the sorrowful conditions of the people, and what would be their conditions on returning to their homes, if they had nothing to eat, I might be able to bring about some understanding by which we might either stop the wholesale shipment of our fruit and other crops to Pearson and Casas Grandez, [*sic*] till the people could arrive or have the proceeds deposited to the credit of the owners of the property, at the store.

The day I came from Pearson, I think I met not less than from fifteen to twenty outfits, either wagons or pack trains, partially loaded with fruit, corn, mellons, [*sic*] etc. from the Colony.

I must confess that I was considerably disappointed with what seemed to me the chilly reception accorded to these ideas. Some few of the Mexicans came up after the meeting and expressed their desire to conform to our wishes, but the great majority went off and the conditions have continued much the same.

The Presidente, Felipe Chavez, seems to have done an excellent part and many of the Mexicans have been looking after the property in their charge to the best of their ability, and all are entitled to credit for desisting from looting our property, as was done in all of the other Colonies so far as reports have come in.

When the brethren reported to Blanco the killing of Bro. Stevens, about seventy soldiers were sent up to investigate and as the brethren have returned sice, [*sic*] we have received reports of their findings about as follows: The soldiers reached Pacheco late Tuesday evening and about six o'clock the next morning, they came down to the Stevens home, which is a short distance out of town to the North and held a sort of inquest. The day before, Omni Porter had discovered that the Mexican dressed in light had died a short distance above where the struggle had taken place. Both bodies were examined by the soldiers, and some date written. They seemed to quesyion [*sic*] at first whether the Mexican had been shot down where Bro. Stevens had been killed as reported by the family, and suggested that he had been killed first by Bro. Stevens, where he lay and that Bro. Stevens had later been killed, but when they examined the Mexican, they found that the blood had run from the wound above the right nipple down his right side, clear to his shoe, showing that he had been on his feet for some time, they seemed to be satisfied with the story of the family. Just as soon as the soldiers had examined the bodies and arranged for the local Mexicans to bury the native, they returned to Pearson. The brethren then arranged for the burial of Bro. Stevens. They had made a rough coffin, because they had no tools. They dug a grave in the Pacheco semitary, [*sic*] and buried the body there, though the boys of the family had already prepared a grave on a knowl [*sic*] in the field, thinking that their father would have to be buried without attracting attention. No temple clothes would be procured, and they simply had to wrap the body in a clean sheet for burial. They held a brief service at the grave, at which several of those present spoke briefly for the comfort of the boys, and then Walter, Bro. Steven's oldest boy, dedicated the grave. The Stevens boys came right down and the other brethren remained two or three days and made a careful investigation of conditions in the town. According to their reports, there is absolutely nothing of worth left in the town, except the houses and these have been considerably damaged by holes chopped in the ceilings and floors with axes, to look for anything that may have been hidden away and by the breaking of windows and doors.

The organs, stoves, chairs, dressers, and in short all kinds of furniture that they have not been able to haul off, have simply been broken into pieces and strewn from one end of the town to the other.

Cattle have been shot down by dozens and the skins never opened.

A clean sweep has been made of all horses, including mares and colts, so much so, that they were only able to find one mare and colt and two colts two years old, all broncos, which they could break and come out with. In walking and riding over the range where they should have been able to locate from two or three hundred head of cattle, they saw in all 19 head, but of course, it should be born in mind that at this season of the year, there may be more cattle than it would seem, as there is water and feed everywhere, and they would naturally be scattered in small bunches and hard to find. Their fences had been cut and what cattle were about the town were in the crops. The rebels had demolished the crops closest to the town, but the brethren think that perhaps of the crops would be saved if the people could now return and take care of them. The Mexicans are reported to have come in from the railroad camps and done much of the damage after the rebels left, and it was two of these who made the attack on the Stevens family, as near as can be found out. The local Mexicans are very much afraid of them, saying that they all come armed with large knives, and that they were very vicious, even driving them out of the houses which had been entrusted to them in many instances. The boys report much land and crop washed away by almost unprecidented [*sic*] floods. It rains every day and the river has been very high ever since we came in.

The brethren have returned from Garcia and report much the same conditions as at Pacheco, though not quite so bad so far as the stoves and cattle are concerned. Bro. Farnsworth things [*sic*] that if they could return right now, they could perhaps save about 25% of the corn crop at Garcia, and perhaps about 80 to 90% of the oats. Many of the potatoes are already rotted, owing to the excessive rains. Many of the pigs are running loose in the town and have pretty well finished up the gardens and potatoes growing on the town site. They saw perhaps a hundred head of cattle or a little more, and they think that not many of these have been killed or driven away, but all of the horses seem to have been taken. They saw only 3 or 4 head and were unable to get any except one small mule, which a Mexican had at work. They had left in the neighborhood of sixty sets of harness, complete, and you would have smiled to see the sum total of harness belonging to Garcia when they returned-- they had made a harness for the two animals which was a combination of leather strings, ropes and bailing wire. They came back in a buckboard, and left Garcia about 11:30 Friday night, and when they crossed the Hop Valley creek, it was so swollen, that it washed their roll of bedding off, and down the creek in spite of the fact that one of them was standing on it, and then began a chase for it down the stream, which ended rather abruptly, when they suddenly found themselves in the midst of a camp of rebels. Two or three of the rebels raised up in their beds, startled by their sudden appearance in the camp, and the brethren beat a hasty retreat, without getting taken in. They continued their journey without the bed. They found a bad bunch of Mexicans in the town in possession, who seemed very suspicious of the brethren and made them feel quite uncomfortable, unarmed as they were, and they have concluded that it is foolish for them to remain there longer under existing conditions. They finally told this bunch that they were going to leave, and that they would like them to look after the town and not allow anyone to bother the place, which the Mexicans agreed to do. While the brethren were at Garcia, a pack train came into the town to load with provisions from the fields and when they saw our people there, they simply went down to the lower end of the fields and loaded up with potatoes and corn, and carried it away to the camps. As at Pacheco, much damage has been done by the floods. They are the worst known there for many years. The reservoir was taken out, the saw mill and shingle mills carried away, and the new pumping plant which some of the brethren were installing, is also carried down the creek. Some of the machinery might be recovered, if peace prevailed. Last Friday two of the Garcia boys thought they would go down to the town of Pacheco and look for the brethren there and see how they were getting along. They failed to locate any of our people, but were met there by an old Mexican, who told them, with tears running down his cheeks, that if they expected to escape with their lives, they had better get out of there, as the rebels were hunting for the Stevens family and had threatened to get even on some of the Mormons for the killind [*sic*] of the mexican. The boys left and that day or night, all of the Garcia boys left for here. After the Stevens boys left Pacheco, a bunch of rebels, eleven in all, came into Pacheco and went over to the Stevens home and made a search for the Stevens boys, with threats of what they would do if they succeeded in finding them, because their father had killed a mexican. The rebels took what flour was left at the house and came back over to town and tried to make our brethren tell where the boys were. These rebels then divided up and five of them came on down to Pearson, and were pardoned, while six of them remained in Pacheco with the intention of awaiting the arrival of two hundred rebels, that they report to be at Gavelan, just west of the town. It is also reported that they expect another bunch from over in the direction of Dos Cabezas near the Sonora line. In Pacheco there were many obscene pictures drawn on the white walls, and one or two of the peculiar things noticable, [*sic*] was that they had taken especial delight in destroying the portraits of women, while leaving sometimes the men's or simply breaking them, they had picked the eyes and mouths out of many of the women's pictures. In a number of places, they found chairs tarred and feathered, and many other evidences of barbarism.

The brethren from Garcia estimate that if they were able to harvest the oats that is left, now, there would be about 400 acres and that at a yield of 10 hectolitros per acre, they would have about 4,000 hectolitros, which would be worth about sixteen thousand pesos, but if these are to be saved, they must be harvested within the next two or three weeks, and we are confronted with the fact that they have neither horses, wagons or harnesses, and worse than all the country is still infested with rebels, and our Federal army shows absolutely no disposition to clean the country up, but on the contrary they are pardoning the very instigators of the revolution and our worst enemies, and refuse to do anything for the relief of the country. It is common talk among the rebels in the mountains, who have come down and received amnesty, that they have worked the Federals pretty smoothly, that they have delivered some old gun and have reserved a good outfit, with which to do execution if their party comes along with any prospect of winning.

A train finally came in from El Paso today and on it a very few more of our people. Huerta was expected in today from the Madera way at two o' clock with thirty cars of coldiers, [*sic*] but I have not yet heard if he arrived.

We learn that yesterday a skirmish took place out along the North Western near Sabinal. We are also now reliably informed that Salazar and his bunch have their headquarters at the Coyote ranch just below the Nogales Ranch, and that they are all through the Marquesote, Janos, Ascencion and Sabinal country.

The federals are building trenches at Nueva Casas Grandes which in itself shows no good for us. If they are calculating on letting the rebels come in there to attack them, the outlook for us is certainly not very reassuring.

I omitted to say that according to the testimony of the mexicans at Pacheco, the whole rebel army hunted for four days for the Stevens family, but failed to find them.

I shall probably go out to El Paso within a few days, if the trains continue to run, but I scarcely know what to do.

Yours very truly,
(signed) Junius Romney.

August 30, 1912. Morning clear and beautiful. Spent the night at Brigham Stowell's with him and Eugene. Soon after arising went over to my own home and took down one hundred lbs. of flour from upstairs, of which I delivered about half to Angel Parra at the Riggz home to pay him for what he says he did in the way of looking after my home during my absence. The rest I left in the bin. Pulled a few weeds from the lot, carried in the tub and stool which the mexicans had taken out to use in the lot and had left them there. Visited mother's and my brother Thomas' homes, which seem to be in good shape. Happened at the Eugene Romney place, now owned by A. P. Spilsbury [*sic*] and occupied by the family of Joshua Stevens since they came down from the mountains, just in time for breakfast and accepted of an invitation to eat with them. Made an appointment to call later and listen to the story of the killing of Bro. Stevens. Returned and assisted Bro. Stowell and Eugene to break a bronco mule to work. After dinner at Stowell's it rained so much in the afternoon that we were unable to handle other broncos, which we had intended to gentle in the afternoon. Called at the shoe-shop and took my typewriter to Rhoda Stowell's, where we expect to make our headquarters for the present. Went with some mexicans and gathered peaches from Charles E. McClellans's lot in the rain and sold to the amount of $4.80 Mex. and sold musk-mellons, [*sic*] water-mellos, [*sic*] and tomatoes from the Duthie lot for Bro. W. Longhurst amounting to $2.50 Mex. It was now late in the afternoon, so I called on the Stevens family, and there found John Allan, who seemed to be much improved in health. Joel H. Martineau and boy were also there. We visited awhile and then I had the girls tell me their story of their recept experiences, while I wrote it for them and then will typewrite it into my journal, and they will all sign it tomorrow. Following is their statement.

Monday, Aug. 26, 1912, Abbie and I were picking berries in the upper black-berry patch about six hundred yards from our home, near Pacheco. About 8:30 A. M. we heard a dog give a warning bark and looking up in the direction of the creek, we saw a Mexican standing at the foot of the black-berry rows, dressed in a yellow suit and with a light colored felt hat on. We saw no weapon of any kind in his hand. After glancing at the man, the first time, we continued with our work without appearing to notice him, and in a moent [*sic*] when we glanced up again, we saw another mexican dressed in black clothing, including a black felt hat, with a knife in his hand, approaching from the willows up the creek to the West of the Mexican, who stood at the end of the rows. The two seemed to discuss something for a few moments, and then, without saying anything to us, they started down the road to the

East and toward the house to a point where the field road passes near a large pine tree. The place where we were at work was just over a low ridge, running North and South between us and the house, on which ridge the black berries grow more rank than in other parts of the patch. From the pine tree to the place where we were, anyone approaching would pass through a low part of the field and would be hidden from view till near us. The mexicans were therefore, out of sight of us for some time, and we expected to see them appear on another rise farther down, if they kept the road which we supposed they would do. Finally one of them raised up in the bushes just over the ridge enough to see us and be seen by us. I did not see him, but my sister Abbie did, and we both heard him speak. We both understood him to speak in English, but I could not hear what he said. Abbie says he said "Come here". Abbie said the man who raised up and spoke was the one who wore the light felt hat. We saw at once that their position was such as to cut off our retreat to the house by the usual trail, but we knew that by running South through the oak brush for short distance, we would come into a road which would lead to the house around the South side of the orchard. This we did, keeping out of view of the Mexicans. When we reached the West end of our upper orchard, we came in full view of the black berry patch where the mexicans were located. We looked back and saw both standing in plain view, and they at the same time seemed to see us. They began to then, to pick berries, where we were, and I suggested to Abbie that she go on to the house and tell father that they were there and I would stay in view of them and keep track of them till father could come. Abbie thought we ought both to go, so I suggested that we would pick the berries on the outside row of the orchard (berries are planted between the trees) as we went and we would have that much of that patch done. We began picking the berries as suggested, and when the mexicans saw that we had stopped in the field, they started toward us. We then started again for the house, and soon passed from view of the mexicans.

On reaching the lower orchard, we found mother and my sister Emma picking fruit there, and while one of the children was sent in search of father, we all remained and picked fruit. Father was not at the house, but was returning from the field, when my sister found him. While we were picking fruit in the lower orchard, and waiting for father, we heard the mexican's dog bark again near the lower end of the upper orchard, so we all went into the house and mother passed on through in search of father, and met him coming to the house. Father took the double barrel shot gun and went up through the field, going along the North side of the upper or large orchard between the first two rows of trees. When father left the house, my sister Emma suggested that we go up and finish the berry picking, while father was in the field, so we two and Abbie started up there. When father reached the lower end of the large orchard, we were about one hundred and twenty-five yards behind him, or about twenty-five yards from the upper end of the lower orchard. When father had gone about twenty-five to thirty yards into the upper orchard and we had reached the upper end of the lower orchard, we saw the two mexicans come out of the trees on the South side of father. They crossed over to where he was and passed by him and started toward us with father following closely behind, with gun in hand. Emma said, "it looks like father is driving them". They passed from view behind a clump of trees at the lower end of the orchard. We stood and watched till they emerged near some poplar trees below the orchard and in full view of us at a distance of about 100 yds. They had only come about four or five yards after coming out of the trees, when we saw the mexican dressed in black turn quickly toward father and strike with his knife. We could not see whether he struck father or not, but as the mexican struck, we heard father call out, but were unable to distinguish what he said. Emma said, "it sounds like pa is calling me". My sister Elmina had run upstairs and was looking out of the upstairs window, where she could see all that passed below. At this time she called out that the mexicans were fighting pa. My sister Abbie ran back to the house to get the pistol and Emma and I ran toward father and the Mexicanso. [*sic*] My oldest brother, Walter, had been gone on the range for two days, and that morning, father had sent the next two brothers, Alden and Ammon, out to fix fence and look for cattle, and father had told Alden to take his pistol, so it was not at the house when Abbie went for it. None of the three boys mentioned had returned, and the oldest boy at home was only ten years old. As emma [*sic*] and I ran toward father, we saw that his clothing was covered in blood. While we were running and were looking where to stop, we heard the report of the gun, but did not observe that it was fired twice, but my sister Elmina had come from the house and was running also in the direction where father and the Mexicans were. She heard both shots distinctly, and says that the reports were just one step apart as she ran. The next we saw of the mexican dressed in light, he was trying to run away and emerged from the opposite side of the clump of trees, holding his right side with his left hand. We saw father and the mexican dressed in black, facing each other, and just about the distance of the length of the gun apart, and father pointing the gun at the Mexican. The ground was somewhat rough and we could not keep our eyes on them constantly as we ran. When we looked up again, they had passed from view behind the poplars, and the next we saw of them, was as we approached them and saw the mexican lying in a water ditch across the gun and father astride of him in a stooping posture with his right hand firmly clenched around the mexican's right wrist. The mexican held a large dagger in his hand with a blade about eight inches long. As we ran toward the men, I picked up a large stick about two and a half inches in diameter, and about four and a half feet long. As we approached, father looked at us such a look as I am unable to describe, but shall never forget. I dropped the stick and ran up and took hold of their hands to try to take the knife, at the same time Emma grasped the blade of the dagger, but we were unable to wrench it from the mexican. I took hold of the gun and managed to draw it from beneath them as they struggled. I carried it a short distance away and laid it on the ground. While I was struggling to get the gun out, Emma picked up the stick I had brought. By this time father had grown weak and the mexican managed to free the hand that held the knife and raised it to strike father again, but was prevented in this by Emma, who gave him a violent poke in the face with the end of the stick, knocking his head down in the bushes. Father must have then fainted from loss of blood, as he pitched forward onto the ground and the mexican, rising, made a pass at Emma with the knife. I reached out and drew her quickly back, so that he missed her, and reaching down I picked up the gun, and pointing it at him I tried to fire, not knowing that both barrels had been fired. The Mexican evidently feard [*sic*] that I would be able to do execution with the gun, for he turned and left, looking back as he went. I followed him a short distance, and then returned to father. We wondered if this man was wounded, because he did not run and we could not understand why he should be frightened enough to leave and yet not be sufficiently afraid to go more quickly than a walk. This man took the same direction as the first one, going along the North side of the upper orchard. The last man left his hat, a black felt, lying on the ground. Emma returned first to father and found him on his knees and elbows with his head bowed. She raised his head and spoke to him, but he did not answer. He soon laid over on the ground with his head resting in Emma's hands. He was in this position when I returned. We secured some water near by and bathed his brow, and I found his wound. We two then picked him up and carried him a short distance, and as we laid him down to rest, we heard a faint grown [*sic*] and we think that he expired at this time. We carried him a short distance again, and while we were resting, Abbie came and we bathed his face again with water which she brought, and then the three of us carried him to the house, not yet certain that he had passed away. We reached the house about 10 A. N. [*sic*] It was about two hours before we were able to locate Bro. S. H. Johnson and get him there, and during all this time, we worked over father, hoping that life was not extinct. During the afternoon, the boys returned and at 12:30 P. M., Bros. Omni Porter and Joseph Porter, arrived. After consultation, it was decided that it was unsafe for the family, except the older boys to remain at the place, and in the morning, Joseph Porter took us to Colonia Juarez while Omni remained to make the coffin and assist the boys in the burial.

Colonia Juarez, August 30th, 1912.

Bishop Thurber reported verbally the conditions at Dublan, as he has just returned from there. Things generally look well so far as a generous rainy season could make them look good. There is also much grain and considerable other property left. Sister Spencer and Josiah have done an excellent work in helping care for things. But there has been very much thieving, looting and wanton destruction. The Mexicans generally, are not very gla-d [*sic*] to see the Mormons return. They are doing no work in the way of caring for things, only as they can sell garden stuff, melons, milk for their profit, etc. Politically the conditions are bad. "The rebels have not left the country and do not intend to", and in his opinion, there is danger of their dashing into Dublan to sack the town, or do other mischief at any time.

Said that an American, Mr. Henry, who had been a prisoner with the rebels for five days, had claimed that the rebels were very much disappointed through the Mormons coming out as they did, thus thwarting a deep laid plot against the Mormon people, and the rebels threaten to get vengeance.

Pres. Romney said the Mexicans who are taking advantage of the amnesty proclamation, are generally of the worst class of men, and are remaining in the district where they are carrying off our property and committing various depradations; [*sic*] that there are various rebel bands in Chuichupa, Mound Valley, Garcia and elsewhere, and their conduct is vicious. Says General Sanjinez and Blanco do not manifest any disposition to pursue the rebels and are apparently indifferent as to conditions. Pres. Romney also read a communication, which he had submitted to General Blanco, in which he had reviewed the situation of the forcible expulsion of our people from Mexico, of our losses and needs, and of future losses, which must aggregate to not less than $100,000.00, unless we can get in there soon, and this we cannot do unless in the meantime, the federals clear the country of rebels.

General Sanjinez told Pres. Romney that he could not put a large garrison in Colonia Juarez, because he did not have forces enough, and he could not put a small garrison there, because they would be in too great danger. Pres. Romney said the federal forces were of service if we could run to them, but of no use, if we have to wait for them to come to our assistance.

Pres. Romney does not feel that it is safe for families to go into the Colonies now. And even those who are there, are taking some risks.

Benediction by David Brown, Jr.

C. E. McClellan, Secretary.

Minutes of Committee meeting held in rooms 8 & 9 Buckler Building, El Paso, Texas, at 5 P. M. September 5th, 1912. Besides the Central Committee, there were a number of Bishops present. Prayer by Pres. H. S. Harris

O. P. Brown said he had just received word from Mr. Metz at Tucson, Arisona, [*sic*] saying he had made arrangements with the Newman Investment Company to bond all the horses expected to be taken to Tucson. Also had a telegraphic communication from the Collector of Customs to the effect that our horses at Hachita are being neglected and lost, and insisting that we must take better care of them or bond them over regularly.

Bishop E. V. Romney from Colonia Diaz reported that the trouble had arisen only with the Diaz horses. He said the men were bothering Mr. Roberson, the Government man at Hachita, about getting horses to use, etc. That they had also neglected the horses, and all had stampeded, but that all had now been recovered except of about twenty. Mr. Roberson told Bishop Romney to-day that things were not so bad as he (Roberson), had reported in his letter to El Paso.

Bishop Romney said the trouble at Diaz was that everybody was herding horses, and what was everybody's business was proving nobody's business. He agreed in the idea that certain ones should be designated to herd the horses, and the owners of the horses should pay the herders, according to the number of horses owned.

A motion was made by O. P. Brown that the committee previously appointed to look after the horses, hire a man at a salary of $50.00 per month to have a general supervision over and responsibility for all the horses. Motion carried. Bro. Jas. A. Jacobson was suggested as a good man for the place.

Pres. Romney and O. P. Brown had a short conference to-day with Consul Llorente, but could not meet General Huerta till tomorrow.

Bishop Romney reported that the guns were not gather in any one place, but were distributed quite generally among the owners.

Discussing the situation in Mexico, Pres. Romney said every man who goes into the Colonies will be impressed with two things: First--that there are Federals along the railroad, where they expect to stay, and second, that there are rebels nearly everywhere else.

After reviewing conditions in detail in the Colonies, Pres. Romney declared emphatically that it is not safe for families to go yet into the colonies or to be there.

After considerable discussion it was moved by Bro. Guy C. Wilson and seconded by BrO. [*sic*] O. P. Brown that it be the sense of this committee that it is not at present safe for men to take their families to the Colonies. Carried unanimously.

Benediction by Bro. Lester B. Farnsworth.

C. E. McClellan, Secretary.

Minutes of meeting of the Central Committee held September 9th, 1912, in rooms 8 & 9 Buckler Building. Also present some of the Bishops. Pres. Junius Romney presiding. Prayer by Bro. A. B. Call.

Bro. O. P. Brown reported that he had received word from Bishop Lillywhite, stating that the refugees at Douglas were having some difficulty, as the U. S. Representative had demanded that they say under oath that they were U. S. Citizens. Bishop Lillywhite asked for instructions regarding the matter. He advised them to make the declaration. Bishop Lillywhite also asked that some one from here go to Douglas and assist them in getting started right. Pres. Romney was appointed to go.

Pres. Romney reported that Mr. Walker of the El Paso Herald desired to write a sketch of the Colonies, and suggested that Guy C. Wilson, Bishop Whetton, and A. B. Call be asked to write some data of their respective colonies and hand same to him, (Pres. Romney.) Pres.

Harris was appointed to collect some photographs of public buildings, etc. of the colonies.

Benediction by Bro. Thos. C. Romney.

A. B. Call, Secretary, pro tem.

Minutes of Committee meeting held in rooms 8 & 9 Buckler Building September 12th, 1912. Pres. H. S. Harris presiding. Prayer by Pres. H. S. Harris.

After some discussion, on motion by O. P. Brown and seconded by Bishop J. T. Whetton, it was unanimously decided that we would not issue any more cheap rates over the Mexico North Western R. R. for the present, and that Bro. H. E. Bowman be asked to return from the colonies to assist in settling with the railroad people.

On motion it was carried unanimously that the extra issue of Herald of this date in which appears a report of the fillibustering [*sic*] expidition [*sic*] to Mexico, be sent to Bishops Thurber and Bentley who are in the colonies, and that a letter be written each of them, setting forth the present conditions here; also a cipher letter with the words "Do not send Peaches" will mean "bring women and children to the line immediately". If the words "Peaches and Apples" are used, will mean, "men, women and children." Adjourned.

Benediction by P. N. Skousen

A. B. Call, Secretary, pro tem.

Minutes of Central Committee meeting held Sunday morning, September 15th, 1912. Pres. H. S. Harris presiding. Prayer by O. P. Brown.

President Harris read a letter from Pres. Romney who is at Douglas, Arizona; also a letter from Pres. C. E. McClellan, who is now in Colonia Juarez.

On motion, Bro. A. B. Call was requested to visit every place, where rations are delivered and take an inventory of supplies on hand, the number of people receiving supplies and determine the state indigency [*sic*] of each and that this same order be followed at the Diaz camp at Hachita by the commissary there, and that a report be rendered this committee at once. This was carried unanimously.

A letter from Mr. Howard Veater was read by Bro. Guy C. Wilson, urging the brethren, especially those from Chuichupa, to return and harvest their crops. It was the sense of the meeting that it is practically safe for a number of the brethren to return to the mountain colonies and save as much of their property as they can in the shortest possible time, and get it out and turn it into money. This policy will also apply to the other colonies in Chihuahua.

It was moved and carried that Bro. David A. Brown be released from his labors with the horses at Hachita, and be allowed to return to the colonies and assist in getting our loose property on the market.

On motion, meeting was adjourned.

Benediction by Bro. Brigham Stowell.

A. B. Call, Secretary, Pro tem.

Minutes of special Meeting of the Central Committee, held in rooms 8 & 9 Buckler building, on September 16th, 1912. Pres. Junius Romney presided. Prayer by Bro. O. P. Brown.

Minutes of last meeting were read. A letter from Senator Reed

Smooth [*sic*] was read by Bro. O. P. Brown, in regard to the bringing of the horses across the line from Mexico.

A report from Bishop E. V. Romney was read in which a request was made by him for a check to cover general expenses.

Bro. O. P. Brown reported that he had again seen General Huerta, who had promised to send some troops to La Ascencion. Bro. Brown read a letter he had written to Bishop Romney at Hachita, instructin [*sic*] him as to how the rations should be distributed, that were given by the Government.

Pres. Romney gave a replort [*sic*] of the people at Douglas, Ariz. Said that the rebels had looted Colonia Morelos, and that the American Consul had advised the people to come and said that it was not considered safe for people to stay in Colonia Morelos. Pres. Romney also told of the Morelos people leaving the colony and going to Douglas. Also reported that he had had good meetings with the people while at Douglas. Said the people felt much better after said meetings. He organized Bishop Lillywhite to preside over the people while in Douglas. Said that arrangements had been made for the children to go to school there. Reported that good conditions prevailed at the refugee camp; that water was being put into the camp, also that Bro. Arnold Huber had been appointed as transportation agent and also to attend to the distributing of the rations. Pres. Romney said that he had left $100.00 with Bishop Lillywhite to cover general expenses. He read a letter he had written to General Sanjinez, requesting that a troop of soldiers be sent in search of Bro. Edward Haymore who had been robbed that day, and it was feared that he had been taken prisoner or killed by the rebels. Later Bro. Haymore was found. Pres. Romney also reported that the general health of the people at Douglas good.

Pres. C. E. McClellan reported on conditions at Colonia Juarez. Said that it was quiet at said Colony, and that the report that 300 men were in Hop Valley was not true; that the Chuichupa crops were good, and that a few rebels were still in the mountains. Said that most of the people in Colonia Juarez feel safe, but that Bro. J. W. Wilson feels that conditions are growing worse and is ready to come out on a minute's warning. Pres. McClellan reported that troops had been sent to Sabinal, La Ascencion and Palomas, and said that the Dublan people all feel that conditions are gradually growing worse.

Benediction by Bro. Gaskell Romney.

D. V. Farnsworth Sec. pro tem.

Minutes of meeting of the Central Committee held in rooms 8 & 9 Buckler Building, September 18th, 1912. Prayer by Bro. Guy C. Wilson.

Pres. Romney reported an interview he had with Dr. Gay last evening. The Doctor explained that his attorney, a Mr. Eugene Harris, was in possession of the affidavits Dr. Gay had made, relative to the danger that threatened the Americans in the Casas Grandes district at the time our people left there. He also suggested that the services of Mr. Harris might be secured by us to our advantage in the matter of collecting claims for damages, etc. Pres. Romney also gave some of the reasons the Doctor advanced for feeling that conditions were serious for the Mormons at the time he left. All of this evidence the Doctor is willing to give us in writing.

The following resolution suggested by the Juarez Stake Presidency was unanimously adopted by the Central Committee:

"In view of the recent visit of Pres. McClellan to the Colonies in the Casas Grandes district and his report, based on the most thorough information he could obtain, we feel that now is an opportune time for men having cattle, farm products, or household good that need caring [missing line in the original document] and look after these interests.

The conditions that make the present time seem opportune for this work are that there are apparently few rebels in that part of the country at present, and but little rebel activity manifest; while Federal garrisons already occupy the towns of Pearson, Nueva Casas Grandes, La

Ascencion, Sabinal and Guzman, while a detachment of 135 Federals are now on their way from Guzman to Palomas. There are many cattle belonging to the colonists in the district and good offers have been made to buy most these cattle. There is much lucern hay, corn, and oats that might be harvest and perhaps sold."

Pres. Romney said that in view of the fact that winter is approaching, making necessary the moving of families from the lumber camp and the tents soon, it will be necessary to advise either that the people return to the Colonies or go to Arizona, Utah or elsewhere to find homes and employment for themselves for the winter. And further he felt that representatives from the Stake Presidency perhaps the Committee should go to Salt Lake City and seek an audience with the First Presidency of the Church, in order to lay before them the conditions now existing with the Juarez Stake and its people, and to make certain recommendations for their approval or disapproval.

After discussing these ideas for a time it was decided to write a letter to the First Presidency, setting forth the present conditions and telling the brethren that we could not recommend our families returning to Mexico now, and the only alternative is to advise them to find homes in some of the nearby Stakes or Missions, at least for the winter, which we shall do unless the First Presidency wishes to counsel differently.

It was the unanimous opinion of the committee that Bro. Guy C. Wilson should be free to make arrangements to teach or attend school in the United States this winter, but that in the meantime while these arrangements are being made, he is to continue in his labors as a member of the Committee.

It was also thought that Pres. McClellan might be released in about ten days from the cCommittee [*sic*] to go to Provo where he is to teach.

The question of securing a room for storing furniture to be brought out from the colonies was discussed. Bro. O. P. Brown said he would take the matter up.

Benediction by Pres. Romney

C. E. McClellan, Secretary.

Minutes of committee meeting held in rooms 8 & 9 Buckler Building, September 18th, 1912. There were also present several of the brethren. Prayer by High Councillor [*sic*] Deronda V. Farnsworth.

Pres. Romney read the insert letter he had prepared according to the resolution passed at the morning meeting, and which had since been approved by the Committee. He read it for the information of the brethren present, but advised that the contents of the letter be not made public except in a general way, until we hear from the First Presidency.

Benediction by Bro. E. C. Eyring

C. E. McClellan, Secretary.

Minutes of meeting of the Central Committee held in rooms 8 & 9 Buckler Building, September 19th, 1912. Prayer by Pres. Romney.

Pres. Harris reported that the Stake Presidency had asked him to take charge directly of the work of having all the refugees still remaining on the border or other localities within reach, visited by good strong men spiritually, to talk with them as ward teachers, to encourage, strengthen and advise them spiritually, especially. This work the Bishops will be asked to look after and follow up vigorously, and have a report made of numbers, conditions, etc. This information will be useful to the Stake Presidency when their representtaties [*sic*] go to Conference as well as Salt Lake.

Pres. Romney said it was expected that he and Pres. McClellan would be present at the October Conference at Salt Lake, leaving Pres. Harris to assist here.

He also asked the members of the Committee to have in mind the matter of what questions should be presented to the authorities at Salt Lake and submit their suggestions before the brethren go north to Salt Lake.

Pres. Romney also discussed the questions of our claims for damages. Told of several attorneys who have suggested plans for our consideration in the matter of claims.

It was decided to hold meetings of the Committee at 4 o'clock hereafter instead of 5 P. M.

Benediction by Pres. H. C. Harris.

C. E. McClellan, Secretary

Minutes of Committee meeting held at 4 P. M., in rooms 8 & 9 Buckler Building, September 20, 1912. Prayer by Pres. H. S. Harris.

Bro. Benj. Judd who has been rendering faithful assistance to Bro. A. B. Call in the commissary was present, and stated that if the brethren were encouraging the men to return to the Colonies to harvest crops, he would like to return if he could be released from the commissary. On motion of Bro. O. P. Brown, Bro. Judd was released from his position with words of appreciation, and given permission to return to Mexico if he desired.

Pres. Harris reported that he had begun the work of visiting assigned to his direction yesterday. Had found a few sick ones. Had also heard that a few from Chuichupa have a spirit of complaint toward the Church. Would try to investigate this matter. Also reported that he had taken steps to safe-guard certain of our girls, who seem to be forming undesirable acquaintances.

Pres. Romney referred to an application for the people's needs at Hachita, that had come through Sister Lucy E. Johnson. Said this application had not come in the proper form and therefore could not be considered. If individuals or families are in need, they should make application through the Bishop or through the head of the family who might arrange for a loan from the committee, or receive charity aid if their conditions justified.

Bro. A. B. Call reported some conditions connected with the commissary. He had refused to grant rations to a Mr. Smith on the grounds that he was not a refugee. A little trouble had arisen over the matter, but the Sargeant [*sic*] had told him, (Bro. Call) that he had done exactly right in this matter.

A letter from Bishop Bentley at Colonia Juarez was read, giving an account of the celebration of the 16th of September in the Colony. The school-house was granted to the natives for their dance in the evening. The day passed off pleasantly, as did the evening; the Mexicans maintaining good order and respecting the schoolhouse by not smoking or drinking in it. About twenty-five of the Mormon people visited the dance. The Bishop hoped we could soon permit families who desired, to return to the Colonies.

At this point, Bro. O. P. Brown, called up General Steever [missing also in the original document] conditions. The General did not think it safe yet to send families to the Colonies, and thought that the present quiet is only a lull before the storm.

It was decided to ask Bro. B. B. Riggs to assist Bro. Call in the commissary in the place of Bro. Judd.

Benediction by Bro. A. B. Call

C. E. McClellan, Secretary

After the above meeting, Bro. Henry Lunt Smith was ordained an Elder in the Church of Jesus Christ of Latter Day Saints by Junius Romney, assisted by Bros. Gaskell Romney and A. B. Call.

Junius Romney.

Minutes of Committee Meeting held in rooms 8 & 9 Buckler Building, September 21, 1912. Prayer by Pres. C. E. McClellan.

Pres. Romney read a letter from Bishop Thurber at Dublan, reporting conditions in that part of the country. Conditions generally are quiet, although there are some rebels still in the country, as only the other day they disarmed the boys who were gathering cattle from Colonias Garcia and Pacheco. There is quite a need of men to take care of property. Does not say anything about women going in, but does not seem very sanguine over the prospects for immediate peace.

Letters and telegram from Bishop E. V. Romney were read, telling of conditions at Hachita and asking some questions. Said no word had yet come from the boys who had gone to investigate conditions at Colonia Diaz.

Also read letter and telegram from Bro. CD. [*sic*] B. Brown at Thatcher, Arizona, reporting conditions of the refugees there, and asking if the families, especially from Chuichupa, might return to Mexico. Said most of the sick were getting better.

Also read a letter from Bro. David Stout, telling of his mental worry over conditions and asking for advice.

The question of what to advise the people about going down to the Colonies and the conditions in the country were discussed at length.

At this point the following telegram was received from the First Presidency.

"Salt Lake City, Utah. Sept. 21, 1912.

Romney & Wilson, No. 8 & 9 Buckler Bldg., El Paso, Texas.

We fully approve course suggested and resolutions adopted. Will write."

(signed) Joseph F. Smith.

Decided to come here tomorrow morning at 11 o'clock, fasting and praying, to further discuss these matters and to decide on answers to the questions that have been asked other brethren.

Benediction by George S. Romney.

C. E. McClellan, Secretary.

Minutes of Special meeting of Committee and leading brethren in fasting and prayer, held Sunday morning 11 o'clock, rooms 8 & 9 Buckler Building, September 22nd, 1912. Those present were, Pres. Romney, H. S. Harris, and C. E. McClellan, High Councillors [*sic*] Guy C. Wilson, O. P. Brown and P. H. Hurst, alternates Geo. S. Romney and James Skousen, Bishop J. T. Whetton and Bishop's Counsellor [*sic*] Thos. C. Romney.

Pres. Romney reviewed certain conditions that have existed ever since our brethren first went down to the colonies to investigate conditions, and showed that there had been all along quite a difference of opinion among the brethren and people of the matter of our returning to the Colonies, some feeling that conditions justify all going back, and other feeling that the danger was still too great to warrant the return of women and children.

Pres. Romney told of the various interviews he had had with the Military officials, Generals Tellez, Sanjinez, Alamo and Huerta to show that their counsel usually had been against our families returning, and to show that the promises made by these officials to do things insuring our protection, had in hardly any instance been kept. These things were related to show the reasons why the members of the Committee have taken the ground of being cautious as they have.

He read the letter written by the Stake Presidency to the First Presidency several days ago, and their telegram in reply.

He also called attention to other reasons that make the return of our families to the Colonies seem an unwise thing. The question of intervention with the probable attitude of the natives toward our people in that case; and the attitude of the R. R. Company, and the Government of the United States in case were forced to flee again,--- all these were discussed.

He stated the purpose of the meeting was to come together in fasting and prayer to seek earnestly the Lord to know His will, to know whether the attitude of the Committee in the past has been wrong, with a determination to change our attitude if the Lord will manifest that we have been wrong; or to continue our stand if the Lord inspires us to condinue [*sic*] to do so.

The brethren all expressed themselves as being willing to lay the matter before the Lord with a willingness to have our personal opinions changed if the Spirit of the Lord so manifests. After this the brethren bowed together in a circle in prayer led by Pres. Romney, as mouth, followed also by Pres. Harris, McClellan, Councillors [*sic*] Wilson, Brown and Bishop Whetton.

After an intermission, during which the principle of faith was discussed, the brethren all knelt again in a circle and were led again in prayer, Bros. Skousen, Hurst, George Romney, Gaskell Romney, and Thomas Romney being mouth in turn.

After this Pres. Harris expressed himself as feeling the same way as before, that it would not be safe for the people to return.

Bro. Jas. Skousen felt that it was his duty to return to the Colonies for the present in order that his child who is now very ill, el [*sic*] El Paso may recover. He is not concerned over his property interests there, any may rent his property for the year.

Bro. Guy C. Wilson said he was deeply interested in the Juarez Stake and in the members of the Juarez Stake Presidency and their future success. Felt these brethren had been inspired in what they had done and safety for the people has lain only in following the course they have outlined. Felt that the suggestion that the people generally refrain from returning to the Colonies this winter is the right plan, but felt also that possible those who had returned had done so under the inspiration of the Lord and possibly for a wise purpose, and should have our faith and prayers.

Bro. James Skousen said he did not think the families now in the Colonies were or desired to be out of harmony with those over them. In regard to returning the people to the Colonies, he felt just as Bro. Wilson had expressed himself.

Bro. Thos. Romney read a line from the Era on sustaining the Priesthood, and felt as though some of the people were not fully sustaining the Stake Presidency.

Bro. George Romney had experienced a little change of feeling, and now feels as though it would be well for those in the Colonies to remain and that perhaps others should return.

Bro. Gaskell Romney felt to sustain the Committee and their position. Personally his business in Mexico had been destroyed and he had nothing to return to now. Did not feel that the people, as a whole should return, but felt that those there now, were perhaps where they should be.

Pres. McClellan said he felt that the minds of the First Presidency would be relieved by knowing that the people, generally, would not be advised to return to Mexico this winter. Did not criticize the families who were in the Colonies for being there, but condemned some for being out of harmony with the Priesthood and criticizing it. Thought all that class should be labored with till they repent. Felt as though some families might remain there and be a great blessing in protecting the homes and property, and might do so with the approval and blessing of the Lord. Felt the resolution to advise the Saints not to return to Mexico, is the only one we can carry out in wisdom.

Bro. Brown said he felt stronger than ever that no families should go down or remain down there this winter; that the dangers are so great that it is suicidal for them to remain. Thought selfish personal interests were the predominating influence that is keeping them there. Did not know that we should ever return to Mexico.

Bro. Gaskell Romney did not agree with Bro. Brown. Did not feel the people had gone to the Colonies against advice; and that they were not sacrificing so much socially for their children, as conditions in El Paso are comparatively worse.

Bro. Wilson spoke again in defense of his views.

Bishop John T. Whetton said he thought that the brethren now in the Colonies had gone down there thinking they were doing so with the approval of the presiding brethren. Felt as Bro. Gaskell Romney, that social conditions in the Colonies with only a half dozen families would be better than they are in El Paso for Latter Day Saint children. Said this was a stronger incentive for him to go back than his property interests. If he went back there he would have to start all over again in a financial way. Said if we ever go back to Mexico to live, we must get rid of the spirit of fight, that we must go only with a spirit of love.

Bro. P. H. Hurst felt he could not return to Mexico and submit to the things he felt he would have to if he returned under conditions as they now exist. Felt to sanction what had been done by the Juarez Stake Presidency.

Pres. Romney felt that the people as a whole would some time go back to Mexico, as they have undoubtedly been a blessing to the Mexican people and can be in the future. "We have never shown fight to the Mexican people and have never killed one of them except in case of just necessity." He was not sure he would, himself, ever return to Mexico to live, but believed that the Lord will chastise the Nation for their sins, and did not think we could live in Mexico under existing conditions and get justice and said, "We must descend to their level. We cannot stand upon our right; they will not give them and we cannot claim them." He believed our coming out of Mexico was right, and thought that Joshua Steven's experience a warning against being a law unto ourselves. He said he did not want to take any responsibility for the people who are in the Colonies if they remain, but expects that the people will have yet to flee from their homes there, and thinks that intervention will have to come before peace comes to Mexico.

In answer to a question by Bro. George S. Romney, Pres. Romney said there was a decided difference between the position of Bro. Joshua Stevens and the men now in the Colonies with their families; that the first acted against counsel; and the latter are acting without counsel.

After some general discussion, benediction was pronounced by Pres. C. E. McClellan/. [*sic*]

C. E. McClellan, Secretary.

Minutes of Committee meeting held in rooms 8 & 9 Buckler Building, September 23rd, 1912. Prayer by Bro. O. P. Brown.

Bro. Josiah Spencer who remained in Colonia Dublan during all the troubles and has just come out for the first time from the Colonies, made a report of his observations and experiences.

Told of the arrival of the first train load of rebels at the Union Mercantil store and their looting. The latter was participated in by local Mexicans who continued the thieving continuously, especially at night. The rebel leaders treated him and his parents well and said the people needed not to have gone, but many rumors circulated among the local Mexico, that the Liberals intended to drive out the Mormons or kill them. There was a hostile feeling among the 'dgers, most of them, against our people. The Federals came first from the South on Sunday and Blanco arrived on Monday. The Federals have not manifested any activity in pursuing the rebels.

Bro. Spencer came from Galeana only last Saturday. The people of that section are principally "liberales".

A native told Bro. Spencer that Rabago had said virtually that he sanctioned what the Liberale had done to our people, and he did not expect to police the country. Bro. Spencer believes from all he has heard and felt, (he speaks Spanish well) that the local Mexicans would prefer to keep us out, or drive us out if we return. Did not think it was wise or profitable thing for all our people to return-- thought the more there the greater the danger.

Bro. Spencer talked with Pancho Mirando, who said he was willing to protect American interests, but could not control the men under him. This was rather a usual condition. Said his father anticipated intervention, in which case he thought that the people would have to come out. So much has been lost that in many cases it will not be profitable for men to remain with their homes this winter-- can do better by working elsewhere during the winter.

Bro. Wilson reported that he had had a long talk with Mr. Ryan of the Mexico Northwestern R. R. Company and had made arrangements by which the cheap rates to the Colonies may continue to be had. Bro. Wilson also discussed the bill the R. R. Company holds against us for bringing people out of the Colonies. Said in view of the facts that the Company sent three special trains down for us/. [*sic*] the bill does not seem so exorbitant.

Bro. A. B. Call reported the need of help for some of the boys who have been aiding in the commissary work, mentioned especially Rulon Schaeffer. It was decided to assist the boys a little.

Benediction by Bro. T. C. Romney.

C. E. McClellan, Secretary.

Bro. Calvert A. Allred ordained to the office of an Elder, President Romney, H. S. Harris and Bro. Guy C. Wilson, placing their hands upon his head. Pres. H. S. Harris was mouth.

El Paso, Texas. September 28th, 1912

Minutes of Central Committee High Councillors, [*sic*] and Bishoprics, held in room 8 & 9 Buckler Building, at 6 P. M. September 28th, 1912. Prayer by Bro. George S. Romney. Bishop A. D. Thurber and Pres. Rey L. Pratt were in attendance, just having returned from Colonia Dublan.

Bishop Thurber reported conditions at the Colonies. Said there are many rumors afloat about bands of rebels coming from the west, and that many rebels are coming. Reported that Neils Larsen and Demar Bowman were taken at the Railroad camp and all their supplies taken: that Bro. Larsen got away by making a long run on foot; Demar Bowman was held upwards of one week and made to walk a long distance and was poorly fed; otherwise not badly treated. Was now released and was given a poor horse to ride from point where released to Cumbre. Bishop Thurber things [*sic*] it was the same bunch who later took Billy Orr and Joe Place prisoners and completely looted their commissary. They beat Orr and according to report went so far as to walk on his prostrate body, till Orr gave them about $2,500.00 and secured his released [*sic*] after begging on his knees to heabe [*sic*] his life spared. Reports are also that rebels are in the hills east of Casas Grandes and Bishop Thurber says that rebels under Silvestre Quevedo burned the bridge at Arroyo Seco and detained Jesse Mortensen and two other of our boys while this was done. He thinks the rebels are surrounding Pearson with the probably [*sic*] idea of taking it. Everything points to the fact that the sentiment among the returning rebels is decidedly anti-foreign. Silvestre Quevedo told Jesse Mortensen, while holding him, that they had many men coming and they would take Pearson.

During this report, Bro. O. P. Brown said one of the high Railroad Officials of the Mexico North Western had just told him that the rebels had yesterday completely destroyed the station buildings and all bridges at and near Aguaje station. They had also turned a new engine loose full speed down grade and it had turned over three times and landed in the bottom of the canyon a complete wreck. Also said this official had told him that it looks as though the Mexico North Western will have to suspend all operations as conditions are steadily growing worse and that their Company are making very strong representations to their English Government and that England will undoubtedly take a hand in the affair in the near future. Also said that a United States secret service man of long acquaintance and undoubted reliability, told him tonight that he has positive information that Huerta and the Federal Commanders in the North are in collusion with the rebels and propose to let them go on till Madero resigns and then they will construct a government to their own liking. Huerta is sore at Madero for interfering after giving him a free hand in military affairs.

Pres. Pratt reported that he had made careful enquiry as to the number of rebels known to be in the vicinity of the Colonies, and believes that the total number does not exceed four hundred. He corroborated the report of Bishop Thurber. He thinks the people are doing the right thing in staying to look after their interests, and says that his brothers are intending to stay and plant wheat.

Bishop Thurber said two Mexicans had lately been shot to death by Federal guards in Casas Grandes and Pearson, for disregarding a command to halt. The letter from the First Presidency dated September 23rd, inst. was read. Discussed as to the best method for Bishops of the Stake to pursue to carry out the suggestion of Stake Presidency to keep track of members of their wards.

Pres. Harris reported that he and associate brethren have visited all members of Chuichupa and Pacheco wards in the City because their Bishoprics were not represented here, and that they found conditions generally good. Most of the people desire to go back to their homes as soon asconditions [*sic*] will permit. Had administered to some sick and comforted them, and all are out of danger except a little babe of Bro. Benj. Judd, which is very low with phneumonia. [*sic*] Spiritually all are feeling well, except some are a little neglectfull [*sic*] of prayer, etc. Special recommendations had been made that all spare time be devoted to teaching and training their children.

Read reports of Bishop E. V. Romney and Bishop C. W. Lillywhite, regarding the conditions of the people under their care.

In report of Bishop Romney, a request was made for permission to be granted to Counsellor [*sic*] Frederickseon [*sic*] to go in search of work. On motion this was granted. Bishop Lillywhite requested aid for some families, stating that the United States had cut off rations. Bro. Brown is to take this matter up at once and if necessary go to Douglas and render necessary aid. Pres. Romney is to refer the matter to the Church authorities while at Salt Lake.

Bro. Orsen [*sic*] P. Brown reported his recent visit to Hachita, New Mexico. While there he received word from the brethren who had gone to make an investigation of conditions at Colonia Diaz. They had met Federals at Ascension, [*sic*]who had promised protection. In connection with Bishop Romney, we advised that the brethren get together all of their live stock and other movable property and get it out to the United States as soon as possible. Bros. Levi Tenney and Alfredo Mortensen were sent as special couriers from Hachita to Colonia Diaz and about fifteen others followed with wagons and teams to bring out what could profitably be moved.

Application of Bro. A. E. Keeler which was endorsed by Bishop E. V. Romney for a loan of $50.00 U. S. Currency to build a house or homestead at Columbus N. M., was granted. The note was made payable in one year, and interest at 8%, to be sent to Bishop Romney for signature or delivery of accompanying check.

Suggested that the Committee prepare typewritten forms, reminding those working to pay Bro. Call a small amount weekly for the delivery boys.

Benediction by F. W. Jones, Jr.

Junius Romney, Secretary.

Edith Jones, daughter of Laura Moffett and F. W. Jones, Jr., was baptized in El Paso, Texas, September 29th, 1912, by Elder F. W. Jones, Jr., and was confirmed by Elder Thomas H. Jones, on the same date.

Minutes of Committee meeting held in Rooms 8 & 9 Buckler Building, El Paso, Texas, October 20th, 1912. Pres Junius Romney presided. Prayer offered by Bro. Lester B. Farnsworth.

Bro. H. S. Harris made a report of the condition of finances. Said that when Bro. Guy C. Wilson left, he left a check for $1,000.00 and that this was at the present time practically exhausted. Had received authority to draw on the Church a sight draft for $1,000.00, but this had not been drawn yet. Many people have been furnished transportation out. Diaz has recently been furnished with $150.00 U. S. in provisions and cupplies. [*sic*]

Pres. Romney thought that the people at Douglas would need about $250.00 and thought a part of this amount should be sent in cash. Said that some bedding had been provided for the refugees by the officers of the Relief Society in Salt Lake City, but these had not arrived and if any one in charge of camps will furnish lists of people known to be in need of these things, an effort will be made to get the bedding to them.

Moved, seconded and carried that $250.00 be sent to Douglas to be distributed by Bishop C. W. Lillywhite and Bishopric and the Committee in charge of those affairs.

Pres. Romney stated that Joseph Duthie who met with an accident breaking both legs has been under doctors care for some time, and that over $100.00 Gold was due for this treatment. Said Sister Duthie had asked for help to pay Sister Lewis and the Doctors who have treated the case. Moved and carried that $60.00 be furnished as charity to kelp [*sic*] defray this expense and that $20.00 each be paid Flora Lewis, Dr. Gay and the El Paso Doctor for services.

Pres. Romney spoke of the duty on provisions to be brought out , and O. P. Brown said he was writing the Department at Washington, D. C. about same.

Pres. Romney stated that he had seen Bro. Ivins just prior to leaving Utah and they had discussed the question of titles and the keeping of the Colonization Co.'s business in order. Also said that he had received a telegram from Bro. Ivins, stating he would be here Saturday.

The question of taxes which become due on property of the Colonists was discussed and it was decided to make an effort to have matters adjusted so that no property will be sold for delinquent taxes. It was suggested that a communication be sent to the Government, asking to remit all our taxes until peace is established. It was decided that the Committee would take the matter up at once.

Pres. Romney stated that all Bishops would be required to make recommends for all people leaving the ward.

It was decided that suggestion be made to the Presiding Bishopric's Office that Bishops make up annual reports and send to Stake Clerk at end of year and that the reports be compiled as usual, that the Bishops allowance and Stake Clerks be allowed to the end of the year.

Benediction by Bro. E. C. Eyring.

Ordination of Richard Parks Harris, son of F. H. and Josephine R. Harris, to the Aaronic Priesthood to the office of Deacon, Bro. Hyrum S. Harris being mouth, was made in room 8 Buckler Building, at El Paso, Texas on November 6th, 1912.

NOTES

1. Michael R. Mullen, "Borderland Saints," newsletter, April 2012, vol 2. issue 1, p. 1.

2. Shirley Taylor Robinson, "Mexico, Mormon Settlements in," *Encyclopedia of Mormonism*, ed. Daniel H. Ludlow (New York: Macmillan, 1992), 2:896–97, notes, "In 1990, there were approximately 4,000 Latter-day Saints in the area, about 500 of them descendants of the original pioneers." William G. Hartley and Lorna Call Alder, *Anson Bowen Call: Bishop of Colonia Dublán* (Provo: Lorna Call Alder, 2007), ix, explains that some Mormon families who returned to the colonies had to flee Mexico repeatedly. Such was thc casc of Lorna Call, who initially fled with her family in the mass exodus of 1912 and then again in 1914 and 1917 as a result of the raids of Pancho Villa and other rebels. On the Call family's 1912 exodus experience, see pp. 239–62; 1914 exodus, pp. 337–76; and 1917 exodus, pp. 461–90. Lorna recalled, "The Call family members were just like swallows. . . . When somebody broke down their nests, they left, and waited until everything was peaceful, and then built them up again and went twittering on" ("Faith learned in colonies fosters life long service," *Church News*, November 15, 1997, 12). However, in a recent lecture presented by Barbara Jones Brown, "'A Very Pitable Site': Mexican Revolution, Mormon Exodus, and the Break-up of Polygamous Families," Brown explained that the 1912 exodus from the Mormon colonies back into the United States caused some polygamous families to be broken up.

(Unpublished paper presented at the Conference on the History of Mormonism in Latin America and the U. S.-Mexico Borderlands, July 28, 2012, El Paso Public Library, El Paso, Texas.) Brown has also authored a forthcoming biography of Lorna Call Alder.

3. Orson Pratt, "Celestial Marriage," in *Journal of Discourses* (London: Latter-day Saints' Book Depot, 1854–86), 1:53–66. Leonard J. Arrington and Davis Bitton estimate that less than 5 percent of all Mormon males practiced polygamy in the nineteenth century and that most of them had only two wives. *The Mormon Experience: A History of the Latter-day Saints* (New York: Knopf, 1979), 199.

4. Blaine Carmon Hardy, "The Mormon Colonies of Northern Mexico: A History, 1885–1912" (PhD diss., Wayne State University, 1963), 67.

5. Ray Jay Davis, "Antipolygamy Legislation," in *Encyclopedia of Mormonism*, ed. Daniel H. Ludlow.

6. Most of the men served time in the Utah penitentiary in Salt Lake City. See Melvin L. Bashore, "Life Behind Bars: Mormon Cohabs of the 1880s," *Utah Historical Quarterly* 47 (Winter 1979): 23–24. Those who served in South Dakota and Michigan were sent there from Arizona, Idaho, and Utah because there was no room for them in the territorial penitentiaries. For information on those incarcerated in Idaho and South Dakota, see Fred E. Woods and Merle W. Wells, "Inmates of Honor: Mormon Cohabs in the Idaho Penitentiary, 1885–1890," *Idaho Yesterdays* 40, no. 3 (Fall 1999): 13–22; Melvin L. Bashore and Fred E. Woods, "Consigned to a Distant Prison: Idaho Mormons in the South Dakota Penitentiary," *South Dakota History* 27, no. 1–2 (Spring–Summer 1997): 21–40. The author and Professor Richard Holzapfel have plans to coedit a book on the story of each of these penitentiaries.

7. Not only were many LDS men forced to hide and flee their homes, but LDS women and children were also impacted by the underground. For articles concerning this topic, see Martha Sonntag Bradley, "'Hide and Seek': Children on the Underground," *Utah Historical Quarterly*

51 (Spring 1983): 133–53; Kimberly Jensen James, "'Between Two Fires': Women on the 'Underground' of Mormon Polygamy" (master's thesis, Brigham Young University, 1981). Some men also chose to disguise themselves as women as they sought to avoid arrest. For instance, by attiring himself like a female in a sun bonnet and a mother hubbard dress and answering to the name of "Aunt Matilida," Mormon Apostle Wilford Woodruff was able to enjoy some quail hunting on the outskirts of St. George, Utah. See Phil Murdock and Fred E. Woods, "'I Dreamed of Ketching Fish': The Outdoor Life of Wilford Woodruff," *BYU Studies* 37, no. 4 (1997–98): 34, 46.

8. Milton R. Hunter, *Brigham Young the Colonizer*, 4th ed. rev. (Salt Lake City: Peregrine Smith, 1973), 373.

9. Brigham Young, in *Journal of Discourses*, 18:356.

10. Daniel W. Jones and Henry W. Brizzee, who spoke some Spanish, were called to prepare to serve missions in Mexico and perform the Book of Mormon translation. Miraculously, the men met Meliton G. Trejo, a Spanish officer from the Philippines, mere months after their calling. Trejo had traveled from the Philippines in search of the Mormons in response to "an impressive dream he had received." Trejo joined the Church and began assisting Jones and Brizzee in translating Book of Mormon passages, which were printed in 1875. Thomas Cottam Romney, *The Mormon Colonies in Mexico* (Salt Lake City: University of Utah Press, 2005), 38. For more information on Trejo, see Daniel W. Jones, *Forty Years among the Indians: A True Yet Thrilling Narrative of the Author's Experience among the Natives* (Salt Lake City: Juvenile Instructor Office, 1890), 220–22.

11. F. Lamond Tullis, *Mormons in Mexico: The Dynamics of Faith and Culture* (Logan: Utah State University Press, 1987), 19. The men called were Anthony W. Ivins (who would later serve in the Quorum of the Twelve and the First Presidency of The Church of Jesus Christ of Latter-day Saints) and Daniel W. Jones, Wiley C. Jones, Helaman Pratt, Robert H. Smith, James Z. Stewart, and Ammon M. Tenney. See Romney, *Mormon Colonies in Mexico*, 38.

12. Jones, *Forty Years among the Indians*, 220. Nephi was "the first of several leaders named Nephi" in the Book of Mormon. See Noel B. Reynolds, "Nephi 1," in *Encyclopedia of Mormonism*, 3:1003–5, for more information.

13. In Romney, *Mormon Colonies in Mexico*, 39.

14. Ibid.

15. Tullis, *Mormons in Mexico*, 26, 31, 36. See also F. Lamond Tullis, "Early Mormon Exploration and Missionary Activities in Mexico," *BYU Studies* 22, no. 3 (1982), 1–2. See also Matthew G. Geilman, "Taking the Gospel to the Lamanites: Doctrinal Foundations for Establishing the Church of Jesus Christ of Latter-day Saints in Mexico" (master's thesis, Brigham Young University, 2011), 27–46. The author thanks Geilman for supplying him with an electronic copy of his thesis.

16. Hardy, "Mormon Colonies of Northern Mexico," 72.

17. Ibid.

18. "Juárez Stake High Council Historical Record, 1895–1903," February 21, 1896, Church History Library, The Church of Jesus Christ of Latter-day Saints, Salt Lake City (hereafter cited as CHL), as cited in http://www.orsonprattbrown.com/Polygamy/polyg-mex-canada-byhardy.html.

19. Stephen Hill, "Politics and Polygamy in Northern Mexico: Porfirio Díaz and Mormon Colonization, 1885–1912" (master's thesis, Tulane University, 1993), 22–23.

20. See Hill, "Politics and Polygamy," chapter 3, for a discussion of the Mexican government's policies and practices concerning foreign immigration.

21. México, Informe que rinde el Secretario de Fomento a la honorable Cámara de Diputados sobre colonización y terrenos baldíos (México City: Oficina Tipográfica de la Secretaria de Fomento, 1885), 196, in Hill, "Politics and Polygamy," 26–27.

22. Hill, "Politics and Polygamy," 82–83.

23. Annie R. Johnson, *Heartbeats of Colonia Díaz* (Salt Lake City: Publishers Press, 1972), 14.

24. Joseph Barnard Romney, "'The Lord, God of Israel, Brought Us Out of Mexico!': Junius Romney and the 1912 Mormon Exodus," *Journal of Mormon History* 36, no. 4 (Fall 2010): 210–11.

25. Hardy, "Mormon Colonies of Northern Mexico," 73–74.

26. Romney, *Mormon Colonies in Mexico*, 62.

27. Romney, "'The Lord, God of Israel,'" 211. Joseph B. Romney further notes that by 1912, there were about "4500 men women and children distributed [in these nine colonies] as follows: Diaz - 750, Dublán - 1,200, Juarez - 800, Pacheco - 275, Garcia - 275, Chuichupa - 275, San Jose - 200, Oaxaca - 64, and Morelos - 625." "The Exodus of the Mormon Colonists from Mexico, 1912" (master's thesis, University of Utah, 1967), 2–3. There is also evidence of a few other small Mormon settlements which will not be dealt with in this work. This book will also not treat the evacuation of the Sonora colonies in detail. For more information on these Sonora colonies, see Romney, "Exodus of the Mormon Colonists," 105–9.

28. Richard E. Turley Jr., interview by author and Martin L. Andersen, February 23, 2012, transcript, 4, in author's possession.

29. Nelle Spilsbury Hatch, *Colonia Juárez: An Intimate Account of a Mormon Village* (Salt Lake City: Deseret Book, 1954), 26–27.

30. See Hatch, *Colonia Juárez*, 67–79, 152–53.

31. Ibid.

32. Ibid.

33. Ibid.

34. Romney, *Mormon Colonies in Mexico*, 57.

35. Romney, ibid., 58–59.

36. Merlo J. Pusey, *Builders of the Kingdom* (Provo, UT: Brigham Young University Press, 1981), 185.

37. Junius Romney, "Was the Exodus Necessary?" 8–9, in Romney, "Lord, God of Israel," 212.

38. Hatch, *Colonia Juárez*, 131–33.

39. Agnes Scott Bluth, interview by Joseph B. Romney, August 30, 1971, transcript, 17, California State College at Fullerton Oral History Program.

40. W. Derby Johnson Jr. diary, December 25, 1887; July 15, 1888; cited in B. Carmon Hardy, "Mormon Polygamy in Mexico and Canada: A Legal and Historiographical Review," in *The Mormon Presence in Canada*, ed. Brigham Y. Card (Edmonton: University of Alberta Press, 1990), 187.

41. Anthony W. Ivins, in Conference Report, October 1902, 28. William G. Hartley and Lorna Call Alder, *Anson Bowen Call: Bishop of Colonia Dublán* (Provo: Lorna Call Alder, 2007), 90–91, reasoned that this lack of assimilation was typical of immigrants who initially encounter a new region. Further, they note that relatively few Mormons learned Spanish or adopted Mexican citizenship. They considered themselves Latter-day Saints and Americans first.

42. "'Mormons' in Mexico," *Deseret Evening News*, October 3, 1891, 4.

43. Hatch, *Colonia Juárez*, 106.

44. Johnson, *Heartbeats*, 137.

45. Tullis, *Mormons in Mexico*, 59.

46. Ibid.

47. Romney, "'Lord, God of Israel,'" 213.

48. Charles Curtis Cumberland, *Mexican Revolution: Genesis under Madero* (Austin: University of Texas Press, 1952). In the end, the

Mexican Revolution would cost a million lives and more than a billion dollars. W. H. Timmons, *El Paso: A Borderlands History* (El Paso: Texas Western Press, 2004), 209.

49. For more information on Villa, see Friedrich Katz, *The Life and Times of Pancho Villa* (Stanford, CA: Stanford University Press, 1998); Brandon Morgan, "Mormon Colonists' Image of Pancho Villa," *New Mexico Historical Review* 85, no. 2 (Spring 2012): 109–29.

50. Several other followers of Orozco had also been educated at the academy. Mike Landon, interview by Fred E. Woods, February 23, 2012, transcript, 7.

51. Colonia Morelos began to feel effects of the Revolution in November 1911. A detachment of rebels passed through the colony with about a hundred *federales* (government troops) in pursuit. The government soldiers camped on the streets of Morelos for two days, confiscating colonists' cattle and hay. Bill L. Smith, "Impacts of the Mexican Revolution: The Mormon Experience, 1910–1946" (PhD diss., Washington State University, 2000), 54.

52. Smith, "Impacts," 52.

53. A stake is an administrative unit within The Church of Jesus Christ of Latter-day Saints. It is composed of several congregations and is roughly equivalent to a diocese in some Christian denominations.

54. Hatch, *Colonia Juárez*, 164.

55. Michael C. Meyer, *Mexican Rebel: Pascual Orozco and the Mexican Revolution, 1910–1915* (Lincoln: University of Nebraska Press, 1967).

56. Junius Romney, "Remarks . . . made in the Rose Park Stake Priesthood meeting . . . July 13, 1966, typescript, 6, in possession of author.

57. Johnson, *Heartbeats*, 306.

58. Joseph C. Bentley, Marion T. Bentley, and Joseph Ivins Bentley, "'Our Hearts Were Touched by Fire': Bishop Joseph C. Bentley and Families in the Mexican Revolution," paper presented to the Mormon History Association, Tucson, AZ, May 16–19, 2002, 10–11.

59. Jesse M. Taylor, Oral History, L. Tom Perry Special Collections, Harold B. Lee Library, Brigham Young University, Provo, UT (hereafter cited as HBLL), 9.

60. Romney, "Exodus of the Mormon Colonists from Mexico," 13–14; Hatch, *Colonia Juárez*, 167–70.

61. Hazel Richardson Taylor, Oral History, HBLL, 17.

62. H. I. Miller to unknown party, May 17, 1912, John H. McNeely Collection, MS 167, box 11, S-1, University of Texas El Paso Special Collections, El Paso (hereafter cited as UTEP). This correspondence of Brown to Smoot had been going on for some time, as attested by several letters, including Orson P. Brown to Senator Reed Smoot, April 1, 1912; and April 2, 1912; April 2, 3, 1912, Collected Letters concerning Church in Mexico Colonies, CHL.

63. Romney, *Mormon Colonies in Mexico*, 168.

64. Ibid., 171.

65. Ibid., 176.

66. Smith, "Impacts," 70.

67. Hatch, *Colonia Juárez*, 185–86.

68. See Nelle Spilsbury Hatch and B. Carmon Hardy, eds., *Stalwarts South of the Border* (California: n. p., 1985), 32.

69. Hatch, *Colonia Juárez*, 185.

70. John Jacob Walser, "My Life," comp. Bonnie Simon, HBLL.

71. Willard Whipple, "The Life of Willard Whipple" (unpublished manuscript, 1977), 13–14, in possession of the author. Thanks to Michael Mullen for bringing this source to the attention of the author.

72. Journal of Hyrum Albert Cluff, submitted by Mrs. Sarah Matilda Cluff Lewis, in Hatch and Hardy, *Stalwarts South of the Border*, 122.

73. Charles Call, interview by Joseph Romney, August 29, 1971, transcript, California State University at Fullerton Oral History Project, 2.

74. Journal of Catherine Auerlia Carling Porter, in Hatch and Hardy, *Stalwarts South of the Border*, 535.

75. John A. Whetten in *John A. Whetten, Pioneer, Patriach*, ed. Thomas F. Peterson, (Mesa, AZ: The John A. Whetten Genealogy Committee, 2001), 23.

76. Vaneese Harris Woffinden, in *Treasures of Pioneer History*, comp. Kate B. Carter (Salt Lake City: Daughters of Utah Pioneers, 1954), 3:248.

77. Charles E. McClellan, in *Treasures of Pioneer History*, 3:242.

78. Romney, *Mormon Colonies in Mexico*, 183; Karl E. Young, *The Long Hot Summer of 1912: Episodes in the Flight of the Mormon Colonists from Mexico* (Provo, UT: Brigham Young University Press, 1967), 9.

79. Edward Christian Eyring, in Hatch and Hardy, *Stalwarts South of the Border*, 149–50. Romney, *Mormon Colonies in Mexico*, 183, notes, "Although the decision had been made to send the women and children to El Paso it was felt by most of us at least that their absence from home would be of short duration." Other views seem to have been influenced by which of the colonies the Mormons were living in, as some areas were impacted more by the rebel confrontations than others.

80. Louise Whipple Skousen, interview by Ivan L. Carbine, November 28, 1959, Mesa, AZ, in private possession of Ivan and Helen Carbine, Provo, UT.

81. Enos Wood, interview by Joseph B. Romney, August 31, 1974, transcript, 2, California State University–Fullerton Oral History Program.

82. Frank and Annie O'Donnal, interview with Karl E. Young, Mesa, Arizona, December 26, 1962, transcript, 11, HBLL.

83. "Three Babes Born on Road," *El Paso Herald*, July 31, 1912, 1.

84. George T. Sevey, "The Story of Chuichupa," Ruby Spilsbury Brown Collection (1880–1985), CHL, in Michael N. Landon, "'We Navigated by Pure Understanding': Bishop George T. Sevey's Account of the 1912 Exodus from Mexico," *BYU Studies* 43, no. 2 (2004): 81.

85. Jesse M. Taylor, interview by Ivan Carbine, November 10, 1959, transcript, 16, HBLL.

86. Jesse M. Taylor, interview, 16. See also Tullis, *Mormons in Mexico*, 94. Some of the men who departed with the women left for their own protection. "They put . . . all the men that were connected with the killing of Juan Sosa on the train, some of them in disguise." John Telford, interview, audio tape in possession of Taylor Macdonald, Pleasant Grove, UT.

87. Extracted by Ellen Beecroft Farnsworth, in Hatch and Hardy, *Stalwarts South of the Border*, 29.

88. President Henry B. Eyring, interview by Martin L. Andersen and Fred E. Woods, May 25, 2012, Salt Lake City, transcript in author's possession.

89. Caroline Eyring Miner and Edward L. Kimball, *Camilla: A Biography of Camilla Eyring Kimball* (Salt Lake City: Deseret Book, 1980), 30. Camilla Eyring would later become the wife of future Church President Spencer W. Kimball.

90. Sarah Jones Payne, in Hatch and Hardy, *Stalwarts South of the Border*, 376.

91. La Vieve Huish Earl, daughter of James William Huish Jr., in Hatch and Hardy, *Stalwarts South of the Border*, 270.

92. George Sevey, in Landon, "'We Navigated by Pure Understanding,'" 82; Hazel Richardson Taylor, Oral History, 18. Contemporary

reports of such rebel attacks can be found in H. I. Miller to Dr. F. S. Pearson, August 6, 1912; and H. I. Miller to Louis Riba, September 27, 1912, UTEP.

93. Prince G. McKenzie, interview by Fred E. Woods, April 13, 2012, Railroad and Transportation Museum in El Paso, where Prince is the director, 1, transcript in author's possession.

94. William Whipple, cited in Pat Henry, "El Paso: Sanctuary to Mormon refugees," *El Paso Times*, February 5, 1984, 1E. Gratitude is expressed to Ellwyn Stoddard, emeritus professor of sociology and anthropology at the University of Texas at El Paso, for bringing this article to the author's attention.

95. Sarah Jones Payne, daughter of Timothy Jones, in Hatch and Hardy, *Stalwarts South of the Border*, 376–77.

96. Young, *Long Hot Summer*, 20

97. "Red Flaggers Drive Americans from their Mexican Homes," *El Paso Morning Times*, July 29, 1912, 1. Although the Mormons were exiting Mexico and entering the United States at this time, "by 1910 El Paso, with more than 10,000 people of Mexican birth or parentage, was the largest Mexican center in the United States." Timmons, *El Paso*, 186. The *Deseret Evening News* noted that Pearson was two hundred miles southwest of the US border. "Hundreds of Refugees Stranded in El Paso," *Deseret Evening News*, August 1, 1912, 10.

98. "Arms Taken from Americans by Rebels," *El Paso Herald*, July 29, 1912, 1.

99. "'Mormons' Flee From Mexico," *Deseret Evening News*, July 29, 1912, 1. These first Mormon refugees who crossed the border were from Colonia Juárez.

100. "Protesting Against Outrages," *Deseret Evening News*, July 31, 1912, 4. Romney, *Mormon Colonies in Mexico*, 215, maintains that the colonists were driven out for economic reasons. He notes, "Officers of the Mexican government took part in the numerous ravages to terrorize

the American people to leave the country, so that their property might be confiscated among the Mexicans" (218). This same reasoning is presented by Jeffrey N. Walker, "Mormon Land Rights in Caldwell and Daviess Counties and the Mormon Conflict of 1838: New Findings and New Understandings," *BYU Studies* 47, no. 1 (2008): 4–56, wherein he argues that a major reason why the Missourians drove the Mormons from the state was to take possession of their lands. Romney, "Exodus of the Mormon Colonists from Mexico," 6–7, notes that by March of 1912, the US secretary of state had advised all Americans to leave Mexico. By August of 1912, 42,000 out of the 75,000 had left Mexico, about 10 percent of which were Latter-day Saints. "More Americans Come to Border," *El Paso Herald*, July 31, 1912, 1, indicated that not only Americans but also many Mexicans and a number of Chinese people sought refuge in El Paso during this tumultuous period.

101. Alonzo L. Taylor, "Record of the Exodus of the Mormon Colonies from Mexico in 1912," typescript, 5, CHL.

102. Hatch, *Colonia Juárez*, 189.

103. In Landon, "'We Navigated by Pure Understanding,'" 82.

104. Taylor, "Record of the Exodus," 7. Taylor was the official clerk of the Juárez Stake when he composed the report, which he presented to Bishop Joseph C. Bentley shortly after the exodus.

105. Young, *Long Hot Summer*, 49.

106. In Landon, "'We Navigated by Pure Understanding,'" 83.

107. George T. Sevey described the Stairs as "an ideal place for a camp, a sort of rolling basin with plenty of good pure water, and protected with high bluffs on the east from where any invasion was likely. There were but two trails entering the basin from the east, they were narrow and easily defended." In Landon, "'We Navigated by Pure Understanding,'" 83.

108. Smith, "Impacts," 75. Sadly, the colonists were not able to locate the records when they returned later.

109. Hatch, *Colonia Juárez*, 199; Landon, "'We Navigated by Pure Understanding,'" 71–72.

110. Hatch, *Colonia Juárez*, 198–99. According to Taylor, "Record of the Exodus," 15, the Juárez Stake presidency had general supervision over the group, while A. D. Thurber was named commander of the expedition. Anson Call was given charge of the home guards and Miles A. Romney took charge of the scouts. Gaskell Romney took the job of quartermaster, with Ed McClellan as his assistant. Finally, George S. Romney was put in charge of camp discipline and moral conduct. Taylor also provides the following names of unit commanders:

Home guard captains:

Company 1: Alonzo L. Taylor

Company 2: Edward C. Eyring

Company 3: Martin L. Harris

Company 4: William Jones Jr.

Company 5: John Bingham

Company 6: F. M. Stock

Scout unit captains:

Unit 1: Nephi W. Thayne

Unit 2: Loren Taylor

Unit 3: N. C. Tenney

Unit 4: Sam Hawkins

Unit 5: Ira Pratt

Unit 6: Edgerton Lunt

Unit 7: Omni Porter

Unit 8: John Beecroft

Unit 9: John A. Whetten

111. Romney, "Exodus of the Mormon Colonists," 101.

112. Ibid. According to Alonzo Taylor, "At 2:30 P. M. the camp moved and traveled north crossing the U. S. Line at 6:20 P. M (Friday 9th) about 3 miles east of Dog Springs where 20 U. S. soldiers were stationed and fortified behind rock walls ready to fire on us thinking we were a band of rebels, but on finding out their mistake they gave the Company the best of treatment and all assistance possible." "Record of the Exodus," 19.

113. In Landon, "'We Navigated by Pure Understanding,'" 85.

114. Ibid., 84.

115. In Landon, "'We Navigated by Pure Understanding,'" 93. Helaman Judd, interview with Joseph B. Romney, August 13, 1971, Colonia Juárez, transcript, 7–8, California State University–Fullerton Oral History Program. Their organization resembled that of the Camp of Israel, which Brigham Young organized as the Saints journeyed to the Salt Lake Valley. For details of the Camp of Israel, see Doctrine and Covenants 136.

116. Romney, "Exodus of the Mormon Colonists," 100.

117. In Landon, "'We Navigated by Pure Understanding,'" 95.

118. In Landon, "'We Navigated by Pure Understanding,'" 97–98.

119. For a general history of Hachita, which lies in southwest New Mexico, see George Hilliard, *Adios Hachita: Stories of a New Mexico Town* (Silver City, New Mexico: High Lonesome Books, 1998).

120. In Landon, "'We Navigated by Pure Understanding,'" 99.

121. Maude T. Schofield to Eva Jane Robeson, May 13, 1960, Eva Jane Robeson Papers (MS 007), Letters, 1959–1960, box 1, folder 4, Archives and Special Collections Department, Rio Grande Historical Collections, New Mexico State University Library, Las Cruces, New Mexico. The letters were collected by Robeson as research for her master's thesis on the exodus (Robeson, "Mormon Exodus").

122. Robeson, "Mormon Exodus," 17.

123. Schofield to Robeson, May 13, 1960, 1; spelling standardized.

124. Schofield to Robeson, 2.

125. El Paso lies near the geographic center of the Borderlands region on the southern border of the United States and played a pivotal role as a refuge from the Revolution. Timmons, *El Paso*, xvii.

126. Hatch and Hardy, *Stalwarts South of the Border*, 73–74.

127. "More Refugees have Arrived," *El Paso Morning Times*, August 1, 1912, 1–2. The Union Depot was constructed in 1906 at the cost of $260,000.00. Timmons, *El Paso*, 193.

128. Preface to *Worley's Directory of El Paso Texas 1912* (Dallas: John F. Worley Directory Co., 1912) estimates that the population of El Paso at this time was 41,212.

129. *The Mormons in El Paso del Norte: History of the members of The Church of Jesus Christ of Latter-day Saints in the Juárez-El Paso bi-national community (1876–2000)*, 39. The book has no author, date, nor place of publication.

130. "Red Flaggers Drive Americans From Their Mexican Homes," 1.

131. "Mormon Refugees Given Assistance," *El Paso Herald*, July 30, 1912, 2, adds that other *Herald* employees soon aided these needy families with a stove and a washing machine. It was also thought that other charitable acts were being rendered throughout the city. In addition, "Refugees Housed in Lumber Sheds," *El Paso Herald,* July 30, 1912, 1, notes, "Through the kindness of the Long Lumber Company, the Mormon refugees were comfortably housed in its abandoned lumber sheds on Magoffin avenue Monday night. C. L. Sirmans, secretary and treasurer of the Long company, arranged for the flooring of the sheds in order that the women and children might not find it necessary to sleep on the ground. The use of these sheds was given free by the lumber company. . . . The city arranged for the lighting and plumbing of the sheds and the committee appointed by the chamber

of commerce to assist the refugees visited the sheds late Monday afternoon and saw that everything was being done that was possible to make the unfortunate people comfortable."

132. "More Refugees Have Arrived," 2, gives the names of many of these charitable drivers: "J. F. Roundtree, Tom Kimpton, Billy Brown, Bill Klondyke, Guy Williams, G. R. Williams, Billy Morris, Bernardo Chappo, Abe Aguilar, Irvin Bowles, I. E. Morris, Whitehead Severance, Ray Harrell, J. E. Ellis, Jack Forrest, Billy Davis, Castleburp, Charlie Smith, Bill Harold, Walter Harold, Frank Keene, Nels Nelson, Kid Richards, Miller Johnson and Dillon. When a refugee train is reported in, these boys drop all work that may be pending, leave the stand vacant of all machines and turn to help the unfortunates."

133. Karl E. Young, *Ordeal in Mexico: Tales of Danger and Hardship Collected from the Mormon Colonists* (Salt Lake City: Deseret Book, 1968), 78.

134. Lucille R. Taylor, interview by Joseph B. Romney, November 27, 1970, Colonia Dublán, transcript, 6, California State University–Fullerton Oral History Program.

135. William Morley Black, in Hatch and Hardy, *Stalwarts South of the Border*, 49–50.

136. Vera Whetten Pratt, interview by the author and Martin L. Andersen, February 2012, at her home in El Paso.

137. William Morley Black, in Hatch and Hardy, *Stalwarts South of the Border*, 49–50.

138. Miner and Kimball, *Camilla*, 31.

139. Walter Frederick Hurst, condensed from original by Ruby Hurst Morgan, in Hatch and Hardy, *Stalwarts South of the Border*, 307.

140. Maude Cluff Farnsworth, in Hatch and Hardy, *Stalwarts South of the Border*, 169.

141. Vaneese Harris Woffinden, in *Treasures of Pioneer History*, 3:248.

142. "Refugees From Colonies in Mexico Being Given Every Possible Comfort," *Deseret Evening News*, August 1, 1912, 1.

143. Pratt, interview.

144. Hurst, in Hatch and Hardy, *Stalwarts South of the Border*, 307. Woffinden, in *Treasures of Pioneer History*, 3:248.

145. Hurst, in Hatch and Hardy, *Stalwarts South of the Border*, 307.

146. Woffinden, in *Treasures of Pioneer History*, 3:248.

147. Hazel Richardson Taylor Oral History, 19–20.

148. William Morley Black, in Hatch and Hardy, *Stalwarts South of the Border*, 49–50.

149. "Colonists Leaving Refugee Camps for Places of Safety Elsewhere," *Deseret Evening News*, August 2, 1912, 1.

150. Mary Viola Stout, in Hatch and Hardy, *Stalwarts South of the Border*, 14. Stout also notes that her father died "August 6, 1912, and is buried in the Evergreen Cemetery in El Paso" (p. 14).

151. "Juarez Stake Relief Committee Minutes," 2, CHL (hereafter cited as "Relief Minutes"). The Relief Committee helped pay for Allred's burial. Relief Minutes, 2.

152. "Refugees Are Fleeing North," *Deseret Evening News*, July 30, 1912, 1.

153. "Heart Rending Recital Given," *El Paso Morning Times*, July 30, 1912, 1. Henry, "El Paso: Sanctuary to Mormon refugees," 1E, identifies the eyewitness who told of the Saints' suffering as Enrique Bowman (Henry E. Bowman), who had been a Church leader in the colonies. According to Henry's article, Bowman told the Chamber of Commerce "about rebel soldiers' riding on the communities' sidewalks and about other insulting behavior. 'We don't want your charity, only your hospitality. We have left everything behind. . . . If not for the women and children we would have killed some of them. We could have fought but—' Bowman's voice broke and he wept. Mayor C. E. Kelly [then] said El Paso was prepared to care for all of the refugees." William

G. Hartley and Lorna Call Alder, *Anson Bowen Call: Bishop of Colonia Dublán* (Provo: Lorna Call Alder, 2007), 241–43, noted that Bowman had been sent to El Paso to help with arranging for train travel and accommodations. He arrived on Sunday, July 28, at 1:00 a.m. Upon arrival, he immediately went to consult with Elder Anthony W. Ivins, who had also just arrived from a visit he made to the colonies. He then woke up the officials of the Mexico Northwestern Railroad, who were very willing to begin sending trains south out of El Paso for transporting the women and children.

154. Judge Eylar was later killed by a Santa Fe "cantaloupe" train near his home in La Mesa, New Mexico in 1939 at age seventy-two. See "A. S. J. Eylar Dies in Crash Near La Mesa," *El Paso Morning Times*, July 31, 1939, 1.

155. "Heart Rending Recital Given," 2. "Pitiful Scenes Among Exiles," *El Paso Morning Times*, July 31, 1912, 1, noted that the abandoned lumberyard was located "on Magoffin avenue, between Cotton avenue and the Texas & Pacific railway tracks." The article also reported that "the [Walter] Long Lumber company which owns the structure, has given it free of charge to the refugees." In addition, it was reported that "the El Paso dairy is furnishing milk for the babies." The president of the El Paso Dairy at this time was J. A. Smith. See *Worley's Directory of El Paso Texas, 1912*, 202.

156. The men chosen for this El Paso relief committee were James A. Dick, chairman; J. H. Nations; Thomas O'Keeffe; J. C. Wilmarth; H. S. Potter; George Flory; D. M. Payne; J. A. Smith; and W. S. Clayton. "Heart Rending Recital Given," 2.

157. "Reading Matter for Refugees Wanted," *El Paso Herald*, July 31, 1912, 1.

158. "Refugee Colony Increased by Fresh Arrivals Fleeing from Rebels," *El Paso Herald*, August 1, 1912, 5, notes, "The Unique theater . . . will give a free matinee . . . for the Mormon children, who will be admitted free of charge." See also Henry, "El Paso: Sanctuary to Mormon Refugees," 1E.

159. Melissa Sargent, interview by the author and Martin L. Andersen, February 19, 2012, at her home in El Paso, transcript, 1.

160. "Refugees from Colonies in Mexico Being Given Every Possible Comfort," *Deseret Evening News*, August 1, 1912, 1.

161. William Morley Black, in Hatch and Hardy, *Stalwarts South of the Border*, 49–50. Pat Henry differs from the high sum calculated by Black, noting, "Mormon headquarters in Salt Lake City took responsibility for the refugees. The United States appropriated $20,000 for their care (which the Mormon Church paid back)." Henry, "El Paso: Sanctuary to Mormon Refugees," 1E.

162. "Colonists Are Riding North," *El Paso Morning Times*, August 7, 1912, 1. The American National Bank was incorporated in January 1905 with a capital of $200,000 and a surplus of $10,000. At the time of incorporation, the president of the bank was A. P. Coles with T. M. Wingo and W. J. Harris employed as vice presidents. See J. F. Worley and Co., *El Paso Directory for 1906* (Dallas, TX: J. F. Worley & Co., 1905), 33. Detailed minutes were kept of the meetings by the Church relief committee from August 1 to October 20, 1912. See appendix C, "Juarez Stake Relief Committee Minutes," for these minutes in their entirety.

163. Hatch and Hardy, *Stalwarts South of the Border*, 316–17, notes, "When evacuation of the colonists actually took place, Ivins was in Ciudad Juárez to meet the first trainload of women, children, and aged men, and stayed until the last evacuees arrived. He helped negotiate with the City of El Paso for food for the homeless and with Fort Bliss for the use of tents as a more adequate shelter than the lumber sheds in which they were temporarily housed. When it looked unfavorable for a return to their homes in Mexico, he was partly responsible for obtaining free rail passage in the United States for all who cared to relocate elsewhere."

164. "History of Anthony W. Ivins, Utah," Online Utah, http://www.onlineutah.com/ivins_anthony_w_history. shtml.

165. *Worley's Directory of El Paso 1912*, 35.

166. In 1903, Brigadier General Frederick D. Grant, son of the former president and Civil War general Ulysses S. Grant and commander of the Department of Texas, predicted that Fort Bliss and other border outposts would prove critical in future conflicts and spoke of the importance of maintaining "military stations in Texas only along or in the immediate vicinity of the Rio Grande, at or near important railroad crossings, beginning with El Paso in the west. . . . One of the first considerations which must enter into the maintenance of military stations along the Mexican frontier is the necessity for absolute command or control in time of war or other public danger of any or all of the great international railroad lines which have so extensively grown in the past twenty years. For this reason El Paso must always be regarded as a strategic point, on account of being the most important railroad junction, next to Fort Worth and Houston, in southwestern United States." "Report of Brig. Gen. Frederick D. Grant, U. S. Army, Commanding the Department of Texas," in *Annual Reports of the War Department for the Fiscal Year Ended June 30, 1903*, vol. 3 of *Reports of Department and Division Commanders* (Washington, DC: Government Printing Office, 1903), 100. By 1911, Brigadier General Joseph W. Duncan, then commander of the Department of Texas, was already asserting that "the value of [Fort Bliss] as a strategical point has been fully demonstrated during the recent Mexican border trouble." *War Department Annual Reports, 1911* (Washington, DC: Government Printing Office, 1912), 114.

167. Perry Jamieson, "A Survey History of Fort Bliss, 1890–1940," Historic and Natural Resources Report No. 5, Cultural Resources Management Program, Directorate of Environment, United States Army Air Defense Artillery Center, Fort Bliss, 1993, 24. Because of Fort Bliss's strategic importance, it saw major expansions during and after the revolution. A full cavalry regiment was stationed there in 1912, and semipermanent barracks were built. The fort then achieved the status of permanent regimental post. By 1915, efforts were being made to expand the fort into a permanent infantry brigade post. Ibid., 25.

168. Ibid., 19. Although the United States was not at war with Mexico, more than five thousand Mexican prisoners of war were held

at Fort Bliss. Jamieson, "Survey History of Fort Bliss," 26. Ironically, in 1914 Inés Salazar, the rebel general whose actions led to the Mormon evacuation, was held as a prisoner of war at the fort. Jamieson, "Survey History of Fort Bliss," 24.

169. Steever was promoted from colonel to brigadier general and took over command of Fort Bliss on August 5, just days after the Mormons began arriving in El Paso. Steever apparently suffered from vision loss, making him unfit to lead troops in the field. However, according to a United States War Department official, he had "won the approbation not only of his superior officers but of the officials and citizens of Texas" thanks to his efficiency in commanding affairs along the Mexican border. In "War Department," *New York Times*, August 6, 1912. The *El Paso Herald*, August 5, 1912, 1, carried three interesting headlines: "Col. Steever Given His Star by Taft: Becomes a Brigadier General" appeared just below articles titled "Mormon Men to Fight to Border: If Their Flight Is Opposed, They Are Ready to Put Up a Scrap" and "Orozco Warns Juárez He Is Going: Says He Withdraws Protection for All Who Fail to Join Him in Fighting." Due to his impaired eyesight, Steever was forced to retire in 1913. "Col. Scott a Brigadier: West Point Ex-head Obtains Promotion on Steever's Retirement," *New York Times*, March 23, 1913.

170. Colonel Edgar Z. Steever to Adjutant General, Army, telegram, July 30, 1912, AG1940278, records of the Adjutant General's Office, 1890–1917, national archives record group 94, United States National Archives, Washington, DC (hereafter cited as AG 1940278, National Archives). National Archives Records were taken from Eva Jane Robeson Papers, (MS 007) Letters 1959–1960, Archives and Special Collections Department, Rio Grande Historical Collections, New Mexico State University Library.

171. Hatch, *Colonia Juárez*, 188.

172. Quartermaster-General, U. S. Army, to Adjutant General of the Army, 30 July 1912, AG 1940278, National Archives.

173. "Concert in Honor of the Refugees," *El Paso Herald*, July 30,

1912, 2, notes, "In honor of the refugees who are in El Paso . . . the 22d infantry band will give a special program in Cleveland square. The program . . . has been arranged by C. F. Waddington." This article also lists nine musical numbers which were to be performed. See also Henry, "El Paso: Sanctuary to Mormon Refugees," 1E.

174. "Colonists are Riding North," 1. Eva Jane Robeson, "The Mormon Exodus From Mexico in 1912 and the Subsequent Settlement in Southern New Mexico" (master's thesis, New Mexico State University, 1960), 13–14, observes, "Since all the incoming refugees would more than fill the shed, the Chamber of Commerce opened a large three story brick building, the Reckhart Building at Main and Putnam Streets, as housing for the remainder." Robeson also notes that the Reckhart Building was a former dance hall. On temporary lodging in the Reckhart building. See also "Red Flaggers Drive Americans from Their Mexican Homes," *El Paso Morning Times,* 1.

175. Robeson, "Mormon Exodus," 17; "Orozco Expected to Burn Juárez Before He Evacuates the Town," *Deseret Evening News*, August 3, 1912, 1. Timmons, *El Paso*, 306, describes the military tradition at El Paso since its establishment in 1854 until the time of the Mexican Revolution: "It served as a frontier outpost during most of the nineteenth century, then as an infantry garrison in the 1890s. Cavalry regiments were added during the Mexican Revolution."

176. Edgar Z. Steever to Adjutant General, Army, telegram, August 12, 1912, AG 1940278, National Archives.

177. "Fort Bliss News," *El Paso Morning Times*, August 3, 1912, 5. The article further states, "They are built for two persons each, but can accommodate three without much crowding. They are equipped with front and rear flaps so that they can be made rain proof."

178. Kerr, Adjutant General, to Commanding Officer, Fort Bliss, Texas, July 31, 1912, AG 1940278, National Archives.

179. Edgar Z. Steever to Adjutant General, Army, telegram, August 12, 1912, AG 1940278, National Archives.

180. Commissary General, Memorandum for the Chief of Staff, July 31, 1912, AG 1940278, National Archives.

181. See Robeson, "Mormon Exodus," 18.

182. Mryl Rowley Day, interview by Christine Day Young, February 19, 1978, transcript, 18, CHL.

183. El Paso Relief Minutes, 1, CHL. Taylor, "Record of the Exodus," 21–34, is also a good source to supplement these Relief Minutes. Both are provided in full in the appendices.

184. "Prest. Jos. E. Robinson leaves for El Paso," *Deseret Evening News*, July 31, 1912, 1; "Leaves for El Paso," *Deseret Evening News*, July 31, 1912, 5.

185. In Romney, *Mormon Colonies in Mexico*, 219–20.

186. "Assisting Refugees," *Deseret Evening News*, July 30, 1912, 2.

187. Relief Minutes, 2. This generous offer to allow the Relief Committee to meet at the American National Bank Building was made under the direction of T. M. Wingo, who was then serving as the bank's president. See *Worley's Directory of El Paso, 1912*, 112.

188. Ibid., 1.

189. Ibid.

190. "Colonists Express Their Thanks to Citizens," *El Paso Morning Times*, August 2, 1912, 1. The committee of five LDS Church leaders who signed the letter included A. W. Ivins, H. E. Bowman, O. P. Brown, Jos. E. Robinson, and Guy C. Wilson. It is probable that A. W. Ivins was the person who penned the letter inasmuch as he presided over the committee and provided the first signature. See also the same letter of gratitude in "Thanks of the Mormons," *El Paso Herald*, August 1, 1912, 5.

191. Relief Minutes, 3.

192. Ibid.

193. Ibid., 4.

194. Ibid., 9. The Mexico North-Western Railway office was located in Ciudad Juárez, just across the border from El Paso. Their general manager at this time was H. C. Ferris. See *Worley's Directory of El Paso, 1912*, 41.

195. Ibid., 13.

196. Ibid., 17, 24.

197. Ibid. 32.

198. Romney, *Mormon Colonies in Mexico*, 220, notes, "Two Mormon families remained behind in the colonies at the time of the exodus deeming the move from the country unnecessary. One of the families at Colonia Dublán and the other one at Colonia Pacheco. The [Stevens] family at Colonia Pacheco particularly felt secure under the shadow of the lofty peaks of the Sierras." However, William G. Hartley and Lorna Call Alder, *Anson Bowen Call: Bishop of Colonia Dublán* (Provo: Lorna Call Alder, 2007), 258, note that there were also other LDS families who chose to remain in Mexico at the time of the 1912 exodus: "Several [Mormon] colonists stayed in Mexico, including Alma Spilsbury, Byron McDonald, and John Allen in Colonia Juárez; the Franklin Spencer family of Dublán; the Joshua Stevens family of Pacheco; and Milton [Meliton] G. Trejo of Chuichupa."

199. Relief Minutes, 29–32.

200. Ibid., 33. See also "El Paso Branch Minutes" (1912), 16, CHL.

201. Ibid., 39.

202. Ibid., 39–40.

203. El Paso Branch Minutes, 16, CHL. Thanks to Mike Mullen for bringing this source to the author's attention.

204. "Colonists Leaving Refugee Camps for Places of Safety Elsewhere," *Deseret Evening News*, August 2, 1912, 1.

205. H. I. Miller to Dr. F. S. Pearson, September 12, 1912, University of Texas at El Paso.

206. "Creel's Business With Refugees," *El Paso Morning Times*, August 2, 1912, 10. Charles E. McClellan recalled, "A very few had a little money and rented rooms for a short time, while fewer still were sent for by relatives or friends in Utah, Arizona, or Idaho who had heard of the situation." Charles E. McClellan, in *Treasures of Pioneer History*, 3:242.

207. Miner and Kimball, *Camilla*, 31–32.

208. Ibid., 32.

209. Lucille R. Taylor, interview by Joseph B. Romney, November 27, 1970, Colonia Dublán, transcript, 6, California State University–Fullerton, Oral History Program.

210. Claudius Bowman III, in Hatch and Hardy, *Stalwarts South of the Border*, 57.

211. Ruby S. Brown, in Hatch and Hardy, *Stalwarts South of the Border*, 71.

212. Lola Allred, in Hatch and Hardy, *Stalwarts South of the Border*, 15.

213. Sarah Geneva W. Richardson, in Hatch and Hardy, *Stalwarts South of the Border*, 762.

214. Henry, "El Paso: Sanctuary to Mormon refugees," 1E.

215. Turley, interview.

216. Joseph F. Smith, in Conference Report, October 1912, 3.

217. Ibid., 7.

218. Ibid., 5.

219. "Flight Means Great Loss to Mormons," *El Paso Herald*, July 30, 1912, 12, notes that this figure was calculated by the presiding

bishop of the LDS Church, who estimated that for seven to eight hundred families in the region, "the average individual property of each family, including improvments, water rights and stock [was] $10,000.00. . . . Meeting houses and other buildings of the church in Mexico [were] said to be worth $145,000." The presiding bishopric member was probably O. P. Miller, who had been sent by the Church to assist the refugees. Parley P. Jones, interview by Eva Jane Robeson, January 29, 1960, transcript, 1, Archives and Special Collections Department, Rio Grande Historical Collections, New Mexico State University Library, notes that "numerous attempts were made to claim redress from the Mexican Government and in some small degrees some small payments were received. Generally speaking, however, people received very little from what they owned in Old Mexico." In September 1935, the US Special Mexican Claims Commission began accepting claims from American citizens who lost property in Mexico between 1910 and 1920. In 1936, Mary L. N. Clayson, widow of Eli A. Clayson, filed a claim with the Special Mexican Claims Commission for the loss of property in Colonia Juárez at the time of the 1912 exodus. The claim included "land, buildings, fences, furniture, growing crops, fruit trees, fruit, household effects and supplies, grain, cattle, poultry, stock investment, saddle, horses, income, rent and expenses," totaling $24,074. Special Mexican Claims Commission, "Memorial and Deposition of Mary L. N. Clayson in behalf of Claimant," 3, in possession of author who thanks Irene McAllister for providing a copy of this document. For details on the special commission, see Louis W. McKernan, "Special Mexican Claims," *The American Journal of International Law* 32, no. 3 (July 1938), 457–66.

220. Fernando Gomez, interview by the author and Martin L. Andersen, February 22, 2012, Mormon Mexican History Museum, Provo, UT. Of the nine major Mormon colonies in northern Mexico, two of those in Chihuahua remain active: Colonia Dublán and Colonia Díaz. See http://en.wikipedia.org/wiki/Mormon_colonies_in_Mexcio.

221. "Mormon Chapel," *El Paso Herald*, February 22, 1975, 3. This chapel is still used by the Latter-day Saint community in El Paso.

222. Mike Mullen, interview by the author and Martin L. Andersen, February 12, 2012, LDS Douglas Street Chapel, El Paso.

223. Karl Murphy, interview by the author and Martin L. Andersen, February 19, 2012, Mount Franklin Stake Center, El Paso. Murphy serves as the president of the Mount Franklin Stake.

224. President Henry B. Eyring, interview.

SELECTED BIBLIOGRAPHY

BOOKS

Arrington, Leonard J., and Davis Bitton. *The Mormon Experience: A History of the Latter-day Saints.* New York: Alfred A. Knopf, 1979.

Bentley, Joseph T. *Life and Letters of Joseph C. Bentley: A Biography.* Provo, UT: Joseph T. Bentley, 1977.

Card, Brigham Y., ed. *The Mormon Presence in Canada.* Edmonton: University of Alberta Press, 1990.

Carter, Kate B., comp. *Treasures of Pioneer History.* Salt Lake City: Daughters of Utah Pioneers, 1954.

Cumberland, Charles Curtis. *Mexican Revolution: Genesis under Madero.* Austin: University of Texas Press, 1952.

Davis, Ray Jay. "Antipolygamy Legislation." In *Encyclopedia of Mormonism*, edited by Daniel H. Ludlow. New York: Macmillan, 1992.

García, Mario T. *Desert Immigrants: The Mexicans of El Paso, 1880–1920.* New Haven, CT: Yale University Press, 1981.

Garner, Paul. *Porfirio Díaz: Profiles in Power*. London: Longman, 2001.

Hart, John Mason. *Revolutionary Mexico: The Coming and Process of the Mexican Revolution*. Berkeley: University of California Press, 1987.

Hartley, William G., and Lorna Call Alder. *Anson Bowen Call: Bishop of Colonia Dublán*. Provo: Lorna Call Alder, 2007.

Hatch, Nelle Spilsbury. *Colonia Juárez: An Intimate Account of a Mormon Village*. Salt Lake City: Deseret Book, 1954.

———, and B. Carmon Hardy, eds. *Stalwarts South of the Border*. California: n. p., 1985.

Hilliard, George. *Adios Hachita: Stories of a New Mexico Town*. Silver City, NM: High Lonesome Books, 1998.

Hunter, Milton R. *Brigham Young the Colonizer*. 4th ed. rev. Salt Lake City: Peregrine Smith, 1973.

Johnson, Annie R. *Heartbeats of Colonia Díaz*. Salt Lake City: Publishers Press, 1972.

Jones, Daniel W. *Forty Years among the Indians: A True Yet Thrilling Narrative of the Author's Experience among the Natives*. Salt Lake City: Juvenile Instructor Office, 1890.

Journal of Discourses. 26 vols. London: Latter-day Saints' Book Depot, 1854–86.

Katz, Friedrich. *The Life and Times of Pancho Villa*. Stanford, CA: Stanford University Press, 1998.

Macdonald, Taylor O. *Jess and Hazel Taylor: A Borderland Family History*. Salt Lake: n. p., 1998.

Meyer, Michael C. *Mexican Rebel: Pascual Orozco and the Mexican Revolution, 1910–1915*. Lincoln: University of Nebraska Press, 1967.

Miner, Caroline Eyring, and Edward L. Kimball. *Camilla: A Biography of Camilla Eyring Kimball.* Salt Lake City: Deseret Book, 1980.

Peterson, Thomas A., ed. *John A. Whetten, Pioneer, Patriarch: Including sketches of his wives Ida Elizabeth Jesperson, Martha Elizabeth Carling, Drusilla Sorenson.* Mesa, AZ: John A. Whetten Genealogy Committee, 2001.

Pusey, Merlo J. *Builders of the Kingdom: George A. Smith, John Henry Smith, George Albert Smith.* Provo, UT: Brigham Young University Press, 1981.

Romney, Thomas Cottam. *The Mormon Colonies in Mexico.* Salt Lake City: University of Utah Press, 1938.

Taylor, Harold W., comp. *Memories of Militants and Mormon Colonists in Mexico.* Shumway Family History Services, 1992.

Timmons, W. H. *El Paso: A Borderlands History.* El Paso: Texas Western Press, 1990.

Tullis, F. Lamond. *Mormons in Mexico: The Dynamics of Faith.* Logan: Utah State University Press, 1987.

Turley, Clarence F., and Anna Tenney Turley. *History of the Mormon Colonies in Mexico (The Juárez Stake), 1885–1980.* 2nd ed. Salt Lake City: Publishers Press, 1996.

Whetten, LaVon Brown. *Colonia Juárez: Commemorating 125 Years of the Mormon Colonies in Mexico.* Bloomington, IN: AuthorHouse, 2010.

Whipple, Willard. "The Life of Willard Whipple." Unpublished manuscript, 1977.

Worley's Directory of El Paso Texas, 1912. Dallas: John F. Worley Directory Co., 1912.

Young, Karl E. *Ordeal in Mexico: Tales of Danger and Hardship*

Collected from the Mormon Colonists. Salt Lake City: Deseret Book, 1968.

———. *The Long Hot Summer of 1912: Episodes in the Flight of the Mormon Colonists from Mexico*. Provo, UT: Brigham Young University Press, 1967.

ARTICLES AND PAPERS

Bentley, Joseph C., Marion T. Bentley, and Joseph Ivins Bentley. "'Our Hearts Were Touched by Fire': Bishop Joseph C. Bentley and Families in the Mexican Revolution." Presented to the Mormon History Association, Tucson, AZ, May 16–19, 2002.

Hardy, B. Carmon. "Cultural 'Encystment' as a Cause of the Mormon Exodus from Mexico in 1912." *Pacific Historical Review* 34, no. 4 (November 1965): 439–54.

Hardy, B. Carmon, and Melody Seymour. "The Importation of Arms and the 1912 Mormon 'Exodus' from Mexico." *New Mexico Historical Review* 72, no. 4 (1997): 297–318.

Jamieson, Perry. "A Survey History of Fort Bliss, 1890–1940." Historic and Natural Resources Report No. 5, Cultural Resources Management Program, Directorate of Environment, United States Army Air Defense Artillery Center. Fort Bliss, TX: 1993.

Landon, Michael N. "'We Navigated by Pure Understanding': Bishop George T. Sevey's Account of the 1912 Exodus from Mexico." *BYU Studies* 43, no. 2 (2004): 63–101.

McKernan, Louis W. "Special Mexican Claims." *American Journal of International Law* 32, no. 3 (July 1938): 457–66.

Morgan, Brandon. "Mormon Colonists' Image of Pancho Villa." *New Mexico Historical Review* 85, no. 2 (Spring 2012): 109–29.

Romney, Junius. "Remarks . . . made in the Rose Park Stake Priesthood meeting . . . July 13, 1966." Typescript.

Romney, Joseph Barnard. "'The Lord, God of Israel, Brought Us Out of Mexico!': Junius Romney and the 1912 Mormon Exodus." *Journal of Mormon History* 36, no. 4 (Fall 2010): 208–58.

AUDIO INTERVIEWS

California State University–Fullerton Oral History Program:

- Bluth, Agnes Scott, by Joseph B. Romney, August 30, 1971.
- Call, Charles, by Joseph Romney, August 29, 1971.
- Judd, Helaman, by Joseph B. Romney, August 31, 1971.
- Taylor, Lucille R., by Joseph B. Romney, November 27, 1970.
- Wood, Enos, by Joseph B. Romney, August 31, 1974.

L. Tom Perry Special Collections, Harold B. Lee Library, Brigham Young University:

- Brown, David, by Karl E. Young, December 21, 1962.
- Lunt, Heaton, by Karl E. Young, December 17, 1962.
- Nielson, Ernest O., by Karl E. Young, March 13, 1962.
- O'Donnal, Frank and Annie, by Karl E. Young, December 26, 1962.
- Pierce, Arwell L., by Karl E. Young, February 22, 1963.
- Whetten, James Elbert, by Karl E. Young, March 5, 1962.

Charles Redd Center for Western Studies, Brigham Young University, LDS Polygamy Oral History Project:

- Taylor, Hazel Richardson, by Ivan Carbine, November 9, 1959.
- Taylor, Jesse M., by Ivan Carbine, November 10, 1959.

University of Utah and California State College at Fullerton Mormon Colonies Project:

- Turley, Clarence, by Joe Romney, November 30, 1970.
- Walser, William, by Joe Romney, August 18, 1971.

Archives and Special Collections Department, Rio Grande Historical Collections, New Mexico State University Library:

- Jones, Parley P., by Eva Jane Robeson, January 29, 1960.

Church History Library, The Church of Jesus Christ of Latter-day Saints, Salt Lake City:

- Day, Mryl Rowley, by Christine Day Young, February 19, 1978.

Private possession of Ivan and Helen Carbine, Provo, UT:

- Bentley, Maude Taylor, 1959
- McClellan, Cal and Arson, 1964
- Richardson, Ray, 1959
- Romney, Junius, 1961
- Shumway, Elva Richardson, 1961
- Skousen, Ida Walser, 1959
- Skousen, Louise Whipple, 1959
- Telford, John, circa 1960

Private possession of Taylor Macdonald, Pleasant Grove, UT

- Macdonald, Ross, 1978, 1990.
- Macdonald, Sadie T., 1991
- Nixon, Charlotte Macdonald, 1986

NEWSPAPERS

Deseret Evening News. "Assisting Refugees." July 30, 1912.

———. "Colonists Leaving Refugee Camps for Places of Safety Elsewhere." August 2, 1912.

———. "Leaves for El Paso." July 31, 1912.

———. "'Mormons' Flee from Mexico." July 29, 1912.

———. "Orozco Expected to Burn Juárez Before He Evacuates the Town." August 3, 1912.

———. "Prest. Jos. E. Robinson Leaves for El Paso." July 31, 1912.

———. "Protesting Against Outrages." July 31, 1912.

———. "Refugees Are Fleeing North." July 30, 1912.

———. "Refugees from Colonies in Mexico Being Given Every Possible Comfort." August 1, 1912.

El Paso Herald. "Arms Taken from Americans by Rebels." July 29, 1912.

———. "Reading Matter for Refugees Wanted," July 31, 1912.

———. "Mormon Refugees Given Assistance," July 30, 1912.

———. "Refugees Housed In Lumber Sheds," July 30, 1912.

———. "Flight Means Great Loss To Mormons," July 30, 1912.

———. "Three Babes Born on Road." July 31, 1912, 1.

———. "Mormon Chapel." February 22, 1975.

El Paso Morning Times. "Creel's Business with Refugees." August 2, 1912.

———. "Heart Rending Recital Given." July 30, 1912.

———. "More Refugees Have Arrived," August 1, 1912.

———. "Red Flaggers Drive Americans from their Mexican Homes." July 29, 1912.

Henry, Pat. "El Paso: Sanctuary to Mormon refugees." *El Paso Times*, February 5, 1984.

New York Times. "Col. Scott a Brigadier: West Point ex-Head Obtains Promotion on Steever's Retirement." March 23, 1913.

THESES AND DISSERTATIONS

Geilman, Matthew G. "Taking the Gospel to the Lamanites: Doctrinal Foundations for Establishing The Church of Jesus Christ of Latter-day Saints in Mexico." Master's thesis, Brigham Young University, 2011.

Hardy, Blaine Carmon. "The Mormon Colonies of Northern Mexico: A History, 1885–1912." PhD diss., Wayne State University, 1963.

Hill, Stephen. "Politics and Polygamy in Northern Mexico: Porfirio Díaz and Mormon Colonization, 1885–1912." Master's thesis, Tulane University, 1993.

Smith, Bill L. "Impacts of the Mexican Revolution: The Mormon Experience, 1910–1946." PhD diss., Washington State University, 2000.

Romney, Joseph Barnard. "The Exodus of the Mormon Colonists from Mexico, 1912." Master's thesis, University of Utah, 1967.

Robeson, Eva Jane. "The Mormon Exodus From Mexico in 1912 and the Subsequent Settlement in Southern New Mexico." Master's thesis, New Mexico State University, 1960.

UNPUBLISHED HISTORIES

Juárez Stake High Council Historical Record, 1895–1903. Church History Library, The Church of Jesus Christ of Latter-day Saints, Salt Lake City.

"Juarez Stake Relief Committee Minutes." Church History Library, The Church of Jesus Christ of Latter-day Saints, Salt Lake City.

Taylor, Alonzo. "Record of the Exodus of the Mormon Colonies from Mexico in 1912." Church History Library, The Church of Jesus Christ of Latter-day Saints, Salt Lake City.

"The Mormons in El Paso del Norte: History of the Members of The Church of Jesus Christ of Latter-day Saints in the Juárez-El Paso Bi-national Community (1876–2000)." L. Tom Perry Special Collections, Harold B. Lee Library, Brigham Young University.

Walser, John Jacob. "My Life." Compiled by Bonnie Simon. L. Tom Perry Special Collections, Harold B. Lee Library, Brigham Young University.

INDEX

Italicized page numbers refer to images.

A

Abegg, Eli 153
Adams, Loren 201
Aguaje station 247
Alamo Hueco 159
Alanis, Colonel 151
Alder, Lorna Call 57, 58, 59, 253, 254
Allan, John 155, 156, 157, 158, 224
Allred, Byron Harvey 38, 173, 269
Allred, Calvert A. 246
Allred, Calvert Lorenzo 49
Alvarez, Melquiades 148, 150, 161
American National Bank 41, *45*, 45 159, 205
Andersen, Martin L. xii
Apaches 177
Arizona. *See* migration, Arizona
arms 76, 86, 124, 135
Arrington, Leonard J. 254
Arroyo Seco 247
Aultman, Otis, images: 10, 17, 25, 26, 36, 39–42, 45

B

babies 26, 37–38, 58, 103, 106, 131, 176, 190, 270
Bautista, Juan 148
Bavispe River 8
Beecroft, John 156, 186, 215, 265
Bench, Susie 142
Bennion, S. O. 185, 187
Bentley, Joseph C. 17, *20*, 20 145
  on returning to colonies 179, 185, 196, 198, 206, 239
  record of exodus 145, 148, 151, 152–55, 164–66, 168, 176–177
Bentley, Joseph T. 17
Bingham, John 155, 265
Black, David P. 111, 157–58
Black, Ed 155
Black, William Morley 38, 41, 111
Bluth, Agnes Scott 11
Bluth, Oscar 181
Boca Grande 202
Book of Mormon 6, 74, 90, 255, 256
Bowman, Demar 247

Bowman, Henry Eyring *39*, 39, 44, 49, 176, 182, 190
Brannan, Samuel 79
Brizzee, Henry W. 255
Brown, David A. 165, 178, 233
Brown, David Brigham 49
Brown, Galbraith 180
Brown, Orson Pratt 19, 35, *35* 44, 172, 199, 202, 205, 209, 260
Brown, Sam 31

C

cabdrivers 70, 94, 268
Calcido, Major 150
Call, Anson B.
  and leaving colonies 23, 119, 155, 165, 265
  commissary work 187, 233, 238–239, 246, 249
  family life of 58
  meeting secretary 231
Call, Charles 23
Call, Julia Abegg 58
Call, Willard 163, 176, 187
Canada 8, 168
Carbine, Helen xi, 24
Carroll, James 165
Casas Grandes
  as gathering place 8, 77
  evacuation from 28, 65
  garrison stationed at 166, 179, 182, 196–98, 211
  military in 146, 223, 235, 247, 248
  rations at 195
  travel to 212–13, 216
Casas Grandes River 95
Castillo, Maximo 148, 150, 153, 161
Catholic 75, 78
Cavada, Felipe A. 148, 150, 152–54, 161
cavalry 42, 149, 272
Cavalry 274
cemetery 8, 81
Cervantes, Candelario 217
Chamber of Commerce *10*, 39, 269, 274
Chavez, Felipe 154, 219
Chico station 26, 86, 199
Chihuahua
  evacuation from 28, 45–46, 116, 118, 174, 178
  evacuation order 10
  modern colonies of 278
  on returning to 182, 189, 211, 212, 233
  rebels in 15, 19, 64, 67, 146
  settlement of 2, 6, 8–10, *9*, 60, 61, 72
Church in Mexico 80, 136
citizenship, Mexican 258
Ciudad Juárez 10, 94–96, 103, 109, 123, 181, 211
claims, for lost property 160, 188–89, 192, 235, 238, 278
Clayson, B. A. 165
Clayson, Ed 155
Clayson, Eli A. 148, 152–53, 155, 278
Clayson, Mary L. N. 278
Cluff, Hyrum Albert 21, 165
Colonia Chuichupa
  colonists in El Paso 238, 240
  evacuation from 26, 31–33, 86, 87, 156, 165, 178
  life in 87–88
  on returning to 49, 233–34
  rebels in 156, 229
  settlement of 8, *9*

Colonia Díaz
- conditions at 240, 249
- evacuation from 33–34
- forces around 116
- rebels in 230
- returning to 187, 201, 211
- settlement of 8, *9*, 11

Colonia Dublán
- evacuation from 20, 23, 28, 30–31, 58, 93, 104, 152
- rebels in 20
- returning to 47, 59
- settlement of 8, *9*

Colonia García 8, *9*, 24, 26, 152, 215

Colonia Juárez
- conditions in 13, 75, 239
- evacuation from 30, 31, 93, 104, 147, 148, 162, 175
- leadership of 41
- life in 109
- on returning to 139, 204, 210, 213, 228, 229, 234, 239
- rebels in 17, 21, 153, 175
- settlement of 8–9, *9*, 11, 13

Colonia Morelos
- defense of 166, 180
- evacuation from 187, 202, 204, 208–9, 234
- rebels in 209, 234, 259
- settlement of 8, *9*

Colonia Oaxaca 8, 10, 257

Colonia Pacheco
- conditions in 240
- evacuation from 31, 156, 162, 165
- on returning to 47, 215, 217, 219, 221–22, 224, 248
- rebels in 152, 175
- settlement of 8, *9*,

Colonia San Jose, 8, *9*, 186, 204

colonies 83, 89, 61, 92, 156

colorados 16, 62

Columbus, New Mexico 34, 95, 249

Concordia Cemetery 81

Congress 4, 42, 44

Cooperative Mercantile Institution 9

Corner, the, New Mexico 34

counter-revolutionaries 124

Creel, Juan B. 49

Croft, B. L. 195

cultivate 179, 213

culture 9, 11

D

dances 11, 21, 108, 239, 274

danger 92
- in returning 166, 241, 246
- threats from rebels and 228–29, 235

Darton, James B. 215

Day, Myrl Rowley 44

death
- by execution 150, 161, 223, 227
- of colonists 38, 180, 216, 219, 228
- of Mexicans 248
- threats 18, 149–50, 162

Deseret Evening News 28, 37, 48

Díaz, Porfirio 7, 10, *10*, 16, 79, 83–85, 113, 122–23, 125, 133–34

Dog Springs, New Mexico 10, 31, 34, 88, 159, 211, 266

Done, Ethel C. 173, 189

Dos Cabezas, Mexico 222

Duncan, Joseph W. 272

E

Edmunds-Tucker Act 4, 5, 75
Edwards, Mr., American consul 174
El Paso
  Church in 99
  culture in 130, 132
  refuge in 1, 141, 267
  state of 127
El Paso and Southwestern Railroad 95
El Paso chapel *53*
El Paso, conditions in 130–31
El Paso dairy 13, 270
El Paso Herald 25, 28, 36, 40, 54, 231
El Paso Morning Times 28, 35–36, 39–40, 43, 45
El Paso, refuge in 96, 98, 100, 112, 119, 127–28, 130, 132, 140
El Paso Union Depot 1, 35–37, *36–37*, 59, 69
El Tigre mines 204, 205
embargo 64, 123
employment 38, 49–50, 127, 140, 179, 184, 187–88, 198, 200, 236
entertainment 130
Escobosa, Colonel 152–53
Europe 7, 85, 127
evacuation 1, 6, 21, 129
  cause of 175, 273
  discussion of 46, 165, 178
  of women and children 23–26, 33, 72, 95, 116, 118, 129, 271
execution. See *death*
exodus
  attitude toward 21, 46, 54, 86, 111, 119, 135 160, 174, 176, 178
  impact of 53, 111, 120, 139
exodus, *continued*
  of women and children 23, 26
  reason for 4, 28, 135
  reception in El Paso 69, 94
  record of 145
  stories about 103
expedition 6, 155, 158, 208, 265
experienced 140
Eylar, A. S. J. 39, 270
Eyring, Camilla 27, 37, 48–49, *48*
Eyring, Caroline Cottam Romney 49
Eyring, Edward Christian 24–25, *24*, 265
  in meeting minutes 165, 202–3, 237, 251
  preparing to leave 150–51, 155, 162–63, 167, 180
Eyring, E. E. 155
Eyring, Henry 116, 138–39
Eyring, Henry B. 54–55, *54*, 72
Eyring, Mary Bommeli 73, 138, 139, 148

F

Fall, A. B. 207
Farnsworth, Deronda V. 176, 189, 193, 235
Farnsworth, Lester B. 165, 197, 200, 214–15, 221, 231, 250
Farnsworth, Mary 214
Farnsworth, Maude Cluff 37
federals 155, 158, 163, 164, 179, 181, 186, 193–94, 211, 223, 231, 236, 245, 249
First Army Division Band 101
Flores Magon brothers 61–62
Fort Bliss 42, 99, 101, 127–28, 130
Frederickson or Fredericksen, Alma 165, 167, 178, 180, 201, 249

G

Galeana 148, 193, 213, 245
Gavelan 222
Gay, Dr. 235, 250
Geilman, Matthew G. 74
Gila River 83
Gomez, Fernando 54, 78
Gonzáles, Andreas 80
Gonzalez, Abraham 215
gospel 6, 76, 78
Grant, Heber J. 188
guns 92
Gutierrez, Captain 152
Guzman, Mexico 166, 236

H

hacendados 65
Hachita, New Mexico *34*
  arms from 200, 204, 208–9
  conditions in 207, 233–34, 238, 240, 249
  government assistance in 43
  horses at 185–86, 190, 198–99, 230
  travel to 32–34, 88, 95, 104
Harris, Eugene 235
Harris, F. H. 251
Harris, Hyrum S. 48, 167, 168, 175–76, 180, 182, 186–87, 200
  and visiting members 237–38, 248
  as photographer 232
  mission to Sonora 189, 202–3
  on returning to colonies 206, 242
Harris, Josephine R. 251
Harris, Martin L. 155, 165, 265
Harris, Richard Parks 251
Hatch, Ernest 148, 154–55
Hatch, John 155
Hatch, Nelle 119
Hawkins, Sam 265
Hawkins, Saul 155
Haws, David 157–58
Haws, George M. 207
Haws, James 156
Haymore, Edward 234
Hillstrom, Brother 157
Hop Valley 218, 221, 234
Huber, Arnold 234
Huerta, General 210, 223, 230, 234, 241, 248
Huish, Ivie 27
Huish, Viva 27
Humphrey, Dayl 155
Humphrey, Fred 155
Hurst, F. H. 37, 163, 165, 176, 202, 209, 241–42, 244
Hurst, Walter Frederick 37

I

International Workers of the World 62
Ivins, Anthony W. *6*, *11*
  and government 196, 197
  and refugee assistance 36, 41, 80, 172–73, 183, 184–85, 270–271
  and relief committee 45, 119, 148, 165–66
  as apostle 16, 159, 255
  as leader of relief committee 119
  as missionary, early colonist 6, 11, 12, 16
  on leaving Mexico 46, 159–60, 162–67, 174–76, 178–179, 181
  on returning to 180–81
  on returning to Mexico 168,

179, 180, 182–83 186–89, 191–92

J

Jackson, Joseph 214
Jacobson, James A. 230
Jameson, Alexander 149, 163, 165, 167, 176–77, 180, 183, 185, 200, 203
Janos River 158
Johnson, Elmer 199
Johnson, Lucy E. 238
Johnson, S. H. 215
Johnson, W. Derby, Jr. 11, 258
Jones, Daniel W. 6, 78, 103, 255
Jones, Edith 250
Jones, F. W. 176, 249–50
Jones, F. W., Jr. 165
Jones, Parley P. 278
Jones, Thomas H. 250
Jones, William, Jr. 155, 265
Juárez, Benito 60, 79
Juarez Stake Academy 9, 80, 88, 92, 140, 172, 180, 259
Judd, Benjamin 238–39, 248

K

Keeler, A.E. 249
Kelly, Charles E. 40, *40*, 70, 99, 101, 130, 269
Kiddney, Patricia 81
Kindrich, Charles W. 13

L

La Ascencion 158, 190, 201, 203, 223, 234–36
Landon, Michael N. 83
Larsen, Neils 247
Lewis, Frank 18, 153, 155
Lillywhite, C. W. 187, 202, 231, 234, 249–50
Lillywhite, Mitchell W. 203, 208, 209
Lincoln, Abraham 4
Llorente, E. C. 160, 189, 197, 201, 205, 230
Longhurst, W. 224
Long's Lumberyard 36–38, 40–43, 48–49, *40*, *42*, 270
Long, Walter 99–100
Loose, Ed 173
lumberyard 59, 70, 99, 107, 129, 131
Lunt, Edgerton 155, 265
Lunt, Edward 215, 217–18

M

Macdonald, Alexander F. 90
Macdonald, Bryan 148
Macdonald, Byron 155
Macdonald, Taylor 90
Madero, Francisco 15, *15*, 17, 19, 62, 64, 85, 114, 122–124, 175, 182, 248, 258, 281
map of Mormon colonies 9
Martineau, Joel H. 117, 202, 215, 224
Masten, Brother 157
McClellan, Charles E. 24, *24*, 173, 185–86, 189, 192, 197, 224, 233–35, 242–43, 277
as secretary 199–209, 229, 231, 234, 236–241, 245–46
McClellan, Ed 176, 265
McClellan, S. E. 154–55, 163, 165–67, 180, 183

McKenzie, Prince G. 95, 263
merchandise, confiscated 17, 149, 194, 214
Merrill, Mary 103–4
Metz, Leon 96
Metz, Mr. 230
Mexican Revolution 1, 16, 60, 67, 259
  causes of 60–62, 122–23, 223
  escaping the 100
  impact of 15, 67, 84–86, 91, 105, 114, 145, 259
  impact on El Paso 96–97, 127, 274
Mexico North Western Railroad Company 28, 46, 47, 186, 189, 190, 200, 232, 242, 246–48, 270
migration
  to Arizona 1, 48, 65, 67, 199, 200, 236, 277
  to California 1, 4, 8
  to Idaho 277
  to New Mexico 1
  to West Texas 67
military 4, 31, 33, 42–43, 46, 55, 127, 128, 168, 211, 248, 272, 274
Miller, H. I. 19, 260, 263, 276
Miller, O. P. 45, 168–69, 173, 181, 185, 187, 191–92, 196, 278
Mirando, Pancho 246
missionary work 5–6, *6*, 11, 74, 77, 78, 89, 103, 133, 136, 256
Moffett, Laura 250
Mormon Battalion 3–4, *3*
Morrill Anti-Bigamy Law 4
Mortensen, Alfredo 249
Mortensen, James 165
Mortensen, Jesse 247
mosquitoes 38, 106–7, 131
Mullen, Michael R. 54, 98, 253, 276, 278
murder 50, 165, 177, 215. See also *death*
Murphy, Karl 55, 279
music 9, 274

N

Nauvoo, Illinois 4, 25, 38, 89
Nephites 6, 74, 77, 155, 256, 265
neutrality, of Americans 16–17, 65, 80, 92, 114, 134–35, 146, 164, 175
Newman Investment Company 230
New Mexico 31, 33–34, 43, 65, 67, 77, 93, 95
Nielson, Ernest 215
Nogales Ranch 201, 203, 223
Nueva Casas Grandes 211–12, 223, 235

O'Donnal, Annie 25
O'Donnell, Lilly 105
Ojitos 151, 158
orchard 121, 194, 225, 226, 228
orchestra 20–21
Orozco, Pascual 16, 17, 62, 64, 85, 88, 114, 122–24, 145, 171, 172, 175, 181, 259, 273, 282
Orr, Billy 247

Pacheco 111

Palomas 190, 195, 235, 236
Palomas Land and Cattle Company Ranch 158
Palotada Creek 158
Palotado 158
Parra, Angel 223
Payne, Ed H. 176, 187
Payne, H. M. 164
Payne, Sarah Jones 27
Pearson 24–26, 28, 59, 93, 106, 119, 147–49, 161, 166, 179, 184, 186, 188, 190, 193–95, 212, 215–219, 222, 235, 247–48, 263, 276
Pearson Company 166, 179
penitentiaries 5, 5, 254
persecution 4, 5, 7, 23, 66, 67, 75, 84, 113, 135
Piedras Verdes River 8
Pierce, Arwell L. 36
pioneers 25, 75, 80–81, 87, 112, 253
Pittard, Dana J. H. 100
Place, Joe 247
plays 108
polygamy 4, 5–8, 66, 74, 86, 106, 131, 133, 137, 254
Ponce, Demetrio 150–51, 163, 177
Ponce, Lino 161, 193
Ponce, Luis 148, 150
Porter, Catherine Aurelia Carling 23
Porter, Joseph 215, 228
Porter, Omni 156, 215, 219, 228, 265
Pratt, Gerald 102
Pratt, Helaman 102–3
Pratt, Ira 155, 265
Pratt, Orson 6
Pratt, Parley P. 102
Pratt, Rey L. 102, 165, 181, 247
Pratt, Vera Whetten 105
prayer 48, 58, 76, 161, 165, 241, 242
preaching 6, 11, 76, 133, 181
priesthood 21, 54, 80, 92, 182, 187, 243
prisoners 5, 5, 42, 47, 148, 153, 158, 229, 234, 247, 272

Q

Quevedo, Silvestre 247

R

railroad 65, 85, 93, 103, 109, 116, 189, 210, 212, 220, 231, 232, 272
Reckhart Building 274
Redd, George E. 148
red flaggers 28, 62, 76, 92, 193, 216, 218, 245, 263, 274
redress 51, 165, 278
relief committee 44–47, 73, 118, 120, 270, 271
Relief Society 9, 250
Richardson, Charles Edmund 93
Richardson, Edmund A. 148, 201
rifles. See *arms.*
Riggs, B. B. 239
Rio Grande 42, 44, 49, 59, 126, 130, 131
Roberson, Mr. 230
Robinson, James H. 190
Robinson, John 204
Robinson, Joseph E. 44, 165, 172, 173, 177, 182, 184, 186, 187, 192, 197, 198
Rodriguez, Balderamo R. 201
Rodriguez, Jesús José 18
Rojas, Antonio 124

Romero, José María 7
Romney, Anna Lucile 108
Romney, Annie M. 214
Romney, Eldon 120
Romney, Eugene 150, 155, 224
Romney, E. V. 200, 204, 230, 234, 240, 249
Romney, Florence Black 111
Romney, Gaskell 155, 165, 235, 239, 242–44, 265
Romney, George S. 152, 155, 176, 180, 241–42, 245, 247, 265
Romney, George W. 54, 136
Romney, Joseph B. 113, 171, 257
Romney, Junius *19*
  and relief committee 183, 190, 197, 231, 233, 249, 250
  and stake records 87–88, 142–43
  as stake president 108, 142, 168, 171
  character of 58, 114
  conflicts with rebels 17, 19, 76, 116, 135, 146
  letters 195, 210, 223
  on evacuating 33, 85–86, 88, 92, 161, 163
  on leaving 164, 175, 176
  on relief committee 192
  on returning 167, 180
  treatment of others 160, 162
Romney, Miles A. 47, 150–51, 155, 187, 189, 195–96, 265
Romney, Mitt 136
Romney, Orin N. 214
Romney, Park 119
Romney, Thomas C. 165, 183, 201, 242–43
Romo, David 122

S

Salazar, José Inés *17*
  as rebel leader 58, 62, 64, 92, 122–24, 195, 273
Salazar, José Inés, *continued*
  at Nogales Ranch 203, 223
  dealing with Mormons 16–17, 19–20, 28, 34, 47, 65–66, 88, 135, 146–48, 152
  demands arms 17, 20, 76, 86, 116, 175
  leader at Nogales 201
  relationship with Mormons 16
  threats 129, 149, 160–162, 178, 190
Salcido, Major 150, 152
Salt Lake City 76, 103, 116, 136, 236, 250, 254, 271
Salt Lake Valley 4, 8, 25, 83, 266
San Jacinto Plaza 41, 130
Sanjinez, General 193, 196, 198, 204, 211–12, 216, 229, 234, 241
San Pedro, Mexico 200, 202
San Pedro River 83
Sargent, Bernie 126
Sargent, Melissa 129
Schaeffer, Rulon 246
Schofield, Maude T. 33–34
Scott, R. L. 155, 157
settlement 90, 134, 135, 136, 137
  in Casas Grandes 134
Sevey, George Thomas 26, 28, 29, 32, 86, 87, 88, 89, 200, 264
Sierra Madre 117, 126
Sirmans, C. L. 267
Skousen, Daniel 152, 155, 163, 165, 176, 189
Skousen, James 163, 176, 243
Skousen, J. W., Jr. 165
Skousen, Louise Whipple 25, *25*
Skousen, P. N. 232

Smith, Henry Lunt 239
Smith, Jesse 157–58
Smith, Joseph 7
Smith, Joseph F. 45, 50, *50*, 210, 241
Smoot, Reed 19, 188, 196, 199, 204, 233, 260
Snow, Erastus 6
soldiers
  American 31, 43–44 101, 118, 159, 193, 234, 266
  federal 85, 179, 211, 217–18, 219, 259
  rebel 17, 30, 85, 116, 129, 150–1, 153, 269
Sonora 186, 202
Sosa, Juan 18, 262
Soto, Marco 190
Sousa, John Phillip 127
Spencer, Josiah 193, 245
Spilsbury, A. P. 155, 158, 215, 224
Stair Canyon *30*, 142
Stairs, the *30*, 31–32, 87–88, 117, 118, 152, 154–56, 162, 264
stake records *30*, 31, 88, 142–43
Steever, Edgar Z. 42–44, 100–1, 188, 204–5, 208–9, 239, 273
Steiner, Bishop 178
Stemer, J. E. 165
Stevens, Joshua W. 47, 215–6, 219, 220, 222, 224, 245, 276
Stocks, F. M. 155, 265
Stout, David 240
Stowell, Brigham 163, 165, 176, 180, 216, 223–24
Stowell, Rhoda 224

T

Taft, William H. 41, 207, 273
Talamantes, Porfirio 212–3
Tamez, Jared 133
Tapicita 32, *32*
Taylor, Adelbert 157–58, 187, 200
Taylor, A. L. 153
Taylor, Alonzo L. 119, 145, 155, 164, 188–89, 191, 193, 196, 264–66
Taylor, E. G. 205
Taylor, Harvey 157–58
Taylor, Hazel Richardson 19, 28, 38
Taylor, Jesse M. 18, 26
Taylor, John 7, *7*, 79, 134
Taylor, Loren 155, 265
Taylor, Lucille R. 36, 49
Tellez, Joaquin 197, 199–200, 203, 211–12, 241
Temple Hill 32
temples 54, 77, 80, 220
Tenney, Ammon M. 149, 157, 164–65, 176, 179–80
Tenney, Ammon M., Jr. 31
Tenney, Levi 249
Tenney, N. C. 155, 208, 265
tent city 34, 43–44, 188, 200, 202–3, 236, 271
tents 99, 109, 120, 130
Thatcher, Arizona 43, 200, 240
Thatcher, Moses 6, 10, 76, 79, 84, 133
Thayne, Nephi W. 155, 265
Thede, Mr. 166
thieving 201, 228, 245
threat, colonization as a 134
Thurber, Albert D.
  and condition of horses 185, 190
  and relief committee 164–65, 208–9
  as commander of expedition 142, 155, 265
  on conditions in colonies 147, 228, 232, 240, 247–48

on leaving colonies 47, 104, 164, 175–77
Thurber, Albert D., *continued*
on returning to colonies 182, 184, 198, 208
tithing 9, 152, 168
Trejo, Meliton G. 255, 276
Treviso, Juan 148
Tucson, Arizona 187, 230
Turley, Clarence 108–10
Turley, Edward F. 109, 153, 155
Turley, Edward Vernon 50, 140
Turley, Isaac 8, 138
Turley, Richard E., Jr. 50, 137
Turley, Vernon 109

U

underground 5, 254
Unique Theater 40, *41*, 270
Utah, migration to and from 1, 4–6, 8, 34, 45, 48, 59, 67, 83, 172, 236, 251, 277

V

Veater, Howard 233
Villa, Francisco "Pancho" 16, 58, 62, 122–24, 253, 282, 284

W

Waddington, C. F. 43, 274
Wall, John Edward 87, 142
Wall, John Edward, images: 29–30, 32–34
Wall, John Ray 142
Walser, Alma 148
Walser, John Jacob 21, *21*, 75, 148, 164–67, 176, 179–80, 260
Walser, William 155
War Department 42–44, 188, 199, 205, 272–73
weapons 134
Whetten, John A. 24, 156, 265
Whetten, J. T. 165
Whetten, Lily O'Donnell 38, 104, 106
Whipple, Brigham Young 29, 49
Whipple, Willard 21, 28, 50
Wilson, Guy C.
and relief committee 44, 165, 172–73, 184, 189, 192, 202, 205, 208–9, 231, 233, 235–36, 241, 250
on leaving colonies 164, 168, 176
on returning 180, 183
on returning to colonies 167, 182, 197, 243
regarding arms 146, 199
Wilson, John W. 155, 163, 165, 176, 234
Wingo, T. M. 271
Wobblies, See *International Workers of the World*
Woffinden, Vaneese Harris 24
Wood, Enos 25

Y

Yaqui Indians 78, 196
Young, Brigham 5, 77, 90, 133
Young, Brigham, Jr. 10, 79

Z

Zion 7, 137
Zion's Cooperative Mercantile Institution (ZCMI) 9

About the Author

FRED E. WOODS IS A professor of Church history and doctrine at Brigham Young University. He held a Richard L. Evans Chair of Religious Understanding from 2005 to 2010, during which time he sought opportunities to build bridges with other cultures and faiths. Professor Woods has lectured extensively in the United States and internationally and has been a visiting professor at several universities. His main area of research is Mormon migration in the nineteenth century, and he is the author of a number of books and scores of articles on this topic. Dr. Woods is the originator, editor, and compiler of the *Mormon Immigration Index* CD. The contents of this CD are now available online at "Mormon Migration" http://mormonmigration.lib.byu.edu. and this database has been enhanced significantly. Fred is married to JoAnna Merrill, and they are the parents of five children and grandparents of four granddaughters.

Use the following link to view the documentary video:
youtube.com/watch?v=7rm_ozZ7_4M
or scan the QR code below.